PSYCHOLOGY
and the
REAL WORLD

Essays Illustrating Fundamental Contributions to Society

PSYCHOLOGY

and the

REAL WORLD

Essays Illustrating Fundamental Contributions to Society

EDITED BY

Morton Ann Gernsbacher
University of Wisconsin-Madison

Richard W. Pew
BBN Technologies

Leaetta M. Hough
The Dunnette Group

James R. Pomerantz
Rice University

Worth Publishers

Publisher: Catherine Woods
Senior Acquisitions Editor: Kevin Feyen
Executive Marketing Manager: Katherine Nurre
Associate Managing Editor: Tracey Kuehn
Developmental Editor: Phyllis Fisher
Media Editor: Eve Conte
Supplements Editor: Andrea Musick
Photo Editor: Bianca Moscatelli
Cover and Text Designer: Kevin Kall
Illustration Services: Casey Sussman, Perfect Pix Studios
Project Editor: Kerry O'Shaughnessy
Production Manager: Sarah Segal
Composition: Northeastern Graphic, Inc.
Printing and Binding: RR Donnelley

Library of Congress Control Number: 2009940244

ISBN-13: 978-1-4292-3043-8
ISBN-10: 1-4292-3043-6

Printed in the United States of America

Third printing

Worth Publishers
41 Madison Avenue
New York, NY 10010
www.worthpublishers.com

About the FABBS Foundation

The FABBS Foundation is an educational, nonprofit organization established to enhance understanding of the sciences of mind, brain, and behavior. Its efforts are focused on educating the public about the contributions of these sciences to the well-being of individuals and society, recognizing scholars who have made significant contributions to these sciences, and facilitating productive dialogue between scientists and relevant stakeholders to inform policies and improve lives.

CONTENTS

Foreword

Malcolm Gladwell

Malcolm Gladwell is a staff writer at the New Yorker *magazine and the author of* The Tipping Point *(2000),* Blink *(2005), and* Outliers *(2008).*

When I was a cub reporter at the *Washington Post*, too many years ago now to mention, I was assigned to the Business desk. Business was not what you wanted to cover at the *Washington Post*. The glamorous desk was National, and three years after I started, a position finally opened on the National desk. It was to be a science writer. I jumped at it.

At the time, I knew nothing at all about science. I did not take a single science course in college. (If memory serves, I took virtually nothing except courses in eighteenth- and nineteenth-century English history.) For that matter—due to an administrative loophole too tedious to go into here—I barely took any science courses in high school. I didn't like science. It seemed arid and technical. But better to be arid and technical on the National staff, I reasoned, than to spend my days in the Siberia that was Business. So I became a science reporter. On the day I started, I went to the mailroom and informed the news clerks that I was now to receive all the mail that had previously gone to my predecessor. They immediately presented me with an enormous box, at the top of which was that month's issue of the *Journal of Personality and Social Psychology*.

I have often wondered how my life might have been different if the magazine at the top had been, say, *Physics Today* or, God forbid, the *Journal of Waste Management*. But fate was shining on me. I sat down at my desk and started reading, and before long I got the prickly sensation that reporters get when they stumble upon a story. This was a different kind of story from the traditional newspaper kind, of course. It didn't involve scandal or outrage or leaked documents. But it was still a story: What psychology was all about, I realized, was an attempt to construct some kind of coherent narrative out of the chaos and jumble of everyday experience. I believe that to this day. And that is the spirit with which to read the essays that follow.

One of things that is so fascinating about academic research is how personal it is. By that I mean, academicians have the freedom to pursue things that interest them, and as a result their career arcs become fundamentally revelatory. You can't look at the cases handled by a corporate lawyer and get a clear sense of what the corporation is like, or what seizes that lawyer's imagination. He or she is required to handle what comes in the door. But the careers of academic scientists very quickly become particularized and idiosyncratic; it is hard not to look at the careers of psychologists psychologically.

One of the essays in this volume, for instance, is by Paul Ekman. Ekman is the father of the idea that expressions of emotion are both meaningful and universal: A smile of embarrassment is the same in Toronto as it is in Timbuktu. We did not always think that. An earlier generation of psychologists and anthropologists thought that emotions were culturally specific, and to make his claim Ekman had to confront some of the most deeply held orthodoxies of his era. If you meet Ekman—as I have had the pleasure of doing—you'll understand why. He came to intellectual maturity in the rebellious 1960s in the Bay Area. He is by nature a persistent man, with a stubborn streak a mile wide. What you see in this volume is an essay written toward the end of a lifetime of accomplishment. But behind that essay are dozens of dogged steps of discovery: papers that no one believed at first, and long years spent painstakingly mastering the subtleties of facial expression of emotion.

There is also an essay by Robert Sternberg on his attempt to construct a college admissions process that more closely reflects the true range of human abilities. That's a very specific and socially useful exercise. But as you read it keep in mind that there's a reason why Sternberg took up this question: He himself was someone who, as a student, did poorly on so-called "predictors" of achievement. The question he's trying to answer is the question at the center of his own career.

This is part of what I mean when I say that I think of academic psychology as telling a story. Stories are narratives about people and their choices, and the kinds of questions that psychologists ask are invariably personal. That's also why we refer to the social sciences as "soft sciences." That word—soft— was originally intended, I imagine, in a condescending way. (The physicists decided that what they did was "hard," which meant that what the psychologists were doing across campus must be "soft.") But I see no reason for psychologists to take offense at "soft." It's actually right on the money. If Ekman was not a stubborn child of the 1960s, it is quite possible that his work might not have turned out exactly the way it did. If society had not told Sternberg that he had no intellectual future, it is quite possible his work might not have turned out the way it did either. "Soft" means a field that is shaped by the experiences and perspectives and idiosyncrasies of its researchers. "Soft" means something that can absorb more than a few blows. "Soft" means something that each new generation can reshape for its own purposes. This is not a volume of scientific commandments, written in stone. Stone is for Moses (and the physicists).

The organizing theme of this volume is "Psychology and the Real World," and as you read through the essays you will, I imagine, be struck by the sheer breadth of topics to which modern psychology has applied itself—from human perception to the use of memory in the courtroom, to teaching children how not to hate, and on and on.

There are many fields in the academy that, as they have gained in sophistication and knowledge, have left the rest of us behind. Just try and read any contemporary literary criticism if you're not a literary critic, or read some political theory if you don't yourself have a doctorate in the subject. Most of the social and institutional pressures inside the modern university are toward specialization—and that fact is probably inevitable. Academicians are supposed to explore the frontiers of knowledge, and intellectual life on the frontier is never going to be as easy or accessible as life in the ordered settlements of the coastal plain.

One of the great joys of psychology, though, is that you can be on the frontier and speak to the middle at the same time. The essay "When You Put Things Out of Mind, Where Do They Go?" is by Daniel Wegner, who is one of the heaviest of the heavyweights in the psychology business. (I read Wegner's book, *The Illusion of Conscious Will*, a few years ago, and I'm still recovering.) But think of where all that intellect has been focused: not on some hopelessly arcane question of interest only to a few, but on something that, I imagine, all of us have asked ourselves from time to time: Where did that thought go? Of course, we couldn't come up with an answer. But Daniel Wegner can. Psychology is the art of giving the most unexpected and thoughtful of answers to the most ordinary of questions. Read on—and enjoy.

Preface

In 2004, a new nonprofit organization was born in Washington, D.C., called the FABBS Foundation. Its parent organization is FABBS (the Federation of Associations in Behavioral & Brain Sciences), a long-standing advocacy group that represents the combined forces of over 20 scholarly groups focused on the behavioral, psychological, cognitive, and brain sciences. The Foundation's mission—to take on the education and communication activities of the parent organization with the goal of enhancing the public's understanding of the sciences of mind, brain, and behavior—frees FABBS to focus on its goal of advocacy.

We created the volume you now hold in your hands to help spread the good word about the contributions of the brain, mind, and behavioral sciences to the larger community and to society in general. This book joins some of our other efforts, such as the Science Café series that we hold periodically in Washington, D.C., and elsewhere, featuring top psychological and brain scientists speaking about their current findings. Videos of these events, along with other materials you may find interesting and useful, are available on the FABBS Foundation's Web site at www.fabbsfoundation.org.

Other publications share the aim of this volume, which is to disseminate more broadly the interesting and useful research findings produced by researchers in the behavioral and brain sciences. However, two distinctive features set this particular book apart from the others.

First, our book puts front and center the relevance and applicability to society of mind, brain, and behavioral science research. We approached leading scientists in our disciplines—those whose work best exemplifies the potential for a positive impact on society—and asked them to write short, personal essays saying plainly what they believe their life work has accomplished and what ramifications it has had, or may have, on society. For these leading scientists, the chance to speak simply and directly to a broad audience is a rare opportunity. For a wide range of readers, from students in introductory psychology courses to members of the general public with interests in human behavior, the opportunity for intimate, personal encounters with some of the most imaginative psychological scientists currently at work is equally rare. These essays put a human face on brain-behavior research and offer a personal glimpse into the thinking of the research scientists who have made these fields what they are today.

Second, this book represents an enthusiastic collaboration between the FABBS Foundation and Worth Publishers. Worth is the premier publisher of introductory psychology texts, and we are delighted that they have taken an active role in helping bring this book to life. Not only has Worth been generous with their time and energy in helping to edit and produce this book, they have provided significant funding to the FABBS Foundation to help support our other activities, including our Science Café series. Worth will make this available at an affordable price to students whose instructors adopt one of Worth's introductory texts and will return all of the revenues so earned directly to the FABBS Foundation. This means that instructors who adopt a Worth introductory text along with this volume of essays are not only providing their students an important extra at a better-than-modest price, they are also helping provide financial support to the FABBS Foundation and thus to their sciences. Of course, this book is also available to instructors adopting texts from other publishers, just as it is available as a stand-alone volume to the general public; in those cases, Worth also returns a significant portion of the revenues to the FABBS Foundation.

Within Worth, we owe our greatest thanks to Kevin Feyen, Senior Acquisitions Editor for psychology. Kevin has been a true believer in this project from its inception. His enthusiasm for and confidence in this effort is equal to that of any of us here at the FABBS Foundation. It is fair to say that without Kevin's efforts and vision, this book would not have appeared in anything resembling its final form or quality.

We also thank Kevin for finding and hiring our talented developmental editor, Phyllis Fisher. Phyllis's efforts to whip this book into shape have been extraordinary and unfailing. Phyllis worked determinedly with each of the authors in this book, scholars who are rightfully called giants in the field. Phyllis's skill as an editor gave us the final result you see here.

We are also grateful to Malcolm Gladwell for his thoughtful foreword to this book. Gladwell's frequent writings, in the *New Yorker* magazine and in books such as *The Tipping Point, Blink,* and *Outliers,* communicate brilliantly the fascinating findings of psychological research as they play out in everyday life. He is the undisputed master of the prose that calls attention to the work our field does, and so it is fitting that he would contribute the foreword to a volume that pursues the same goals as his own written work.

Several members of the FABBS Foundation board made significant contributions of time and effort to help bring this book to life. Besides ourselves as FABBS Foundation presidents, other members of the FABBS Foundation Board also contributed many suggestions and guidance. FABBS/FABBS Foundation Treasurer Robert Feldman, Board member Lawrence Erlbaum, and friend Zick Rubin helped enormously on the business end. Our organization's executive directors, first Barbara Wanchisen and now Paula Skedsvold, as well as able staffers Meghan McGowan and Steve Schwark, have provided logistical support for all of our efforts. We also thank the many supporters of the FABBS Foundation who have given to us generously over the years since our inception. Your names appear on our Web site at www.fabbsfoundation.org.

We save our final and deepest thanks for the authors of the essays contained within these pages. They all donated their time and effort to the FABBS Foundation. Their generosity signals loudly and unambiguously their strong support for the efforts of the FABBS Foundation. We cannot thank them enough for their contributions and for their good cheer in working with us to produce this book. They, along with their colleagues, are the drivers of our field and the ones who have helped make our disciplines what they are today. We thank them for what they have done throughout their careers.

We thank you as well for taking the time to read the essays that appear here. We hope they will inspire you to appreciate the importance of psychological sciences in the real world.

May 2009

Morton Ann Gernsbacher, President elect, FABBS Foundation

Susan T. Fiske, President, FABBS Foundation

James R. Pomerantz, Past president, FABBS Foundation

Introduction

James R. Pomerantz and Morton Ann Gernsbacher
Psychology and the Real World: An Introduction

Psychology and the Real World: An Introduction

James R. Pomerantz
Rice University

Morton Ann Gernsbacher
University of Wisconsin-Madison

Certain readers of this book—the great majority we hope—are convinced of the importance of psychological research and its contributions to society. We welcome you and anticipate your finding this book filled with fascinating, even delightful, examples of how psychology improves our lives. Other readers may be less sure about psychology and will take some convincing. We welcome you, too, and suggest that if you've been waiting to be persuaded, this book may alter your view of how thought and behavior can be analyzed and understood.

Pick up a newspaper and scan the front page. On a typical day, you'll find a story or two on politics (sometimes defined wittily as what happens whenever two or more people enter a room) and articles on war and crime, people with influence and power, tragic accidents, the ups and downs in the economy, the state of education, and more. These events and their antecedents and consequences are all the purview of psychology, because what people (and other animals) do and why they do it is the domain of psychology, the science of mind and behavior. In fact, it is hard to think of any significant area of human activity that is not intertwined with psychology. Psychologists study the underlying causes and cures for human violence, the elements that combine to create leaders and heroes, the human errors that cause accidents and the consequences of such mistakes, the forces that make people more effective in their work, the best ways to foster learning, to name a few.

Psychology and its practitioners are all around us, working to understand what makes people tick. Of course, nonpsychologists are also curious about the people around them, and over the years most of us learn a lot about how others' minds work and how they are likely to behave. We spend time reflecting on our own minds and behaviors as well. In our "studies" of ourselves and of others, we come to know people as individuals, and we also learn about human behavior in general. For example, when we meet someone new, we can anticipate his or her response to a smile or scowl.

Because daily life makes us reasonably expert in understanding the human mind and in predicting and explaining human behavior, what can we truly learn from a course in psychology? The one-word answer is: Plenty! As the essays in this volume demonstrate, vast areas of behavior are hidden from the casual observer. More importantly, some of what we think we know is wrong.

(Students of psychology are not alone in this regard. Most people have serious misconceptions about basic aspects of the world around them. Consider, for example, the laws of motion. When students who have taken physics courses are asked to predict, say, the path that a ball will follow when it rolls off a desk, most of their estimates won't even be close to correct. Merely living in the world and observing it does not necessarily lead to understanding it or even making reasonable predictions.)

Psychology and Common Sense

If you think understanding and predicting human behavior consists mainly of using common sense, think again. Folk wisdom—manifested in the wise sayings that you have heard all your life from your elders—is supposed to reflect universal truths. Take the adage "birds of a feather flock together," which is intended to remind us that people prefer to spend their time with others who are similar to them. This seems to be such a universal law of human behavior that you might wonder why anyone would bother doing research to confirm the obvious. Why would we need to conduct research in the laboratory, or even in the field, to verify what we already know? The adage is based on years of intuition, and isn't that all that psychology is— well-known intuition?

Well, consider another bit of folk wisdom: "Opposites attract." This saying aims to remind us that we are attracted to, and so spend our time with, people quite different from ourselves. This saying, too, is based on years of thoughtful intuition; it, too, is considered a universal law. But these two wise sayings contradict one another and so cannot both be true. Which intuition correctly represents the way people actually behave: Do birds of a feather flock together, or do opposites attract? The most direct way— perhaps the only way— to learn which pearl of wisdom is correct is through close, objective observation or through carefully controlled experiments. That is what psychologists do to learn the answers to questions that casual observation does not supply accurately. If we were to tell you that research has shown that opposites attract, would you be surprised? You should be, because research has shown just the reverse: Birds of a feather do indeed flock together!

If belief in the supposed truth of "opposites attract" in the face of the supposed truth of "birds of a feather flock together" were an isolated example, we might have little reason for concern. But belief in scientifically unsupported truisms is anything but isolated. Moreover, as you can see in Table 1, for many deeply held truisms, there is a conflicting truism 180 degrees opposite in meaning. You can probably think of other examples of strongly held beliefs, assumed to be universal and intuitive, that stand in stark opposition to other strongly held beliefs, also assumed to be universal and intuitive. As satisfying and comforting as folk wisdom may seem, in the end it is research—properly designed and executed—that will give us the valid and reliable answers we seek about human behavior.

Psychology and Subjective Experience

Students new to psychology sometimes wonder how anything as subjective and unobservable as the mind can be studied scientifically. After all, can

TABLE 1 Contradictory Aphorisms

1. Absence makes the heart grow fonder, but out of sight is out of mind.
2. Look before you leap, but he who hesitates is lost (or, strike while the iron is hot).
3. A penny saved is a penny earned, but don't be penny-wise and pound-foolish.
4. Haste makes waste, but a stitch in time saves nine.
5. Turn the other cheek, but an eye for an eye.
6. Charity begins at home, but love thy neighbor.
7. Better safe than sorry, but nothing ventured, nothing gained.
8. All things come to those who wait, but the squeaky wheel gets the grease.
9. The grass is always greener on the other side of the fence, but there's no place like home.
10. Too many chefs spoil the broth, but many hands make light work (or, the more the merrier).
11. Once burned, twice shy, but if at first you don't succeed, then try, try, try again (or, hope springs eternal).
12. Birds of a feather flock together, but opposites attract.
13. United we stand, divided we fall, but it's a dog-eat-dog world.
14. Good fences make good neighbors, but no man is an island.
15. Never put off until tomorrow what you can do today, but let's cross the bridge when we come to it.
16. Seek and ye shall find, but curiosity killed the cat.
17. A rolling stone gathers no moss, but stop and smell the roses.
18. The pen is mightier than the sword, but actions speak louder than words.
19. Don't judge a book by its cover, but the clothes make the man.
20. Half a loaf is better than none, but a miss is as good as a mile.
21. All that glitters is not gold, but where there's smoke there's fire.
22. What's good for the goose is good for the gander, but one man's meat is another man's poison.
23. The best things in life are free, but there's no such thing as a free lunch.
24. You are never too old to learn, but you can't teach an old dog new tricks.
25. Never look a gift horse in the mouth, but beware of Greeks bearing gifts.
26. Slow and steady wins the race, but time waits for no man.
27. Hitch your wagon to a star, but don't bite off more than you can chew.
28. The early bird gets the worm, but better late than never.
29. Variety is the spice of life, but never change a horse midstream.
30. The devil is in the details, but don't sweat the small stuff.

anyone ever truly know what is going on in someone else's head? This excellent question has good—and often clever—answers. Take for example a question many people thought unanswerable not long ago: Do infants see color the same way adults do? You cannot simply ask infants about this— any more than you could ask your family dog or cat whether it sees color.

The solution to this problem illuminates a key point: Psychology combines the study of the mind (not only perceptions but also sensations, memories, thoughts, feelings, and so forth) with the study of behavior (observable actions). Behavior, therefore, serves as a window, sometimes the only window, into the mind.

If you show infants a clear, bright patch of color, they will usually look directly at it (that is, they will fixate the patch of color, and their pupils will dilate perceptibly) until they get bored. Then they will look away, at least until a new and distinct color pops up. Knowing this allows researchers to tell what colors (wavelengths) infants can see and which colors they perceive as different from other colors. Armed with this tool, psychologists have learned a lot about babies' vision, including that they appear to see the rainbow similarly to adults, with about the same bands of color. (Note that those bands are illusory; the rainbow simply consists of a smooth continuum of wavelengths. We learn a lot about the mind by studying such illusions.)

Consider another example. Can you recall the number of windows in the house in which you grew up? Many people report that in answering this question they "mentally walk" through that house, taking a tour in their mind's eye, counting windows as they go. In other words, they use mental imagery to answer a factual question. Is it possible to study such a subjective process objectively when it seems so inherently private? The answer is "yes" because mental imagery can be measured in terms of outward (public) behavior: We can measure the time it takes people to count the windows. It turns out that the larger the house you grew up in, the longer it takes you to finish counting. Thus, by timing a behavior associated with the mind's eye, its operation is revealed. You can demonstrate this yourself: Ask some friends to remain silent until they can name either the twentieth or the fortieth word in the Pledge of Allegiance, and time their responses.

People also wonder whether psychologists can measure the properties of the mind, brain, and behavior with a degree of numerical precision sufficient to allow mathematical modeling. Most of us are familiar with intelligence tests that measure IQ on a scale centered on 100. We know that the higher one's IQ score, the more likely the person is to perform well in school, but we probably don't think that the quantification of IQ is so precise that we can perform basic math on it. For example, we wouldn't expect a person with an IQ of 160 to solve a problem exactly twice as quickly or accurately as a person with an IQ of 80. Although that certainly is true, psychologists have become quite skilled at accurate measurement of many other aspects of mental life. We know quite well, for example, how much more physically intense we must make a sound for it to seem twice as loud to the human ear (hint: far more than simple doubling is required). We now know with some precision the rate at which people forget information they learn and how people's problem-solving abilities change as they age.

Predictability of Human Behavior

Looking at baby pictures, it's hard to tell who is going to turn out to be a Nobel Prize laureate or a selfless hero and who is going to turn toward a life of crime or experience debilitating depression. As random as these outcomes might appear, however, psychological and biological studies (including genetic studies of identical versus nonidentical twins) have revealed a lot about such matters. Take this question: Who among us is most likely to die in a roadway accident? Traffic deaths often appear so open to chance, so dependent on coincidence and bad luck, that none of us seems safe on the road. Statistics provide a clearer picture of risk. For example, men between the ages of 21 and 24 who drive motorcycles between midnight and 4 A.M. face a road fatality risk that is 45,000 times higher than the norm. So, who dies on the road is far from random, as anyone working in a hospital emergency room can verify. In fact, human behavior is so nonrandom that people cannot behave randomly even when asked. For example, if people are asked to call out random numbers, the sequences they produce turn out to be very systematic. Alas, we cannot be truly random even when we try.

Who Are Psychologists and What Do They Do?

Who are the people who study the mind, the brain, and behavior for a living? If asked to name a psychologist, many people think first of Sigmund Freud, although in truth he was instead a neurologist and psychoanalyst. However, his reputation does accurately convey the notion that the most populous group of psychologists, namely, clinical psychologists, treat people who are experiencing psychological difficulties or who wish to understand themselves better. But psychology is also a scientific discipline: Many psychologists work in laboratories—in colleges and universities, in hospitals and medical centers, and in private industry—trying to understand the workings of the mind and brain and to predict everyday behavior.

Some research psychologists focus on health, even though they themselves are not treating patients. The reason for their interest is clear: The U.S. Centers for Disease Control estimates that 50 percent of the variance in U.S. health outcomes—who is healthy and well versus who is sick and dies—is attributable to human behaviors such as smoking, failure to wear seatbelts, alcohol consumption, and other risky but voluntary behaviors. In contrast, only 20 percent of the variance in health outcomes stems from our environment, and only 20 percent arises from our genes. Determining the causes and best preventive measures for these behaviors is obviously of paramount importance to us all, and psychologists lead that effort.

Other researchers seeking to discover the best ways for people to learn and remember new information have encountered some critical and surprising results. For example, giving people hints often hurts their recall performance (for example, supplying people with the names of 25 U.S. states actually hurts their ability to recall the remaining 25); repeated studying and rereading is a poor way to learn new information—testing yourself rather than further studying is far superior; and making learning conditions easy and comfortable rather than difficult and unpleasant can be the best way to lock in new memories. Psychologists studying different cognitive functions—such as language, perception, thinking, and decision-making—often supplement their behavioral experiments with neuroimaging techniques such as fMRI, which tracks brain activity by monitoring blood flow. These scientists argue that a combination of psychological and biological measures will converge to create a clear picture of the mind at work.

Social psychologists look at the behavior of people in groups, showing that, for example, individuals perform better in the presence of others than when they are alone, but that people also try less hard when they are on a team than when they are performing solo (the more people pulling on the rope in a tug-of-war game, the less hard each one pulls). Developmental psychologists look at how all kinds of mental activities and behaviors change as we age. Eleanor Gibson (1910–2002), a leading researcher in perceptual development, discovered in the 1950s that babies have visual (3-D) depth perception, and recently other researchers have determined that even 3-month-old infants can mentally rotate objects in their minds. Other psychologists study how people behave in the workplace—a topic that has significant implications for improving human efficiency and productivity—and how people work with artificial devices such as airplanes, where the consequences of human error can be severe.

So please join us in the coming pages of this book as many of today's foremost psychologists discuss personally and directly their life's work and its contribution to society. We find their stories fascinating and illuminating, and we hope you will too.

Methods of Psychology

John H. Krantz

Can the World Wide Web Be Used for Research?

Paul R. Sackett

Integrity Testing for Personnel Selection: The Role of Research Methods

Can the World Wide Web Be Used for Research?
John H. Krantz
Hanover College

▶ *Please describe your current position and research interests.*
I am currently a professor in the Department of Psychology at Hanover College. I am still doing research on using the Web for psychological research, in particular about how images and media can be used as psychological stimuli over the World Wide Web.

▶ *How did you get interested in the Web as a possible source for research participants?*
Frankly, my location at Hanover College suggested the idea. The Web was still quite new and mostly still an academic tool at the time I first became involved. I could see its potential to reach much larger and more diverse populations of participants than were available at Hanover, a school with a fairly homogenous population of only about 1,000 students. The Web has opened up many new possibilities not only for my colleagues and me but also for many of our students.

▶ *What has been the real-world impact of this work?*
The Web offers a new tool for research. It allows us to ask new questions and re-examine old questions in new ways. The real world impact is and will be two-fold: First, many more people have the opportunity to participate in and know about psychological research. Before the Web, most research was done with college students. Now, many studies are available to a much more general population, giving them access to the ways that psychologists learn about human nature. Second, with new tools come new understandings. Exactly what will be learned is very hard to predict, but the way we ask questions impacts what we can know.

Many introductory science texts make the scientific method sound like a fixed set of steps directly leading to discovery. Science sounds mechanical, automatic, and even rather boring. In the real practice of science, deciding on how to do a study is complex, calling on a range of decisions, all of which can impact the quality of the data. To use the common euphemism, doing science is also an art. In addition, scientists are always developing new ways to collect data in order to better learn about nature. But with each innovation, the scientist must know that good data have been collected. The method itself must be tested. In this essay, I will describe efforts to verify the potential of a new source of data for psychological research: the World Wide Web.

The Web attracted research psychologists' attention because it offered a solution to one of the great problems they face: the availability of appropriate participants (Birnbaum, 1999). At many colleges and universities, researchers have long recruited experimental subjects from among their students, most often from introductory psychology classes—a practice that has led to quips about psychology being "largely the science of the behavior of sophomores" (McNemar, 1942, p. 333). Typically, researchers don't want to know about the students' behavior; they are using them as stand-ins for people in general. However, if their student-participants are in any way different from the general population, their findings can be misleading. Given this limitation, research psychologists are always trying to find better ways to access a more general population. Toward that end, the World Wide Web presents a new means of accessing a pool of potential research participants whose characteristics are more varied than those of college students (Reips, 2000).

First Thoughts About the Web as a Source of Data

Starting in 1993, the Web became accessible to the general population with the introduction of the first general browser, Mosaic. Before Mosaic, Web documents only had links that allowed movement within and between documents. No images, movies, or sounds were available, nor were there any of the other kinds of media that now enliven the Web. With the introduction of Mosaic and then Netscape, the capabilities of the Web expanded rapidly. One of the most important innovations, from the point of view of those who might want to use the Web for psychological research, was the development of forms that permit the person reading a Web page to fill it out and send it to another computer for storage (Musch & Reips, 2000). If you've ever bought anything from a Web site, you'll be familiar with these forms. Buyers enter their name and other information, and those data are sent to the seller's computer, where they are stored.

With the introduction of these forms, psychological researchers realized that the Web could be used to access participants who were *not* college students (Musch & Reips, 2000). But before they could undertake such studies, they needed to determine the quality of the data that would be obtained—information of paramount importance, given that collecting low-quality data would simply be a waste of their time.

In articles written at the time, my colleagues and I and a number of other researchers discussed reasons why the Web might *not* be a good way to collect psychological data (Birnbaum, 1999; Krantz, Ballard, & Scher, 1997; Reips, 2000). This essay highlights one particularly important possibility that concerned us: lack of control over the environment.

For findings from a psychological experiment to be useful, the environment must be controlled very carefully—that is, all features of the environment must be the same for all people participating in the experiment. In setting up their studies, researchers make predictions about cause-effect relationships among variables. (A variable is anything that can vary.) The only feature of the experiment that can change is the variable being studied (the independent variable), which the researcher systematically varies from condition to condition. This requirement that the environment remain constant is essential if researchers are to understand why participants respond the way they do. If the person's behavior differs in different conditions, and the only difference between conditions is the independent variable, then the researcher can conclude that the independent variable caused the change in behavior.

When using the Web, such environmental control is not possible. One volunteer might be working in a quiet room using a computer connected via a slow phone line. Another person might be seated at a computer with a high-speed connection in a crowded, noisy university laboratory. Of course, leaving the study online for a long time can attract a large population of participants, and if the group is large enough, variations between the environments might just average out. That is, among the varied conditions in which a cause-effect relationship is being tested, no differences might exist *on average* other than the independent variable. To test this notion, my colleagues and I decided to use the Web to gather—and then evaluate—psychological data.

Our Early Study Using the Web

In one of the very first, if not the first, true experimental studies conducted on the Web, we repeated two earlier psychological studies of determinants of female attractiveness (Krantz, Ballard, & Scher, 1997). (For simplicity's sake, I will only discuss the first study.) To begin, we asked ourselves: What method is appropriate to determine if the data from a Web study are of high enough quality for scientific research? The solution, we decided, was to collect data from both the laboratory and the Web. If the data from both the laboratory version of the experiment and the Web version of the experiment gave similar results, then the Web would likely be a valid source of data for this type of experiment.

In the original experiment, the researchers presented participants with nine outlines of female figures, varying in body type from very thin to obese. The participants were asked several questions about the outlined figures, including one that asked them to choose the one that represents the ideal weight for females. An interesting finding was that the female participants chose a thinner ideal than did the males (Fallon & Rozin, 1985).

In our experiment, we modified the outlined figures to change the ratio of bust to hips, although the same nine weight levels were used. In some outlines, the bust-to-hip ratio was larger, in others it was the same, and in others it was smaller. Two examples are shown in Figure 1.

In both the laboratory and Web versions of our experiment, the outlined figures were presented one at a time and each participant saw all 27 variations (9 weight values by 3 hip-to-bust proportions). Instead of picking their ideal, our participants rated the attractiveness of each figure. A standard figure, shown in Figure 1a, was given an attractiveness rating of 200, and participants were asked to compare each of the other outlines (for example, Figure 1b) to this standard. For example, if Figure 1b was rated as half as attractive as Figure 1a, the person was instructed to give it a score of 100; a score of 400 would mean that it was twice as attractive as Figure 1a. This traditional way of collecting data is called magnitude estimation. In the early study, participants were asked only to pick the ideal-weight figure.

Figure 2a shows how female participants rated the three outlines that showed equal-size bust and hips, and Figure 2b presents men's ratings of the same outlines. The horizontal axis of the graph shows the weight-value of the

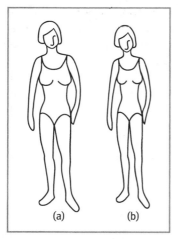

FIGURE 1 Sample figure outlines from the study. Note that (a) is also the standard. (Fallon & Rozin, 1985)

figures, with 10 being the thinnest and 90 being the heaviest. The vertical axis is scaled so that 100 represents the most attractive figure that each participant chose: The higher the number, the more attractive the figure.

Notice that the data from the laboratory and the Web versions of our study are nearly identical despite differences in environmental conditions, computers, and characteristics of the two groups of participants. One hundred percent of the laboratory participants were between the ages of 18 and 22, whereas only 24 percent of the Web participants were in this age range. All of the lab participants were from the United States, most from three states. Web responses came from six continents, although the majority of participants lived in the United States. Statistical analyses confirmed conclusions

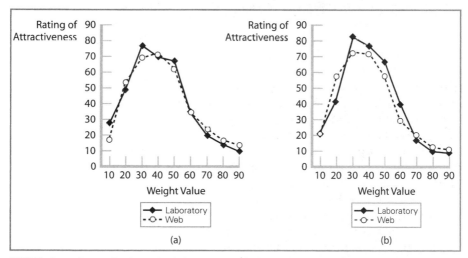

FIGURE 2 Sample results from the laboratory and Web. Note that (a) is female participants' data and (b) is male participants' data. (Krantz, Ballard, & Scher, 1997)

based on visual inspection of the data. In fact, one type of analysis, linear regression, indicated that the data from one version of the experiment can be substituted for the other version (Krantz, Ballard, & Scher, 1997). The data shown in Figure 2 are consistent with the rest of our findings.

One conclusion from the original study differed from ours. In the first study, which took place in the early 1980s, women chose a thinner ideal than did males. Although we did not ask which outline was ideal, analysis of ratings of the most attractive weight-value did not show a gender difference. Our male respondents chose a mid-range weight-value of 30 as most attractive; most women picked either 30 or 40; and the difference between the genders was not statistically significant. We were unable to determine whether the inconsistency in results between our research and the earlier study is due to methodology or changes over time in perceptions of ideal weight.

Where Do We Go from Here?

No matter how provocative the findings, one study that uses Web-obtained data to produce conclusions similar to those of an earlier laboratory study does not demonstrate that the Web can be used for all types of psychological research. Nonetheless, we were encouraged—especially because in the years that followed, our findings were replicated in many other studies. However, exceptions have been reported, and some of the differences between data gathered via the Web and that collected in the laboratory are very interesting. In fact, the differences between Web and laboratory findings have sometimes revealed features of people's behavior that would be missed by either kind of study alone (see Krantz & Dalal, 2000, for an early review of Web studies).

In one interesting study, researchers adapted to the Internet the *lost-letter technique* of social psychologist Stanley Milgram (1933–1984). In the original study, Milgram and his students "lost" a lot of stamped, addressed, return-addressed envelopes and counted the rate of returns. The few that got back to him were sent to the originally intended address instead of to the sender, suggesting an altruistic impulse on the part of the finders. In the Internet version, e-mail appeared to have been misdirected. The person getting the e-mail could send it to the originally intended recipient by forwarding or returning it to the sender. (Both addresses went to the researchers.) Those few e-mails that made their way back to the researchers came by way of the return-to-sender route. In snail mail, the easiest way to send on a letter is to drop it into a box and let it go to the originally intended recipient. In e-mail, returning it to the original sender is easier because the address is entered automatically; forwarding requires typing or cutting and pasting the address. So in both situations, altruists made the low-effort choice—a finding that recast the results of the original study (Stern & Faber, 1997).

The use of the Web for psychological research has grown tremendously. In fact, textbooks are now available that teach methods for collecting data over the Web (see, for example, Birnbaum, 2001). In the mid-1990s, only a handful of Web-based studies had been published. A decade later, hundreds of Web-based psychological studies are being conducted at any one time on a wide range of topics. In fact, many sites exist where researchers can post links to their studies to help potential participants find participant opportunities. The Department of Psychology at Hanover College has sponsored one such list since 1996—the *Psychological Research on the Net* list at http://psych .hanover.edu/research/exponnet.html (Krantz, 2007). At its inception, this site hosted links to fewer than two dozen studies. Currently, it has more than 200 links. In 2007, over 120,000 people visited the site looking for experiments in which to participate.

Despite the large number of links, many topics in psychology are not suitable for Web research. An examination of the *Psychological Research on the Net* page shows that topics in social and cognitive psychology seem to be the easiest to do. Web-based research exploring emotions and sensation and perception are much less common because they usually require complicated stimuli. Emotions researchers often use images of faces and even films—a particularly difficult medium requiring lengthy downloading time and uninterrupted presentation. A long or slow download can cause people to leave a study, substantially reducing participation. More troubling is the possibility that the movie might stop at the wrong place. A glitch like this could change the users' interpretation of the movie and therefore the results of the experiment without the researcher knowing what happened. In sensation and perception research, stimuli must usually be very precisely controlled. The variability of monitors makes that control impossible. So, the Web is not particularly useful in these instances.

The availability of the Web for research has enhanced psychology in many ways. It allows greater access than was previously possible to a wider range of participants (Krantz & Dalal, 2000) and to groups of people who have been hard to study in the past (Mangan & Reips, 2006). It saves time for the research team and often reduces costs (Reips, 2000), and it can allow for the collection of data from a far larger number of subjects, permitting researchers to do more subtle data analyses than would be possible in lab-based experiments (Birnbaum, 1999; Reips, 2000). Most importantly, the proliferation of studies demonstrates the constant effort in the research community to improve methods of data collection. But as our experiment illustrates, researchers using new tools must examine the quality of their data. Research is subtle and interesting, and discovery is exciting.

Suggested Further Reading

Birnbaum, M. H. (2001). *Introduction to behavioral research on the Internet.* Upper Saddle River, NJ: Prentice Hall.

Krantz, J. H., & Dalal, R. (2000). Validity of Web-based psychological research. In M. H. Birnbaum (Ed.), *Psychological experiments on the Internet* (pp. 35–60). New York: Academic Press.

References

Birnbaum, M. H. (1999). Testing critical properties of decision making on the Internet. *Psychological Science, 10,* 399–407.

Birnbaum, M. H. (2001). *Introduction to behavioral research on the Internet.* Upper Saddle River, NJ: Prentice Hall.

Fallon, A., & Rozin, P. (1985). Sex difference in perceptions of desirable body shape. *Journal of Abnormal Psychology, 94,* 102–105.

Krantz, J. H. (2007). *Psychological research on the Net* [Online]. Retrieved August 25, 2009, from http://psych.hanover.edu/research/exponnet.html.

Krantz, J. H., Ballard, J., & Scher, J. (1997). Comparing the results of laboratory and World Wide Web samples on the determinants of female attractiveness. *Behavior Research Methods, Instruments, & Computers, 29,* 264–269.

Krantz, J. H., & Dalal, R. (2000). Validity of Web-based psychological research. In M. H. Birnbaum (Ed.), *Psychological Experiments on the Internet* (pp. 35–60). New York: Academic Press.

Mangan, M., & Reips, U.-D. (2006). Sleep, sex, and the strengths and weaknesses of the Web in surveying a difficult-to-reach clinical population. Paper presented at the 2006 Society for Computer in Psychology conference, Houston, TX.

McNemar, Q. (1942). Opinion-attitude methodology. *Psychological Bulletin, 43,* 289–374.

Musch, J., & Reips, U.-D. (2000). A brief history of Web experimenting. In M. H. Birnbaum (Ed.), *Psychological experiments on the Internet* (pp. 61–88). San Diego, CA: Academic Press.

Reips, U.-D. (2000). The Web experiment method: Advantages, disadvantages, and solutions. In M. H. Birnbaum (Ed.), *Psychological experiments on the Internet* (pp. 89–117). San Diego, CA: Academic Press.

Stern, S. E., & Faber, J. E. (1997). The lost e-mail method: Milgram's lost-letter technique in the age of the Internet. *Behavior Research Methods, Instruments, & Computers, 29,* 260–263.

Integrity Testing for Personnel Selection: The Role of Research Methods

Paul R. Sackett
University of Minnesota

▶ *Please tell us about your current position and research interests.*
I am a professor of psychology at the University of Minnesota, where my research focuses on the use of psychological testing for employment decisions and for academic admission decisions.

▶ *What got you interested in studying the quality of tests of employee honesty and integrity?*
My interest in the topic of integrity testing arose out of an inquiry from an employer wondering whether integrity tests were useful. There was little research on the topic at the time, and I began studying the topic.

▶ *What has been the real-world impact of this work?*
Integrity testing is widely used, having grown from a new and little-understood form of testing to a relatively mature field with an extensive body of supporting research.

Employers often face a complex problem when trying to choose among many applicants for a limited number of jobs. Under such circumstances, some employers turn to psychologists for help, asking whether psychological tests are available that will help them identify those applicants most likely to be effective employees. Psychologists typically respond with a wide range of possible employee-selection tests, including measures of ability, personality, interests, values, knowledge, integrity, and skill.

The goal of most testing in employment settings is the identification of applicants most likely to perform well on particular jobs. However, in some settings, employers have a different goal: They want to *avoid* hiring employees who might engage in various forms of counterproductive work behavior (for example, theft). In settings where employees have access to money or merchandise and work with limited monitoring or supervision, employers are highly motivated to avoid hiring anyone likely to steal. Several decades ago, employers with such concerns commonly administered polygraph examinations in an attempt to learn about applicants' possible past history of wrongdoing.

As the polygraph came under scrutiny and was eventually made illegal for most employers, paper-and-pencil tests of "honesty" or "integrity" emerged as alternatives. One test type is commonly called an overt, or clear-purpose test. This type of test focuses on respondents' beliefs about theft: how often it occurs and how widely; how it should be punished; how easy theft is; what respondents' thoughts are about theft and whether they agree or disagree with common rationalizations for theft; and how they assess their own honesty. A second type of test is commonly called a personality-oriented, or disguised-purpose test. This type of test is closely linked to normal-range personality assessment measures, is not explicitly aimed at theft, and includes items dealing with dependability, conscientiousness, social conformity, thrill seeking, trouble with authority, and hostility.

The market for these tests is huge: Several million applicants are tested each year. Many test vendors have entered the market; at one point, they were offering over 40 tests. Mainstream psychological test publishers developed a few of these tests; many others had little to no research backing. Given the extensive interest in and use of the tests, the obvious question is whether they work: Do the tests, in fact, predict behavior on the job?

My involvement in this area began with such a question. In 1977, I received a phone call from an organization asking whether a particular test was valid. Knowing nothing about the test in question, I set out to research the topic. A colleague and I gathered up all the research studies we could find and published an article summarizing what was known about integrity tests (Sackett & Decker, 1979). Little did I know that 30 years later I'd still be interested in the topic of employee honesty and integrity. Over the years, I've published four more reviews of the state of our knowledge about integrity tests (Sackett & Harris, 1984; Sackett, Burris, & Callahan, 1989; Sackett & Wanek, 1996; Berry, Sackett, & Wiemann, 2007). In 1979, I could locate only a handful of research studies; by the time I wrote the later reviews, I was able to examine and critique hundreds of studies.

Research Strategies for Evaluating the Effectiveness of Integrity Tests

To gain an understanding of integrity tests and how well they work, researchers have employed a wide variety of research methods. Among the most widely used are criterion-related validity studies in which tests are administered to a sample of job applicants or current employees and measures of on-the-job behavior (or whatever criterion you are attempting to predict) are obtained. Various statistical measures are used to index the degree to which test scores are related to job behavior. In other words, data are examined to determine whether individuals with high test scores do better on the job than those with low test scores.

Early studies of integrity testing used scores on a polygraph examination as the criterion. The question in this research was whether individuals with low integrity test scores were more likely than those with high scores to fail a polygraph exam, and research found this to be the case. However, critics were skeptical of these findings, questioning the accuracy of the polygraph method. If the polygraph is not a credible measure, showing that integrity test scores correlate with polygraph scores is not persuasive.

In response to this criticism, researchers conducted studies that did not use the polygraph as the criterion. Instead, test-takers underwent questioning directed at getting them to admit to prior theft from employers. Researchers using this strategy found that test scores are correlated with admissions of theft (that is, those with high integrity test scores admit less prior theft). Again, this evidence was met with skepticism. Among the complaints was the suggestion that test scores don't really predict theft, but merely predict willingness to admit to theft. In other words, high and low test scorers may be just as likely to steal; they may merely differ in their willingness to admit to wrongdoing.

So, researchers tried yet another approach. Because self-reported theft was not seen as a credible measure, the focus shifted to measures of theft detected on the job. In these studies, firms would keep track of all employees caught stealing over the course of a year and then the test scores of employees who were caught stealing would be compared with those of employees who were not caught stealing. These studies showed that those caught stealing were very likely to have low test scores. At the same time, though, only a very small number of employees were caught in a given year, thus raising questions about how to interpret the test scores of those not caught. Skeptics could point out that many people with low integrity test scores were not caught stealing, and thus assert that the test mislabeled innocent people. Most importantly from the employer's point of view, those caught stealing may represent only a fraction of those actually stealing. And it's even possible that those caught stealing are not a random sampling of those who steal, but instead represent those who simply aren't very good at it. So, if we use theft-detection as the criterion measure, we're left with the interesting finding that those caught stealing do tend to have low test scores, a finding consistent with what we'd expect if the tests worked as intended, but also with uncertainty about the issue of undetected theft.

Researchers continued exploring alternative research strategies. The idea of an objective measure of wrongdoing was attractive, but difficulties in detecting theft led to the use of indirect measures. In one creative study, researchers looked at the behavior of a sample of Salvation Army bell-ringers at Christmas time (Jones & Terris, 1981). The researchers gave an integrity test to all bell-ringers at the start of the holiday season, but they did not score the test or use it in the hiring decisions. They then measured the average amount of money collected each day for each bell-ringer. They had historical data for each location, and so each bell-ringer's dollar intake could be compared with the historical average for that location.

At the end of the holiday season, those with low integrity test scores turned in less money than those with high integrity test scores, a finding that they interpreted as evidence that dishonest bell-ringers were pocketing some of the money collected. However, low-integrity bell-ringers could have been taking longer breaks, working fewer hours, and thus soliciting less money. Of course, taking extended breaks can be seen as a form of counterproductive behavior, and thus the integrity test is effective in identifying those prone to taking in less money, regardless of whether it is due to extended breaks or to theft. Nonetheless, we are left unsure of exactly why those with low integrity test scores turn in less money.

These methodological difficulties led to yet another approach, namely to move from on-the-job field settings to research carried out in the psychologist's laboratory. The appeal of laboratory research is the degree of control available to the researcher. Here researchers can design settings where opportunities for forms of wrongdoing or misbehavior are arranged and where settings are designed in such a way that the researcher knows with certainty how each participant behaves. In one study, participants took an integrity test and then engaged in a number of experimental tasks for which they were to be paid a certain amount (for example, $5). When they were finished, they were told, "Here's your $5," and handed an envelope containing two $5 bills. Not unexpectedly, those with high integrity test scores were more likely than those with low scores to report the extra money. Findings from these kinds of studies are consistent—for example, those with low integrity test scores are more likely to cheat on an experimental task or to give themselves more points than deserved when self-scoring a test they've taken (cf. Berry, Sackett, & Wiemann, 2007).

I find this approach an interesting inversion of the typical research strategy as advocated in textbooks. The common sequence is for research to begin in a laboratory and later to move into field settings to examine whether lab findings generalize to real-world settings. In the area of integrity testing, the question of interest is inherently an applied one (Do these tests predict wrongdoing on the job?), and thus most research has been done in applied settings. The use of a lab setting, with its accompanying degree of control over the situation, proved a useful supplement in response to questions about possible flaws in the measures obtained in field settings.

Lessons Learned

This story illustrates several important issues regarding psychological research methods. One is that in settings where research outcomes have significant real-life consequences (for example, the investigation of a type of test affecting the job opportunities of millions of people), research will be scrutinized very closely. Critics will examine the work carefully to determine whether possible alterative explanations for the results can be identified. This kind of analysis can be frustrating to the individual researcher whose work is being critiqued, but it is clearly good for the advancement of knowledge: Criticism prompts additional research to address the concerns raised by critics.

Second, evidence from a single study is rarely seen as fully persuasive. As developments in the investigation of integrity testing illustrate, triangulation across multiple research methods is crucial. Each method has strengths and weaknesses, and convergence of findings across methods plays a large role in the eventual acceptance of research findings. Note that the research on integrity testing has found that integrity tests are predictive of (a) polygraph exam performance, (b) self-reports of theft, (c) detected theft in organizational settings, (d) objective measures of various forms of wrongdoing in organizational settings, and (e) objective measures of various forms of wrongdoing in carefully controlled laboratory settings. This consistency in findings is quite convincing. It would have been quite a different matter had the results been different (for example, had the tests proven to predict polygraph exams but nothing else). A body of work showing that a research finding is *not* specific to one research setting or to one way of measuring the variables of interest is far more persuasive.

Other Research Issues in Integrity Testing

When psychologists assess the quality integrity tests, a wide range of other important research questions arise: Do integrity scores vary by features such as race or gender? Can applicants raise their scores by giving distorted responses (that is, by faking)? Are the test scores reliable (that is, would a test-taker get the same or nearly the same score if he or she retook the test after a short interval)? For what range of jobs are the tests effective (that is, is predictive power limited to entry-level jobs, or are these tests also useful for higher-level jobs)? How do integrity test scores relate to other psychological measures (that is, are they correlated with measures of central personality traits)? The answer to the last question is yes; they correlate with three measures: conscientiousness, agreeableness, and emotional stability.

Important practical issues also influence employers' decisions as to whether or not to use an integrity test. One key notion is that the opportunity to be selective is a scarce resource. Consider an employer with, say, two applicants for each opening. The employer could choose to use an integrity test and screen out the lowest 50 percent of the applicant pool. But the employer may also want employees who learn quickly and solve problems effectively, and so another option would be to use a cognitive ability test and screen out the lowest 50 percent of the applicant pool on that measure. "Spending" your opportunity to be selective on screening for integrity prevents screening on cognitive ability, and vice versa. Alternately, the employer could use both tests but be less selective on each (that is, screen out the bottom 25 percent on both cognitive ability and integrity). A further research question is whether it is more useful to screen for one characteristic than for another.

Conclusion

In sum, psychologists have made great progress in understanding how well integrity tests perform as predictors of counterproductive work behavior. Over several decades, our knowledge base has moved from a handful of studies to hundreds. And, as is typical with research evidence, no single grand study answers all questions; rather, each smaller study serves as a piece in a larger puzzle. Researchers identify potential weaknesses in existing studies and work to design additional studies to remedy these weaknesses. For this to occur, they must not only be highly knowledgeable about their specialty area but also well versed in research methodology. Thus informed, they can effectively evaluate the strengths and weaknesses of existing research studies and design and conduct studies that further understanding of issues that affect the lives of all of us.

Suggested Further Reading

Berry, C. M., Sackett, P. R., and Wiemann, S. A. (2007). A review of recent developments in integrity test research. *Personnel Psychology, 60,* 270–301.

Sackett, P. R. (1994). Integrity testing for personnel selection. *Current Directions in Psychological Science, 3,* 73–76.

References

Berry, C. M., Sackett, P. R., and Wiemann, S. A. (2007). A review of recent developments in integrity test research. *Personnel Psychology, 60,* 270–301.

Jones, J., and Terris, W. (1981). Predictive validation of a dishonesty test that measures theft proneness. Paper presented at the XVIII Inter-American Congress of Psychology, Santo Domingo, Dominican Republic, June, 1981.

Sackett, P. R., Burris, L. R., & Callahan, C. (1989). Integrity testing for personnel selection: An update. *Personnel Psychology, 42,* 491–529.

Sackett, P. R., & Decker, P. J. (1979). Detection of deception in the employment context: A review and critique. *Personnel Psychology, 32,* 487–506.

Sackett, P. R., & Harris, M. M. (1984). Honesty testing for personnel selection: A review and critique. *Personnel Psychology, 37,* 221–245.

Sackett, P. R., & Wanek, J. E. (1996). New developments in the use of measures of honesty, integrity, conscientiousness, dependability, trustworthiness, and reliability for personnel selection. *Personnel Psychology, 49,* 787–829.

3

Neuroscience

Bruce S. McEwen

Neurobiology of Stress and Adaptation: Implications for Health Psychology, Behavioral Medicine, and Beyond

Michael I. Posner and Mary K. Rothbart

Applying the Mechanisms of Self-Regulation

Neurobiology of Stress and Adaptation: Implications for Health Psychology, Behavioral Medicine, and Beyond

Bruce S. McEwen
The Rockefeller University

▶ *Please describe your current position and research interests.*
I am Alfred E. Mirsky Professor and Head, Harold and Margaret Milliken Hatch Laboratory of Neuroendocrinology at The Rockefeller University. My research interests are as follows: (1) stress effects on the brain and its relationship to adaptation and maladaptation—for example, depression, anxiety disorders, unsuccessful aging; (2) sex differences in the brain and actions of sex hormones on higher brain centers and cognitive function, as well as mood and other aspects of behavior not directly related to reproduction, including how gender and sex hormones affect the response to stress; and (3) effects of the social environment on brain and body function, especially socioeconomic status and health in adults and also during development, related to the allostatic load concept that I helped to introduce.

▶ *How did you get interested in brain-body interactions?*
This is explained in my essay: It was a combination of having Neal Miller as a mentor in my early faculty days at Rockefeller and having Alfred Mirsky and Vincent Allfrey, mentors during my graduate student years, helping to focus me on hormone action and regulation of gene expression in brain, which was a new area of neuroscience when I began.

▶ *What has been the real-world impact of this work?*
Our studies on stress and sex hormone action on hippocampus have helped focus human-oriented studies on the central role of the brain as a target of stress and also on the nonreproductive actions of sex hormones that are relevant to age-related changes—for example, hormone therapy for cognitive and motor functional decline. The allostatic load model is having increasing influence in health psychology, epidemiology, psychiatry, and medicine, and it is helping social scientists better understand the biology of stress and the enormous influence of the social environment on the health of people with different income and education levels.

Stress, one of the most common words in many languages, has both positive and negative connotations. "Good stress" generally refers to situations where the successful response to a challenge is at least somewhat rewarding. In contrast, "being stressed-out" means that hard-to-handle experiences are producing distress—a sense that we lack control over the circumstances of our lives and are under great time pressure. The brain is central to stress both as interpreter of events and as regulator of behavioral and physiological responses to those events. Although adaptive in the short run, responses to stress can be damaging when they become chronic or dysregulated. For example, grabbing a cigarette or a drink or a donut may be initially soothing, but too much of that kind of comfort can have serious negative consequences. Physiologically, a sudden, sharp rise in a person's level of cortisol, a glucocorticoid that is one of the primary stress mediators, has immediate beneficial effects. By contrast, chronically high levels of the hormone are implicated in such potentially damaging health consequences as suppression of the immune system and metabolic syndrome (a group of indicators of increased risk for heart disease and diabetes). Thus, many of the same mediators are involved in both acute adaptation and chronic pathophysiology. Of course, individuals differ in the qualitative nature of their response to stress, which is influenced by their genetic constitutions, early experiences, and adult life history. Furthermore, the brain is itself a target of stress. Structural and functional changes brought about by acute and chronic stressors can alter how the brain processes information and responds to potential stressors.

My own research on stress began in the laboratory of Neal E. Miller at The Rockefeller University in 1966 and was shaped by his integrative view of brain-body interactions, which inspired our serendipitous discovery in 1968 that glucocorticoids are taken up and bind to receptors in the brain's hippocampal formation, where they influence a wide variety of both cognitive functions and generative, energy-conserving bodily processes. Since then, numerous studies with animals have produced findings relevant to such human stress-related disorders as depression and cognitive decline due to aging.

Moreover, through my involvement in the activity of the MacArthur Research Network on Socioeconomic Status and Health, the concept of stress has been reworked through introduction of the terms allostasis and allostatic load, which emphasize that the same mediators that protect the body and brain and help it adapt to acute stressors also participate in wear and tear that contributes to diseases of modern life. The allostatic load concept is helping bridge the gap between biological knowledge and investigations of health-related topics in epidemiology and health psychology, among other disciplines, with the expectation that findings will influence public- and private-sector policies that can improve health and well-being (see Figure 1).

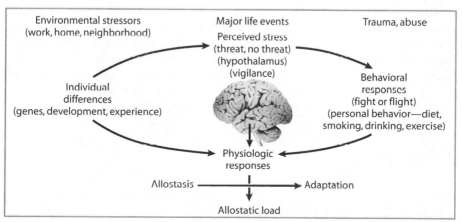

FIGURE 1 The allostatic load concept: Central role of the brain in allostasis and the behavioral and physiological response to stressors. (McEwen, 1998)

Hormone Access to the Brain

Our work on stress began with simple questions about whether the adreno-cortical stress hormone in the rat, corticosterone gains access to the brain and whether there are receptors in the brain for this hormone. Indeed, first with rats and later in the rhesus monkey, we demonstrated that steroid hormones—no doubt because of their greater lipid solubility—gain ready access to the brain, where receptors that have a high affinity for them retain them beyond the time that free steroid is cleared from the brain and body. Hormones active upon the brain include not only glucocorticoids like cortisol and mineralocorticoids like aldosterone, but also reproductive hormones like estradiol, testosterone, and progesterone, as well as vitamin D. The finding of glucocorticoid and mineralocorticoid receptors in the hippocampus triggered the eventual broadening of our concept of how even higher cognitive brain regions respond to external influences via hormones and other mediators.

The long-held belief that peptide and protein hormones cannot reach the brain has been revised on the basis of growing contrary evidence. We now know that the hippocampus has receptors for insulin-like growth factors (IGF-1) and insulin, and that it responds to circulating insulin to translocate glucose transporters to cell membranes. Circulating IGF-1 is a key mediator of the ability of physical activity to increase neurogenesis in the hippocampal formation. IGF-1 is taken up into brain via a transport system different from that which transports insulin. IGF-1 is a member of the growth hormone family, and growth hormone is implicated in cognitive function and mood regulation.

Another peptide hormone, ghrelin, one of the pro-appetitive hormones (those that keep us eating and performing other functions necessary to life), has been shown to increase synapse formation in hippocampal neurons and to improve hippocampal-dependent memory. Another metabolic hormone, leptin, has been found to exert antidepressant effects when infused directly into the hippocampus. Leptin is transported into the brain, and both glucose and insulin mediate the ability of fasting to increase leptin transport into the brain. Leptin receptors are found in hippocampus, among other brain regions, and leptin has actions in hippocampus that reduce the probability of seizures, enhance aspects of cognitive function, and improve mood.

Furthermore, metabolic factors involving glucose regulation play a role in mild cognitive impairment with aging and in shrinkage of the hippocampus. Obese Zucker rats (a widely studied strain prone to obesity and insulin resistance) have poorer hippocampal-dependent memory than do lean Zucker rats, as well as impaired translocation of an insulin-dependent glucose transporter to hippocampal membranes. Moreover, a diet rich in fat has been shown to impair hippocampal-dependent memory, and a combination of a high-fat diet and a 3-week predator exposure (a high-stress situation) causes dendrites and axons in the hippocampus to retract, even though neither treatment alone has this effect. This topic will be revisited below.

Stress Throughout the Life Course

Stressful experiences and stress hormones have effects throughout life. The "weathering hypothesis" recognizes the common observation that a hard life accelerates the aging process. Research on "weathering" effects indicates that increased anxiety and decreased exploration in a novel environment are associated with decreased lifespan of male and female rats compared with animals that show lesser anxiety and greater exploration. The hippocampus is vulnerable to "weathering" with age, and older individuals whose cortisol levels increase over time show more rapid decrements of cognitive function, as well as actual shrinkage in size of that portion of the brain as compared with people of the same age whose cortisol levels are not elevated. Besides cortisol, poor glucose control and factors related to diabetes are also involved in loss of cognitive abilities.

One very productive direction of this research has been the investigation of the role of maternal care and early life stress. For example, "handling" studies of newborn rats have revealed that maternal caretaking can change the way genetic information is expressed, and the effect can persist across generations. One of the mechanisms involves DNA methylation, in which a group of carbon and hydrogen atoms attaches to regions of DNA that influence gene activity. This finding and other advances in developmental neuroscience provide the beginnings of a biological understanding of the effects of abuse, neglect, and trauma in childhood on the development of depression and antisocial behavior. A chaotic home life and lack of verbal stimulation have been shown to impair later self-regulating behaviors and cognitive function.

Protective and Damaging Effects of Stress Mediators: Allostasis and Allostatic Load

Contrary to popular belief, stress and stress hormones are not all bad. Mediators of the biological and behavioral stress response exert adaptive effects in the aftermath of acute stress; their negative effects occur when over- or underproduction of these chemicals chronically impairs mechanisms that govern metabolism, immune response, or organ function. For example, cortisol elevation in times of acute stress promotes certain forms of memory and enhances immune responses to injury and infection, but chronic exposure to even moderate levels of cortisol impairs memory, suppresses immune responses, and contributes to the metabolic syndrome.

The concepts allostasis and allostatic load incorporate this paradox and draw attention to the protective, as well as the damaging, effects of these mediators, which act in a nonlinear manner and influence simultaneously the brain and multiple body systems. By nonlinearity, I mean that the mediators of allostasis (such as cortisol, sympathetic and parasympathetic nervous systems, and cytokines—the substances that activate the white blood cells of the immune system) each regulate the output of the other mediators, which often results in U-shaped or otherwise nonlinear dose-response relationships. In addition, because the mediators of allostasis act simultaneously on many tissues and organs in the body, disorders such as depression, diabetes, and mild cognitive impairment in aging often occur together.

The allostasis and allostatic load framework has been helpful in integrating the biology of stress with the psychosocial factors that promote stress-related disorders and pathophysiology. Tests have been developed that permit prediction of stress effects in aging and health effects of socioeconomic status and social support. Findings from studies of the relationship of allostatic load to a positive life outlook have moved us closer to establishing a biology of resilience and positive health and expanding the concept of allostasis to include the biology of resilience.

The collaboration among neuroscience, biomedicine, and psychology made possible by this new conceptual framework has led to enormous progress in understanding brain-body relationships. For example, cumulative stress among caregivers of autistic children and in conditions such as obesity and diabetes has been shown to affect DNA, reducing the length and activity of a structure at the end of chromosomes. In one provocative observation, hippocampal volume was found to be related to low self-esteem and also to a failure to shut off cortisol secretion efficiently after a public speaking challenge. Low self-esteem is also a possible contributing factor in explaining how subjective ratings of socioeconomic status are frequently as powerful predictors of health as are objective socioeconomic rankings. Research into positive factors in health has identified factors such as positive affect and positive social relationships along with quality sleep as factors that reduce allostatic load.

The Brain as the Central Organ of Stress and Adaptation

The line of research that began with the discovery of adrenal steroid receptors in the hippocampus has reinforced the notion that the brain is the key organ of the stress response for three principal reasons: (1) The brain interprets what is threatening and, therefore, stressful; (2) It regulates behavioral and physiological stress responses, the latter through the autonomic, immune, and neuroendocrine systems; and (3) It is a target of stress and of hormones related to stress and metabolic control (as summarized above) and undergoes structural and functional remodeling that affects its function. Thus, the amygdala and prefrontal cortex are now known to be vulnerable to stress, and stressful experiences are recognized as having an impact on the formation and extinction of fear-related memories, the ability to focus attention, and the cognitive functions that are necessary for goal-directed behavior. Stress-induced brain changes are reversible and are amenable to alteration by pharmaceutical agents and also probably by lifestyle factors such as exercise, diet, and social support, and, very likely, by policies that encourage individuals to adopt healthier lifestyles and reduce stress.

Implications for Interventions and Policy

As the general public and policymakers in the public and private sectors learn more about the science of stress and adaptation, researchers in the field are hoping to see the adoption of rational policies that help people of all levels of income and education move towards healthier and more satisfying lives— lives enhanced by programs that promote education, recreation and social support, and preventative health care. One recent example, the Experience Corps, trains elderly volunteers as teachers' assistants for neighborhood elementary schools. This program benefits the children and also the elderly volunteers by enhancing their physical and mental health and slowing age-related decline of cognitive function. Given the central importance of the brain in "stress," it will be interesting to determine how programs like this reduce measures of allostatic overload, as well as alter the function of the brain circuits that are responsive to chronic stress and allostatic load.

Acknowledgments

I am indebted to the late Neal E. Miller because my own research on stress began in the Miller laboratory at The Rockefeller University in 1966 and was shaped by his integrative view of brain-body interactions. My thinking about brain-body interactions was further shaped by Eliot Stellar of the University of Pennsylvania, first through his textbook *Physiological Psychology* with Clifford Morgan, which I used as a student at Oberlin College under the tutelage of psychologist Celeste McCollough, and later by Stellar recruiting me into the MacArthur Health and Behavior Network, where I began to broaden my thinking about how the social environment shapes what is stressful.

Suggested Further Reading

McEwen, B., with Lasley, E.N. (2002). *The end of stress as we know it*. Washington, DC: Joseph Henry Press.

Sapolsky, R.N. (2004). *Why zebras don't get ulcers*. New York: Owl Press.

References

Acheson, S.D. (1998). Independent inquiry into inequalities in health report. London: The Stationery Office.

Caspi, A., McClay, J., Moffitt, T.E., Mill, J., Martin, J., Craig, I.W., et al. (2002). Role of genotype in the cycle of violence in maltreated children. *Science, 297*, 851–854.

Epel, E.S., Blackburn, E.H., Lin, J., Dhabhar, F.S., Adler, N.E., Morrow, J.D., & Cawthon, R.M. (2004). Accelerated telomere shortening in response to life stress. *Proceedings of the National Academy of Science, 101*, 17312–17315.

Evans, G.W., Gonnella, C., Marcynyszyn, L.A., Gentile, L., & Salpekar, N. (2004). The role of chaos in poverty and children's socioemotional adjustment. *Psychological Science, 16*, 560–565.

Fried, L.P., Carlson, M.C., Freedman, M., Frick, K.D., Glass, T.A., Hill, J., et al. (2004). A social model for health promotion for an aging population: Initial evidence on the Experience Corps model. *Journal of Urban Health: Bulletin of the New York Academy of Medicine, 81*, 64–78.

Geronimus, A.T., Hicken, M., Keene, D., & Bound, J. (2006). "Weathering" and age patterns of allostatic load scores among blacks and whites in the United States. *American Journal of Public Health, 96*, 826–833.

Gold, S.M., Dziobek, I., Sweat, V., Tirsi, A., Rogers, K., Bruehl, H., et al. (2007). Hippocampal damage and memory impairments as possible early brain complications of type 2 diabetes. *Diabetologia, 50*, 711–719.

McEwen, B.S. (1998). Protective and damaging effects of stress mediators. *New England Journal of Medicine, 338*, 171–179.

McEwen, B.S. (2007). The physiology and neurobiology of stress and adaptation: Central role of the brain. *Physiological Review, 87*, 873–904.

McEwen, B.S., & Alves, S.H. (1999). Estrogen actions in the central nervous system. *Endocrine Review, 20*, 279–307.

Pruessner, J.C., Baldwin, M.W., Dedovic, K., Renwick, R.M.N.K., Lord, C., Meaney, M., et al. (2005). Self-esteem, locus of control, hippocampal volume, and cortisol regulation in young and old adulthood. *NeuroImage, 28*, 815–826.

Ryff, C.D., & Singer, B. (1998). The contours of positive human health. *Psychological Inquiry, 9*, 1–28.

Sapolsky, R. (1992). *Stress, the aging brain, and the mechanisms of neuron death.* Cambridge, MA: MIT Press.

Seeman, T.E., Crimmins, E., Huang, M.-H., Singer, B., Bucur, A., Gruenewald, T., et al. (2004). Cumulative biological risk and socio-economic differences in mortality: MacArthur studies of successful aging. *Social Science & Medicine, 58*, 1985–1997.

Szyf, M., Weaver, I.C.G., Champagne, F.A., Diorio, J., & Meaney, M.J. (2005). Maternal programming of steroid receptor expression and phenotype through DNA methylation in the rat. *Frontiers in Neuroendocrinology, 26*, 139–162.

Applying the Mechanisms of Self-Regulation
Michael I. Posner and Mary K. Rothbart
University of Oregon

▶ *Please tell us about your current position and research interests.*
Michael I. Posner: I am Professor Emeritus of Psychology, University of Oregon. I do research on the physical basis of attention networks, including their anatomy and connectivity and how they are shaped by genes and environment to reflect differences among individuals.

Mary K. Rothbart: I am Professor Emerita of Psychology, University of Oregon. I study the development of individual differences in temperament over the life span, including both their reactive and self-regulatory aspects.

▶ *What got you interested in studying the brain networks underlying attention and self-control?*
Our joint work in development began in the 1980s when we sought to determine how attentional networks begin in infancy and change in childhood. As new methods became available, we began research on how genes and environment interact during development to influence individual differences in the efficiency of attentional networks.

▶ *What has been the real-world impact of this work?*
Our work has been applied to understanding differences between typical and atypical development, in the design of clinical and educational interventions, and in understanding how differences among individuals arise in development.

Life often requires us to act in the service of some important or distant goal, even if we'd rather avoid getting involved. We are also required to inhibit actions, thoughts, and feelings in order to respond in ways that may be the opposite of what we'd really like to do or say. When someone says something that makes you angry, you may need to avoid acting on your anger or showing any sign of it; you may even need to substitute a smile. Self-control, or self-regulation, is basic to our adaptation as a species living in groups and essential to fostering civil interactions.

In our research, we have focused on understanding the brain mechanisms involved in self-regulation, how they differ among individuals, and how they develop. Even with the relatively little we currently know, self-regulation can be improved in children and in adults who suffer from conditions that affect their regulatory functions. In this essay, we trace the methods used to study brain mechanisms involved in self-regulation and then describe findings that, when applied, can help children and adults improve their self-control.

The Brain During Self-Regulation

The anatomy of self-regulation can be studied using functional magnetic resonance imaging (fMRI) to see which brain areas are active when adults and children are exercising self-control. The fMRI works like this: Active neurons change the local blood supply, resulting in an increase in red blood cells, and the hemoglobin contained in blood cells can be sensed using a magnetic field such as that produced in MRI. Thus, when we ask participants in our studies to respond to instructions or to resolve conflict between different courses of action, fMRI makes it possible to examine the brain areas that are active (Bush, Luu, & Posner, 2000).

In one such task, the Stroop—an attention test that takes advantage of adults' ability to read words more quickly and automatically than they can name colors—participants are asked to name the color of the ink in which a word is printed (e.g., blue), a response that can conflict with their automatic impulse to read the actual printed word (e.g., red). The arousal of such conflict activates an area in the anterior cingulate region of the brain (see Figure 1) that appears to be related to regulating the strength of other brain networks that support the naming task and that connect closely to other areas involved in cognition (Bush, Luu, & Posner, 2000). If a word meaning has a negative emotional tone (e.g., cancer), the area activated is also in the anterior cingulate but more toward the front of that structure, a region that interacts with areas involved in emotion. When regulating emotion, the cingulate and limbic (emotional) parts of the brain are active together, while cognitive regulation involves the cingulate and frontal or parietal (cognitive or sensory) brain areas. Findings such as this have led to the idea that the anterior cingulate is a part of the mechanism that regulates other brain areas (Posner & Raichle, 1994).

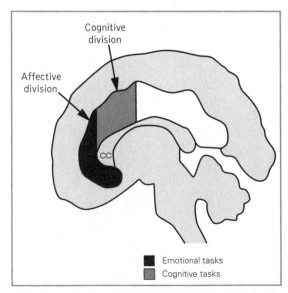

FIGURE 1 Anatomy of conflict arousal. Cognitive and emotional control systems are found in adjacent areas of the anterior cingulate gyrus. (Bush, Luu, & Posner, 2000)

Development of Conflict Regulation

In one of the tests used to study conflict regulation and activation of the anterior cingulate, participants look at a central stimulus (the target) and surrounding flanker stimuli (Fan et al., 2002). Conflict resolution can be measured by comparing participants' reaction time when the flanking stimuli indicate a response different from that of the target (incongruent) and when the flankers indicate the same response as the target (congruent). We have used a child-friendly version of this test with children as young as 4 years of age (Rothbart & Rueda, 2005). Four-year-olds have long reaction times and also take much longer than older individuals to resolve conflict. Children's scores on conflict tasks improve until about age 7 or 8, and beyond that age they seem stable. This finding led us to suppose that major development in the brain network involved in conflict resolution would occur until about age 8. In a related task, the identity of an object and the spatial location of the response conflict. Ability to resolve this kind of conflict develops between ages 30 and 48 months.

The anterior cingulate is also active when a person makes an error in tasks such as those we have described. In this case, the tendencies to make the correct response and a wrong response conflict, and, not surprisingly, this also activates the cingulate. When people notice that they've made an error, they slow down their performance on the trial that follows, and they regulate their behavior to avoid or reduce future errors.

Activation of the anterior cingulate in error detection produces a change in electrical activity of the brain as measured from the scalp. Because scalp electrodes can be used easily with infants and young children, we have been able to measure their anterior cingulate function. One study took advantage of the fact that infants as young as 7 months look longer at visual displays that contain errors than at displays that are correct. When infants wearing a large number of scalp electrodes were tested to see what brain system is involved in detecting errors, clear signs of anterior cingulate activity were evident even at this early age (Berger, Tzur, & Posner, 2006). This finding suggests that the brain network underlying self-regulation is present in some form even in infancy. However, parents don't see self-regulatory behaviors in everyday life until their children are older.

Parents of children between 3 and 8 years of age can observe their children's ability to regulate behavior and emotions, and their descriptions have been widely studied. A number of regulation skills have been found to be related to a single overall factor that we call effortful control and define as the ability to inhibit a dominant response and perform a subdominant response, detect errors, and engage in planning (Rothbart & Rueda, 2005). Results of studies of young children's ability to resolve conflict in the Stroop, flanker, and spatial conflict tasks are consistent with parental reports of effortful self-control in their offspring (Rothbart & Rueda, 2005). These findings suggest that development of the neurological network underlying self-regulation and the ability of the child to regulate behavior in everyday life are related.

Other studies have shown that effortful control is related to the empathy that children show toward others, their ability to delay an action and to avoid such behaviors as lying or cheating when given the opportunity in laboratory studies (Rothbart & Rueda, 2005). We have also found evidence that high levels of effortful control and good ability to resolve conflict are related to fewer antisocial behaviors, such as truancy in adolescence (Ellis, Rothbart, & Posner, 2004). These findings tie the development of the brain areas underlying self-regulation to behaviors one might wish to foster in children and adults.

Genetic Influences on Individual Differences

Because the brain networks that underlie self-regulation are the same in all members of our species, genetics heavily influence their development. Individual genetic makeup is also implicated in the efficiency of a network, which also depends in part upon an individual's specific life experiences. The genes responsible for a portion of these individual differences in efficiency are also likely to be important in the common development of the brain network that supports self-regulation.

The anterior cingulate is one of a number of frontal brain areas whose neurons are modulated by the neurochemicals dopamine and serotonin. Thus, it's possible to determine whether some of the differences in the efficiency of self-regulation among individuals have a genetic basis (Posner, Rothbart, & Sheese, 2007). To find out whether they do, adults were genotyped for several important dopamine-related genes, and two genes were identified (*MAOA* and *DRD4*). When individuals with different forms (alleles) of these genes were compared, they differed in their effectiveness in resolving conflict as measured by their response time in dealing with incongruent- and congruent-flanker tasks. When scanned in the fMRI machine while resolving conflict between incongruent flankers, the two groups differed in activation of the anterior cingulate (Fan et al., 2003). A number of other dopamine and serotonin genes have recently been found to be specifically related to efficiency in resolving conflict (Posner, Rothbart, & Sheese, 2007).

Applications of Self-Regulation Research

Our increasing understanding of the brain mechanisms underlying self-regulation offers hope in treating those with brain injury or psychopathology involving deficits of self-regulation and in strengthening the regulatory abilities of typically developing children.

Damage to the anterior cingulate area can bring permanent or temporary changes that at their most dramatic represent a loss of all volitional activity, even when the person is alert and able to move the head and eyes to orient to strong environmental input. Less dramatic deficits due to lesions of this area can be seen in an inability to regulate the complex activities of daily life. For example, a stroke involving the anterior cingulate can change a well-controlled person into a reckless gambler who can no longer hold a job (Damasio, 1994). Lesions of this area can also produce the belief that an alien force is in control of a hand on one side of the body. Smaller lesions of this area, sometimes made deliberately in individuals with intractable pain, can produce minor or more transient deficits such as difficulty in resolving conflict.

Deficits in regulatory functions due to stroke, tumor, or other brain lesions can show improvements following training of cognitive functions such as attention. In addition, a number of psychopathologies whose cause is unknown—for example, schizophrenia and depression—also involve a loss of regulative abilities. In schizophrenia, the regulation deficit might cause cognitive problems such as the feeling of being controlled by an alien force, paranoia, or deficits of thought and of emotional control. In depression, which often consists of an inability to control negative thoughts and feelings, remediation can be either a form of training called cognitive-behavioral therapy or drugs that influence the utilization of the neurochemical serotonin. Both methods produce improvement in about half of the cases studied.

Brain scans before and after therapy suggest that cognitive-behavioral therapy works by restoring self-regulatory functions of the cerebral cortex and anterior cingulate, while the drugs work primarily upon subcortical areas that connect to the cingulate and that also show deficient activation during depression (Mayberg, 2003). As these findings illustrate, knowledge of brain networks can help guide successful remediation. In the future, we may be able to see how differences in genetic alleles are related to the success of different forms of therapy and thus develop remediation designed specifically for a person's genetic makeup.

Educational applications of our knowledge of the mechanisms of self-regulation are also possible (Posner & Rothbart, 2007). Exercises can teach children how to attend to incoming stimuli, and to select, remember, and resolve conflict between objects. Several studies have shown improved performance in brain areas related to self-regulation following training, as well as generalization to cognitive tasks remote from those trained. Some studies have involved children with known deficits in self-regulation, and others have been designed to assist preschool children during the time when the control mechanisms underlying self-regulation are developing. These efforts have resulted in the development of a number of exercises that have proven effective in improving regulatory functions. Although additional research is needed to tune these exercises to the specific difficulties of the individual child and to discover how long their effects last, some are available free on the Web at http://www.teach-the-brain.org/learn/index.htm.

Our studies of the cognitive and emotion networks underlying self-regulation are only one example of how applied neuroscience can improve the lives of children and adults. Other areas of application include understanding brain mechanisms related to language development and the acquisition of reading, arithmetic, and decision-making skills (Posner & Rothbart, 2007).

Suggested Further Reading

Posner, M.I. & Rothbart, M.K. (2007). *Educating the human brain*. Washington, DC: American Psychological Association.

Rothbart, M.K. (in press). Becoming who we are: Temperament, personality and development. New York: Guilford.

References

Berger, A., Tzur, G., & Posner, M.I. (2006). Infant babies detect arithmetic error. *Proceedings of the National Academy of Science USA, 103,* 12649–12553.

Bush, G., Luu, P., & Posner, M.I. (2000). Cognitive and emotional influences in the anterior cingulate cortex. *Trends in Cognitive Science, 4/6,* 215–222.

Damasio, A.R. (1994). *Descartes'error.* New York: Grosset/Putnam.

Ellis, E., Rothbart, M.K., & Posner, M.I. (2004). Individual differences in executive attention predict self-regulation and adolescent psychosocial behaviors. *Annals of the New York Academy of Science, 1031,* 337–340.

Fan, J., McCandliss, B.D., Sommer, T., Raz, M., & Posner, M.I. (2002). Testing the efficiency and independence of attentional networks. *Journal of Cognitive Neuroscience,* 3(14), 340–347.

Mayberg, H.S. (2003). Modulating dysfunctional limbic-cortical circuits in depression: Towards development of brain-based algorithms for diagnosis and optimized treatment. *British Medical Bulletin, 65,* 193–207.

Posner, M.I., & Raichle, M.E. (1994). *Images of mind.* New York: Scientific American Books.

Posner, M.I., & Rothbart, M.K. (2007). *Educating the human brain.* Washington, DC: American Psychological Association.

Posner, M.I., Rothbart, M.K., & Sheese, B.E. (2007). Attention genes. *Developmental Science, 10,* 24–29.

Rothbart, M.K., & Rueda, M.R. (2005). The development of effortful control. In U. Mayr, E. Awh, & S.W. Keele (Eds.), *Developing individuality in the human brain: A tribute to Michael I. Posner* (pp. 167–188). Washington, DC: American Psychological Association.

Sensation and Perception

Donald D. Hoffman
Human Vision as a Reality Engine

Jeremy M. Wolfe
Visual Search: Is It a Matter of Life and Death?

Human Vision as a Reality Engine

Donald D. Hoffman
University of California, Irvine

▶ *Please tell us about your current position and research interests.*
I am a professor of cognitive science at the University of California, Irvine. I also have appointments in the Departments of Philosophy and Computer Science. This might sound like an odd combination, but there is a simple reason: I want to understand how human vision works, hence the cognitive science. I am also interested in how our subjective perceptions are related to objective reality, hence the philosophy. Finally, I am interested in creating models of perception and reality that are precise enough to build working robotic-vision systems, hence the computer science.

▶ *What got you interested in studying vision?*
My first interest has been to understand conscious experiences, such as the experience of pain, the taste of mint, or the blue color of a clear sky. Do our conscious experiences arise from brain activities? If so, precisely how? If not, what is the relationship between conscious experiences and brain activities? Vision provides a concrete and fascinating arena to study these questions.

▶ *What has been the real-world impact of this work?*
It is natural for us to wonder what kind of creatures we are and what, if anything, makes us special in the universe. For me, the most exciting possible impact of the work on conscious visual experiences is that it might illuminate these perennial questions and help us better understand ourselves. As an added benefit, however, vision research can lead to practical applications such as automatic vision systems for driving, manufacturing, homeland security, medical image processing, and the visually impaired.

Vision feels easy. We simply open our eyes and look. Without apparent effort, we see a three-dimensional world packed with objects, colors, textures, and motions. This apparent ease leads naturally to the assumption that vision is a simple process, no more complex than taking pictures with a camera. But research in cognitive neuroscience reveals that roughly half of the brain's cortex, perhaps 50 billion neurons and 10 trillion synapses, are engaged when we simply open our eyes and look. Why should half of our most sophisticated computational power be engaged in vision? This is overkill if vision is, like a camera, just taking pictures. A digital camera needs nowhere near that much circuitry.

Why does vision engage all this computing power? Research in psychophysics and computational vision provides a remarkable answer. Your visual system is a reality engine: It creates all the depths, shapes, objects, colors, textures, and motions that you see. The term reality engine is borrowed from the field of virtual reality, where it refers to the powerful computers and sophisticated software used to generate the impression of immersion in a virtual world. In the case of human vision, enormous computing power is needed to create the visual worlds in which we find ourselves constantly immersed. That's why roughly half of your most sophisticated computing power is recruited for the job.

Admittedly, we don't feel as if we're constructing the visual world; it seems to always be there with us. We feel this way because our reality engine is so fast and effective that it creates what we see as fast as the eye can move. Thus, the very power and efficiency of the reality engine blocks our awareness of its existence. We can, however, find telltale signs of its operation if we know where to look.

For example, check out the two boxes in Figure 1. Are their gray tops the same shape, or are they different? They certainly look different. The one on the left looks long and narrow, the one on the right short and fat. Nevertheless, they are identical. You can verify this with a ruler, or by using tracing paper to copy the top of one box, and then placing it on the top of the other. You'll see that it fits perfectly. So why does it look to us like the tops have different shapes? The reality engine of vision is at work, creating impressions of shape and depth, using rules that normally work well. But in this figure, the normal operation of the reality engine constructs a visual reality that contradicts what we can measure.

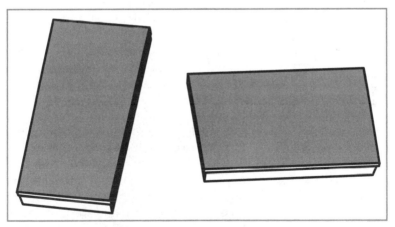

FIGURE 1 Identical box tops. The gray top of the box on the left has the same length and width as the gray top of the box on the right. Yet they look different. This unmasks an operation of our visual reality engine and shows that it can construct realities that contradict what we measure with a ruler. This figure was inspired by a similar demonstration with tables created by Roger Shepard (1990), which first appeared in Kubovy and Pomerantz (1981).

Another illustration of your reality engine at work is shown in Figure 2. When you view this figure, you see a ghostly cube floating in front of black disks. The white lines of the cube are sharp, and brighter than the background. But if you cover two adjacent black disks, you will see that no line extends between them. If you then uncover those two disks, you will again see a line between them. That line is entirely the creation of your reality engine.

FIGURE 2 The subjective Necker cube. The white edges of the cube are entirely constructed by your visual reality engine. So also are the cubes that you see. Drake Bradley and Heywood Petry (1977) created the first subjective Necker cube figure.

To understand what's happening, think of the reality engine as trying to create the most probable interpretation of the image. It notices the precise alignments of the white cutouts on adjacent black disks and decides that this alignment is probably not accidental but is due instead to white lines that occlude the disks. So it hallucinates these lines, making them a bit brighter than the background.

Once your reality engine has constructed the illusory lines between the black disks, it notices that these lines have a regular pattern, consistent with being the projection of a cube. It decides that this is probably no accident, concluding instead that a cube probably occludes the black disks. So it hallucinates the cube and makes it float in front of the disks.

If you watch the cube for a while, you might see it suddenly flip. Sometimes you see a cube with corner A in front and sometimes a cube with corner B in front. Call these *cube A* and *cube B*. Your reality engine decides that cube A and cube B are both likely interpretations of this image, and so it first constructs one, then the other, repeatedly in an infinite loop. But there are more cubes here. Think of the black disks as holes in a white sheet of paper. You look through these holes, and behind them see a white cube (it might take a little time to see it). Again, you sometimes see a cube with corner A in front and sometimes with corner B in front. So here are two more cubes that your reality engine constructs. Call them *cube A'* and *cube B'*.

Now comes a strange question: Which of the four cubes is there when you don't look? Cube A, or A'? Cube B, or B'? The answer must be that no cube is there when you don't look. After all, each cube you see looks three-dimensional, but the page on which Figure 2 appears is flat. Therefore, a three-dimensional cube is only there when you look; its existence depends on your reality engine (Hoffman, 2000).

One last observation. Notice that when you see the cubes in front of the disks, the edges have a ghostly quality, but when you see the cubes behind, the edges are no longer ghostly, but instead have a paradoxical quality of being invisible and yet substantial or solid. This quality of ghostliness versus solidity is also the creation of your reality engine.

Evolution and User Interfaces

Our reality engine constructs everything we see. So the question naturally arises: What is the relationship between our visual constructions and the world that we don't construct, the world that exists whether or not we exist?

This question has a clear answer in evolutionary theory: Our sensory systems are shaped by natural selection to allow *Homo sapiens* to survive long enough to reproduce within its niche. *Homo sapiens*, like, say, the cockroach, is a species whose sensory systems guide adaptive behavior within a particular niche. We don't expect the sensory systems of a cockroach, or a maggot, or a nematode to give detailed insight into the true nature of reality. Instead, we expect those systems to give simple signals, suited for a particular ecological niche, that help avoid predators and find mates. Similarly for *Homo sapiens* (Pinker, 1999).

Evolutionary theory leads us to think of our sensory systems as constituting a species-specific user interface. A user interface, like the Windows interface on your laptop, is useful because it does *not* resemble what it represents. For instance, a file icon on your computer screen might be red, rectangular, and in the upper left corner of the screen, but this doesn't mean that the file itself is red, rectangular, or in the upper left corner of the screen. The icon is there to guide behavior, not to resemble the file. The icon *hides* the complexity of the computer, all of its diodes and resistors and megabytes of software. That's what makes the user interface useful. And that's what makes the sensory systems of *Homo sapiens* useful. Our sensory systems don't resemble the complex reality that they represent, but instead present a greatly simplified set of icons that let us behave adaptively in our niche (Hoffman, 2000).

Medical Implications

If our visual system is a species-specific reality engine, then damage to the visual system should impair our ability to construct visual realities. The neurological literature provides many fascinating case histories of people struggling to live with such conditions.

For instance, activity in an area of cerebral cortex called the lateral fusiform gyrus is correlated with the perception of faces. If the fusiform face area, or FFA, is damaged, say, by a stroke, the patient may be normal in every respect except one: He or she may be unable to recognize faces by looking at them—even the faces of family members, old friends, or the patient's own face seen in a mirror (Bruce & Young, 1998). Patients can still recognize people by voice, indicating that the specifically visual ability to recognize faces is the impaired function. Many people with FFA damage can still recognize facial expressions. Activity in a different area of cerebral cortex in the posterior superior temporal sulcus (PSTS) is correlated with the perception of facial expression. A patient with damage to the PSTS but not the FFA can usually recognize facial identity but not facial expression. This condition leads to serious social difficulties because we are so dependent on the ability to quickly read facial expressions in our daily social interactions.

Damage to other visual areas of cerebral cortex is correlated with other visual deficits (Behrmann, 2001). Bilateral damage to visual area V8 is correlated with achromotopsia, an inability to see color, in which the world appears only in shades of gray. Some people with achromatopsia can no longer dream in color or imagine colors. Similarly, damage to visual area V5 is correlated with an inability to see motion, while area V1 damage is correlated with scotomas, regions of the visual field in which the patient is blind.

Because damage to specific areas of the visual cortex and particular behavioral deficits are so closely correlated, visual deficits can be invaluable in diagnosing neurological disorders. For instance, some people with undiagnosed Alzheimer disease (AD) first complain that they cannot see. Ophthalmological examination reveals that their eyes are fine, but further examination reveals that regions of visual cortex are probably damaged with the plaques and tangles of AD. Research is in progress to use visual deficits, and concomitant changes in brain activity as measured by electroencephalograms (EEGs) to diagnose AD before clinical symptoms appear, so that medical interventions can be introduced as early as possible (Sneddon et al., 2005).

Technological Implications

If the visual system is a sophisticated reality engine that constructs our visual worlds, then we should be able to study its operation, reverse engineer it, and build computer systems that mimic it. To reverse engineer a complex system means to study its structure and function to try to understand how it works, often with the goal of trying to build a new system that has the same capabilities. To reverse engineer human vision means to study it through psychophysical, neurophysiological, and brain imaging experiments to learn the secrets of its operation.

Indeed, this is proving possible. We now have computer vision systems, inspired by insights from biological visual systems, that take images streaming in from video cameras and construct depth, shapes, colors, motions, and objects (Shapiro & Stockman, 2001). These systems are advanced enough to autonomously drive cars on highways, using only computer vision to "see" the road.

Currently, the big open problem in computer vision is object recognition. It has proved remarkably difficult to recognize three-dimensional objects from arbitrary viewpoints, under arbitrary lighting, and with other objects obscuring them. The reason is that a single object can lead to dramatically different images as it is rotated, occluded, or presented under different lighting. A computer vision system must recognize that these widely different images are, in fact, images of precisely the same object. These technical difficulties make neuroscientists admire the speed and accuracy with which human vision solves this problem.

Efforts to reverse engineer visual object recognition, both in humans and other primates, has led to the surprising discovery that biological visual systems can recognize a three-dimensional object by using neural representations of just a few of its two-dimensional views. This insight has led to the discovery of theorems and algorithms for recognizing three-dimensional objects given only a few two-dimensional views. In this way, reverse engineering biological vision has provided key insights for solving a difficult technological challenge.

Computer vision systems are already in use in industry, the military, homeland security, and medical image processing. Once the problem of object recognition has been sufficiently resolved, we can expect computer vision systems to serve as prosthetic devices for the visually impaired, to be used widely in industry for flexible automated assembly, and, inevitably, to be used for smart bombs and other military applications.

Philosophical Implications

What is the relation between our perceptions and the world that exists independent of us? This question has puzzled philosophers at least since Plato and remains puzzling to this day. Advances in understanding human visual perception and the human visual system have helped to sharpen this question and to provide the basis for rigorous experiments that constrain our ideas. The question can now be posed as follows: What is the relationship between brain activity and conscious experience?

Vision researchers are now studying many neural correlates of consciousness. Detailed information about conscious visual experiences and their neural correlates may enable neuroscientists to fashion a scientifically rigorous theory (Blackmore, 2003). I have already mentioned the correlations between neural activity in V8 and conscious color experiences, neural activity in V5 and conscious motion experiences, and neural activity in the FFA and conscious recognition of faces. These and other similar correlations are now being studied in great detail using brain-imaging techniques such as EEG, functional magnetic resonance imaging, positron emission tomography, and magnetoencephalography.

This problem is fascinating in part because we do not yet have a single scientific theory that can explain how neural activity could cause, or be, conscious experiences. If you find this surprising, just consider what neural activity is: It is primarily various ions, such as sodium and potassium ions, passing through holes in neural membranes; it is various neurotransmitters, such as serotonin and dopamine, diffusing across synaptic clefts and binding to receptors. How can ions running through holes or neurotransmitters diffusing through clefts cause, or be, my conscious experience of the smell of garlic or the sound of a flute? Why shouldn't such neural activity, whether of single neurons or interacting systems of neurons, go on without any conscious experiences at all? These difficult and open questions currently engage many vision researchers.

SETI Implications

Are we alone in the universe, or might there be other intelligent beings on other planets? The Search for Extraterrestrial Intelligence (SETI) program has, for decades, been looking for evidence of extraterrestrial intelligence. Suppose that SETI succeeds. How will we communicate with the extraterrestrials? Should we use Greek? English? French? Given that humans have enough trouble understanding foreign human languages, extraterrestrials aren't likely to do any better. Perhaps, then, we can use the same strategy that many traffic signs use: Instead of presenting the information in a specific language, present it by means of images. All humans, despite their linguistic differences, understand such images; perhaps they will also be universally understood by sufficiently intelligent extraterrestrials. With this hope in mind, the *Pioneer 10* and *Voyager 1* and *2* spacecraft were sent into space with many images of life on Earth (Drake & Sobel, 1992).

But if vision is a species-specific user interface, shaped by the selection pressures of a particular ecological niche, it is unlikely that images will have the same interpretation for a civilization near the star Alpha Centauri as they have on Earth. Instead, our interfaces will probably differ, and considerable effort will be required to translate between them (Hoffman, 2007). The difficulty we have communicating with, say, dolphins, suggests how complicated such translation can be. If SETI does make contact, vision researchers may be at the forefront of efforts to establish reliable means of interstellar communication.

Conclusion

Vision is full of surprises. Its apparent ease hides its astonishing complexity and computational power. As we better understand vision, we better understand ourselves, our evolutionary history, and the nature of our conscious experiences. We learn to create automatic vision systems for driving, manufacturing, homeland security, medical image processing, and the visually impaired. Perhaps, too, we will learn to succeed at interstellar communication.

Suggested Further Reading

Hoffman, D.D. (2000). *Visual intelligence: How we create what we see*. New York: W. W. Norton.

Pinker, S. (1999). *How the mind works*. New York: W. W. Norton.

References

Behrmann, M. (2001). Disorders of visual behavior. In F. Boller & J. Grafman (Eds.), *Handbook of neuropsychology* (2nd ed.). Amsterdam: Elsevier Science.

Blackmore, S. (2003). *Consciousness: An introduction*. Oxford: Oxford University Press.

Bradley, D.R., & Petry, H.M. (1977). Organizational determinants of subjective contour: The subjective Necker cube. *American Journal of Psychology, 90*, 253–262.

Bruce, V., & Young, A. (1998). *In the eye of the beholder: The science of face perception*. Oxford: Oxford University Press.

Drake, F., & Sobel, D. (1992). *Is anyone out there? The scientific search for extraterrestrial intelligence.* New York: Delacorte Press.

Hoffman, D. D. (2007). Images as interstellar messages. In D. Vakoch (Ed.) *Between worlds: The art and science of interstellar message composition.* Cambridge, MA: MIT Press.

Kubovy, M., & Pomerantz, J. (1981). *Perceptual organization.* Hillsdale, NJ: Erlbaum.

Shapiro, L. G., & Stockman, G. C. (2001). *Computer vision.* New York: Prentice Hall.

Shepard, R.N. (1990). *Mind sights.* San Francisco: W.H. Freeman.

Sneddon, R., Shankle, W. R., Hara, J., Rodriquez, A., Hoffman, D.D., & Saha, U. (2005). EEG detection of early Alzheimer's disease using psychophysical tasks. *Clinical EEG Neuroscience, 36,* 141–150.

Visual Search: Is It a Matter of Life and Death?

Jeremy M. Wolfe

Brigham and Women's Hospital and Harvard Medical School

▶ *Please describe your current position and research interests.*

For a psychologist, I have a somewhat unusual position. I am a professor of ophthalmology at Harvard Medical School, and I run a lab that is part of the Department of Surgery at Brigham and Women's Hospital. I teach psychology classes at Massachusetts Institute of Technology and Harvard University. My lab is interested in problems in vision and visual attention.

▶ *What drew you to studying how the human brain copes with visual information, and particularly with the overload of information with which we're constantly confronted?*

I became interested in vision when I got a summer job in a vision lab at Bell Telephone Laboratories when I was in high school. I became interested in visual attention and visual search when I tried and failed to replicate a basic finding in the search literature. That was about 25 years ago, and stimulating questions keep presenting themselves and we keep trying to answer them.

▶ *What has been the real-world impact of this work?*

As I hope my essay makes clear, our lives involve hundreds of search tasks each day, and our civilization asks us to perform some very difficult artificial visual search tasks like finding signs of cancer in a mammogram or a threat in a piece of luggage. Our goal in my lab is to understand the basic mechanisms of search and the specific problems raised by artificial search tasks. We want to use that knowledge to improve performance on those search tasks that can really be a matter of life and death.

How do you find what you are looking for in a visual world filled with things that you are not looking for? This is the problem of visual search. Most of the time, it does not seem like much of a problem. I am sitting in my visually cluttered study. I look for my coffee mug and there it is to my right. I look for my cell phone and find it on my left. Of course, some searches are more difficult. If I want to locate my cat, I will need to get up and wander around the house, checking warm spots and assorted hiding places, but that isn't quite the problem of interest here because locating the cat starts from a position outside my field of view.

Why do we need to search at all? The answer is obvious enough in the case of the cat who is outside the field of view, but why do I need to search for that piece of paper that is just lying there, clearly visible in front of me? The answer is that the eye provides us with too much input for the brain to process. The brain has attentional mechanisms that allow it to restrict processing to some subset of the input. As one quick illustration of this point, try reading two texts at the same time. Even if the letters are big enough that you can resolve both at the same time, you can't read them both. You can let your attention jump back and forth between them but you are limited to one at a time.

My lab is devoted to understanding how humans search. Most of the time, we pursue this interest in experiments that use simple stimuli presented on the computer screen. Figure 1 is an example. We collect behavioral responses and use the patterns in the data to deduce the underlying processes. Our hope and assumption is that studies with simple stimuli tell us something about how human observers search in the real world of cats and coffee mugs. On a practical front, results from basic research can be used to improve performance on some of the critical artificial search tasks that our civilization has invented. The security guard checking your bag for weapons and the radiologist scanning a mammogram for cancer are performing very demanding visual search tasks. We would like to make their jobs a bit easier.

How Do We Search for a Target in an Array of Distracters?

Look at Figure 1. It's designed to illustrate the fact that a search through the current contents of the visual field can be a problem.

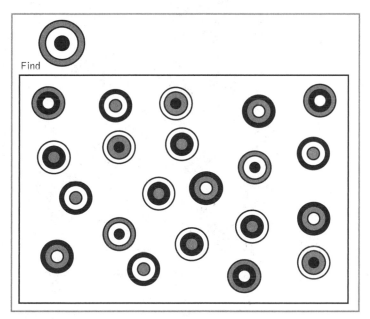

FIGURE 1 Finding the target item is difficult, even though it is visible when you first look at the image.

Your task is to find the item illustrated at the top of the figure: a black disk inside a white disk inside a gray disk. If you found it quickly, look for the other one—there are two. After completing the task, two facts should be introspectively obvious: All of the items are clearly visible, and you still need to search through them before you can find what you are looking for.

If we were to measure the time you needed to find the target item and if we made you search through hundreds of displays that have different numbers of items like this, we would discover that your reaction time would increase something like 30 to 60 milliseconds (1/1000 of a second) for each additional item in the display. Depending on how we model the search process, we could estimate the number of these items that you processed each second to be somewhere in the vicinity of 15 to 30. That is quite fast. But look at the world around you. How many "items" are there in your current field of view? Actually, that seemingly obvious question turns out to be a surprisingly hard to answer, but the number must be pretty large under most circumstances. Suppose the number was just 100. Finding something would take you several seconds. Imagine trying to do this while driving down the interstate at 65 miles an hour; this could be a disaster.

You must be doing something a bit cleverer than just searching at random through the set of all visible items. Figure 2 gives some insight into part of that cleverness.

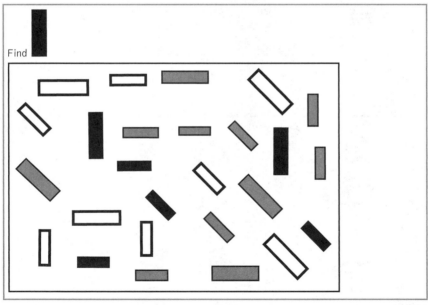

FIGURE 2 Finding the big, black, vertical targets is easy because you can use the basic features to guide attention toward likely target items.

The task is to find the big, black, vertical items. Why is this visual search so much easier than the first? The answer begins with Anne Treisman's influential feature-integration theory (Treisman & Gelade, 1980). She noted that search tasks in which the target is defined by a single basic feature like color, size, or orientation are trivially easy. If you are looking for a green item in a field of red items, you don't need to search. Treisman argued that for anything more complicated than a basic feature search, you would need to attend to the item in order to "bind" its features into a coherent object. Thus, in Figure 2, where items are defined by conjunctions of color, size, and orientation, you would need to attend to an item in order to determine if it has the right combination of black, vertical, and big.

Treisman distinguished between "preattentive" searches like green among red, in which all items could be processed at once, and attentive searches for targets that required binding. In these, attention would have to be directed to one item at a time. In our guided search model, we elaborated on Treisman's theory, adding the idea of guidance to explain why tasks like the one illustrated in Figure 2 are so easy (Wolfe, 1994, 2006; Wolfe, Cave, & Franzel, 1989). We agreed that you need attention to bind big, black, and vertical features into a big, black, vertical object, but we added the notion that preattentive features could be used to guide attention toward the items that might possibly be the target. In the Figure 2 example, guiding attention to items that are black would immediately eliminate most of the items. If you can guide to bigness, blackness, and verticalness, most of your work is done. Figure 1 is hard because guiding isn't possible. All the Figure 1 items have the same shape and the same colors, so you need to attend to one item after another until you stumble on the target.

In the real world, virtually all searches can be guided in some manner. If I am looking for that coffee mug, I can use color, size, and a few other basic attributes to eliminate most of the objects in my field of view as candidate mugs before directing my attention to the remaining mug-like blobs.

The set of guiding attributes seems to be limited to be between one and two dozen (Wolfe & Horowitz, 2004). These include properties like color, size, and orientation as illustrated in Figure 2, and a number of less obvious properties like a variety of depth cues. The field continues to debate some candidates for the status of guiding attribute. Faces are a good example. Some people think that you can guide attention to faces (Hershler & Hochstein, 2005), while others disagree (Vanrullen, 2006).

Most properties cannot guide attention in the way that color or orientation can. So, in Figure 3, you need to search for the two "chickens" among the strange collections of chicken parts (Wolfe & Bennett, 1997). Before attention

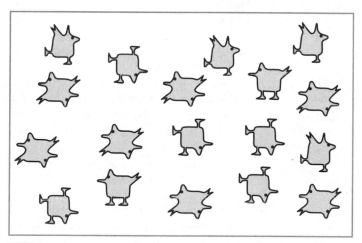

FIGURE 3 Even though the "chicken" targets are easily discriminated from the odd mutants, this cannot be done until attention binds the local features into a coherent object.

is deployed, these items are just an unbound collection of chicken-like features with all of the items roughly equivalent. Once attention arrives, telling a chicken from a mutant is easy.

Bottom-Up and Top-Down Guidance

We distinguish between two types of guidance: bottom-up and top-down. The differences can be illustrated with the help of Figure 4.

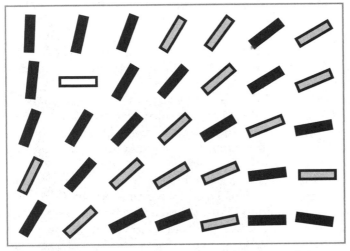

FIGURE 4 The white horizontal item attracts attention in a bottom-up manner. Other possible targets await top-down guidance.

If you look at Figure 4, the white horizontal bar in the upper left will quickly attract your attention. The differences between it and its neighbors make it salient in a *bottom-up*, stimulus-driven manner–no matter what you thought you were looking for. On the other hand, if you are asked to look for gray horizontal items, you will rapidly guide your attention to the item in the lower right. *Top-down*, user-driven guidance allows you to reconfigure your visual system so that you can look at the same display and yet direct your attention away from the most salient item and toward a new goal. You may even find that the gray horizontal item seems to gain in perceptual salience.

To summarize the basic guided search story: Faced with a stimulus and a desire to find something in that stimulus, a set of bottom-up processes direct your attention toward salient items in the scene, while a set of top-down processes guide your attention toward items possessing the attributes of the target. These various sources of information are summed together to form an overall guiding representation that we call the priority map. The contributions of each guiding factor are weighted depending on the task. So, in Figure 4, when you are looking for gray horizontals, the bottom-up weights would be set as close to zero as possible since the bottom-up guidance is actually misleadingly pointing you toward the white horizontal item. Every few milliseconds, attention is redirected to the currently most active spot in this priority map and the search proceeds until the target is found or the search is abandoned.

From the Lab to the Real World

Even if visual search is a vital part of normal visual function, how could study of this topic ever be considered a matter of life and death? Of course, the title of this essay is deliberately a bit melodramatic. Nevertheless, many search tasks—from finding your child on the playground to finding your din- ner—really are quite important. Moreover, our civilization has created a number of artificial search tasks that are, at once, very hard and very impor- tant. Figure 5 illustrates one of these tasks.

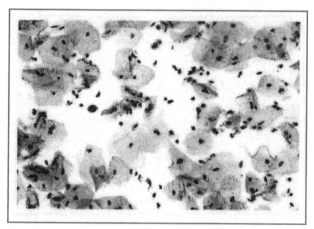

FIGURE 5 A small part of a cervical cancer screening specimen. Where is the target?

Figure 5 shows a small part of the collection of cells that a technician trained in cytotechnology would examine in a Pap test for cervical cancer. In this case, the target is the black item that is bigger than the other black spots, on the left near the horizontal midline. This artificial search task is difficult (Evered, 2005), and errors are potentially very serious—quite literally a mat- ter of life and death. Other tasks could have been used as examples: cancer screening tests like mammograms; X-ray scans of carry-on bags for threats like guns, bombs, or knives; aerial surveillance for survivors when a fishing boat sinks in thousands of square miles of ocean. These tasks are difficult on purely visual grounds. Cancerous cells do not pop out of displays the way that a green dot pops out of a field of red dots.

Bringing the Real World Back to the Lab

In our lab, we have become interested in another common feature of all of these tasks—the search for rare items. In most real-world searches, the target is frequently present. If my coffee cup or my cat were present in only a small fraction of the instances when I looked for them, I might learn not to bother to look. However, in screening for cancer or searching for threats to air safety, we want the searchers to keep searching, and we don't want them to miss the rare targets that do appear.

To study the effect of rarity on performance in visual search, we ran a simple experiment. Using a rough approximation of a baggage-search task, we asked observers to find tools in a display of other objects placed on a visually noisy background. Like the contents of an X-rayed carry-on, the display objects could overlap transparently, making the task a bit harder than the usual search task, although not as hard as the real baggage-screening task. Our observers were untrained, not professional screeners. We simply manipulated target prevalence. The target could appear on 50 percent or 1 percent of the trials.

This conceptually simple experiment poses a methodological challenge: If you want to know the percentage of targets that an observer misses, you need a reasonable number of target-present trials. Unfortunately, a reasonable number of target-present trials requires a quite unreasonable number of target-absent trials. At 1 percent target prevalence, to get a mere 20 target-present trials, we needed to mix those with 1,980 target-absent trials. This was a pretty boring experience for our observers.

The results are not boring. In this experiment, the 50 percent target-prevalence condition produced a rather standard 7 percent rate of misses. When prevalence was reduced to 1 percent, the miss error rate shot up to over 30 percent (Wolfe, Horowitz, & Kenner, 2005). To get a sense of this striking finding, imagine 20 images with targets present. If you embed those in a stack with 20 images that have no target, an observer in this experiment will miss 1 or 2. If you take the same 20 images and embed them in a series of 2,000 images, observers will now miss 6 or 7 of those 20. We were doing this in the lab with untrained observers, but generalized to the real world, this sort of "prevalence effect" could mean many more missed security threats or cancers.

Are observers just being careless? They do come to respond "no" more quickly, but there is more to this than simple carelessness, we discovered. We had two observers independently look at the same series of 1,000 bags, using 2 percent prevalence and stimuli that looked like real X-rays of real luggage. If the two observers were just making careless errors, they'd be unlikely to make the *same* careless errors. In fact, if you have observers making careless errors, having two observers is a good way to improve overall performance. If each observer misses 30 percent of the targets, both observers should miss only 30 percent times 30 percent, or 9 percent, of the targets. When we ran this experiment, however, we found that the combined error rate was only a little better than the individual error rates. You could predict the combined error rate quite well by looking at the error rate for the better of the two observers. If the better observer missed a target, the other observer probably missed it, too. Remember, the same observers would probably find that same target if it were part of a 50 percent prevalence condition (Wolfe et al., 2007).

What is going on here? In the language of signal detection theory, this is a criterion effect. As used here, the term criterion refers to an internal cut-off value above which you will say, "Yes, it is there," and below which you will say, "No, it isn't." When you aren't sure what you are seeing, your criterion depends on the specifics of the situation. For example, you catch a quick glance of someone in the supermarket. Was that the president of the United States? Was that your next-door neighbor? The visual stimulus would be the same in both cases, but you should set a very "conservative" criterion for the president decision. That is, you should require more evidence for the unlikely event that the president is in aisle 4 than for the more likely possibility that it is your neighbor.

We see this in the lab. When you are doing a hard task, you are going to make mistakes. Sometimes you will say "no" when the target is present (a miss error). Sometimes you will say "yes," mistakenly reporting a target when none is present (a false alarm). You will choose (quite unconsciously, perhaps) what kind of errors to favor. Our data show that when targets are very rare, people tend to move their criterion toward "no" responses. This is reasonable. If the target is very rare, you should demand a lot of evidence before you say that you see it. That is the president in aisle 4 case. The problem is that this "rational" approach is maladaptive if it is important to avoid miss errors.

The relative costs of different forms of errors also influence criterion, although some evidence suggests that prevalence is a stronger driver of criterion than cost (Maddox, 2002). Unfortunately, we don't know for sure how prevalence influences behavior at the airport or in medical screening. The studies haven't been done yet. We do know that visual search poses real problems in the real world. For example, in routine screening for breast cancer, if you find a tumor, you can go back to the image from 6 months or a year ago and ask if the tumor is "retrospectively visible" in the older image, now that you know where to look. Quite often the answer is "yes," meaning that, in principle, the cancer could have been detected earlier if the visual search had been successful (Nodine et al., 2001).

We still have a lot to learn about visual search and related questions of visual attention—some fascinating as basic science, others matters of life and death—as we try to help people with difficult and important search tasks to do those tasks more effectively.

Acknowledgements

This work was supported by the National Eye Institute, the National Institute of Mental Health, the Air Force Office of Scientific Research, and the Department of Homeland Security.

Suggested Further Reading

Wolfe, J. M., & Horowitz, T. S. (2004). What attributes guide the deployment of visual attention and how do they do it? *Nature Reviews Neuroscience, 5*(6), 495–501.

Wolfe, J. M., & Horowitz, T. S. (2007). Visual search. *Scholarpedia, 3*(7), 3325. www.scholarpedia.org/article/Visual_search.

References

Evered, A. (2005). What can cytologists learn from 25 years of investigations in visual search? *British Journal of Medical Science 62*(4), 182–192.

Hershler, O., & Hochstein, S. (2005). At first sight: A high-level pop out effect for faces. *Vision Research, 45*(13), 1707–1724.

Maddox, W. T. (2002). Toward a unified theory of decision criterion learning in perceptual categorization. *Journal of Experimental Analysis of Behavior, 78*(3), 567–595.

Nodine, C. F., Mello-Thoms, C., Weinstein, S. P., Kundel, H. L., Conant, E. F., Heller-Savoy, R. E., et al. (2001). Blinded review of retrospectively visible unreported breast cancers: An eye-position analysis. *Radiology, 221*(1), 122–129.

Treisman, A., & Gelade, G. (1980). A feature-integration theory of attention. *Cognitive Psychology, 12*, 97–136.

Vanrullen, R. (2006). On second glance: Still no high-level pop-out effect for faces. *Vision Research, 46*(18), 3017–3027

Wolfe, J. M. (1994). Guided Search 2.0: A revised model of visual search. *Psychonomic Bulletin and Review, 1*(2), 202–238.

Wolfe, J. M. (2006). Guided Search 4.0: Current progress with a model of visual search. In W. Gray (Ed.), *Integrated Models of Cognitive Systems*. New York: Oxford University Press.

Wolfe, J. M., & Bennett, S. C. (1997). Preattentive object files: Shapeless bundles of basic features. *Vision Research, 37*(1), 25–43.

Wolfe, J. M., Cave, K. R., & Franzel, S. L. (1989). Guided Search: An alternative to the Feature Integration model for visual search. *Journal of Experimental Psychology: Human Perception and Performance, 15*, 419–433.

Wolfe, J. M., & Horowitz, T. S. (2004). What attributes guide the deployment of visual attention and how do they do it? *Nature Reviews Neuroscience, 5*(6), 495–501.

Wolfe, J. M., Horowitz, T. S., & Kenner, N. M. (2005). Rare items often missed in visual searches. *Nature, 435*, 439–440.

Wolfe, J. M., Horowitz, T. S., VanWert, M. J., Kenner, N. M., Place, S. S., & Kibbi, N. (2007). Low target prevalence is a stubborn source of errors in visual search tasks. *Journal of Experimental Psychology: General, 136*(4), 623–638.

5

Learning

Elizabeth L. Bjork and Robert Bjork

Making Things Hard on Yourself, But in a Good Way: Creating Desirable Difficulties to Enhance Learning

Henry L. Roediger, III, Kathleen B. McDermott, and Mark A. McDaniel

Using Testing to Improve Learning and Memory

Making Things Hard on Yourself, But in a Good Way: Creating Desirable Difficulties to Enhance Learning

Elizabeth Ligon Bjork and Robert A. Bjork
University of California, Los Angeles

▶ *Please describe your current position and research interests.*
Elizabeth Ligon Bjork: I am Professor of Psychology and Immediate-Past Chair of the University of California, Los Angeles, Academic Senate. My research interests have included visual attention and developmental processes but now focus on practical and theoretical issues in human memory and learning, particularly the role that inhibitory processes play in an efficient memory system.

Robert A. Bjork: I am Distinguished Professor and Chair of Psychology at the University of California, Los Angeles. My research focuses on human learning and memory and on the implications of the science of learning for instruction and training.

▶ *How did you get interested in studying the facilitating effect of apparent impediments to learning?*
Elizabeth Bjork: My interests in optimizing learning were triggered by interactions with students lamenting during office hours how hard they had studied, only then to perform poorly on a just-given exam. This motivated me to examine why students' study activities were sometimes so ineffective.

Robert Bjork: My interests go back to my efforts—as a graduate student—to understand the relationship of forgetting and learning, especially why inducing forgetting often enhances subsequent learning. My interests in the application of "desirable difficulties" were fanned by my experiences teaching and coaching and from what I learned as Chair of the National Research Council Committee on Techniques for the Enhancement of Human Performance (1988–1994).

▶ *What has been the real-world impact of this work?*
Overall, the impact has been slight. There are multiple indications, however, that the impact of basic research findings on educational practices is increasing and that, in particular, optimizing instruction will require unintuitive innovations in how the conditions of instruction are structured.

As teachers—and learners—the two of us have had both a professional and personal interest in identifying the activities that make learning most effective and efficient. What we have discovered, broadly, across our careers in research, is that optimizing learning and instruction often requires going against one's intuitions, deviating from standard instructional practices, and managing one's own learning activities in new ways. Somewhat surprisingly, the trials and errors of everyday living and learning do not seem to result in the development of an accurate mental model of the self as learner or an appreciation of the activities that do and do not foster learning.

The basic problem learners confront is that we can easily be misled as to whether we are learning effectively and have or have not achieved a level of learning and comprehension that will support our subsequent access to information or skills we are trying to learn. We can be misled by our subjective impressions. Rereading a chapter a second time, for example, can provide a sense of familiarity or perceptual fluency that we interpret as understanding or comprehension, but may actually be a product of low-level perceptual priming. Similarly, information coming readily to mind can be interpreted as evidence of learning, but could instead be a product of cues that are present in the study situation, but that are unlikely to be present at a later time. We can also be misled by our current performance. Conditions of learning that make performance improve rapidly often fail to support long-term retention and transfer, whereas conditions that create challenges and slow the rate of apparent learning often optimize long-term retention and transfer.

Learning versus Performance

This apparent paradox is a new twist on an old and time-honored distinction in psychology—namely, the distinction between learning and performance. Performance is what we can observe and measure during instruction or training. Learning—that is, the more or less permanent change in knowledge or understanding that is the target of instruction—is something we must try to infer, and current performance can be a highly unreliable index of whether learning has occurred.

Learning Without Performance and Performance Without Learning

Decades ago, learning theorists were forced to distinguish between learning and performance because experiments revealed that considerable learning could happen across a period when no change was apparent in performance. In latent-learning experiments with animals, for example, periods of free exploration of a maze, during which the animal's behavior seemed aimless, were shown—once reward was introduced—to have produced considerable learning. Similarly, in research on motor skills, investigators found that learning continued across trials during which the build-up of fatigue suppressed performance.

More recently, a variety of experiments—some of which we summarize below—have demonstrated that the converse is true as well: Namely, substantial improvements in performance across practice or training sessions can occur without significant learning (as revealed after a delay or in another context). To the extent, therefore, that people interpret current performance as a valid measure of learning, they become susceptible to misassessing whether learning has or has not occurred.

Storage Strength Versus Retrieval Strength

At a theoretical level, we (Bjork & Bjork, 1992) distinguish between the storage strength and the retrieval strength of information or skills stored in memory. Storage strength reflects how entrenched or interassociated a memory representation is with related knowledge and skills, whereas retrieval strength reflects the current activation or accessibility of that representation and is heavily influenced by factors such as situational cues and recency of study or exposure. Importantly, we assume that current performance is entirely a function of current retrieval strength, but that storage strength acts to retard the loss (forgetting) and enhance the gain (relearning) of retrieval strength. The key idea for present purposes is that conditions that most rapidly increase retrieval strength differ from the conditions that maximize the gain of storage strength. In other words, if learners interpret current retrieval strength as storage strength, they become susceptible to preferring *poorer* conditions of learning to *better* conditions of learning.

Introducing Desirable Difficulties to Enhance Learning and Instruction

So what are these better conditions of learning that, while apparently creating difficulty, actually lead to more durable and flexible learning? Such desirable difficulties (Bjork, 1994) include varying the conditions of learning, rather than keeping them constant and predictable; interleaving instruction on separate topics, rather than grouping instruction by topic (called blocking); spacing, rather than massing, study sessions on a given topic; and using tests, rather than presentations, as study events.

Before proceeding further, we need to emphasize the importance of the word *desirable*. Many difficulties are undesirable during instruction and forever after. Desirable difficulties, versus the array of undesirable difficulties, are desirable because they trigger encoding and retrieval processes that support learning, comprehension, and remembering. If, however, the learner does not have the background knowledge or skills to respond to them successfully, they become undesirable difficulties.

Varying the Conditions of Practice

When instruction occurs under conditions that are constrained and predictable, learning tends to become contextualized. Material is easily retrieved in that context, but the learning does not support later performance if tested at a delay, in a different context, or both. In contrast, varying conditions of practice—even varying the environmental setting in which study sessions take place—can enhance recall on a later test. For example, studying the same material in two different rooms rather than twice in the same room leads to increased recall of that material (Smith, Glenberg, & Bjork, 1978)—an empirical result that flies in the face of the common how-to-study suggestion to find a quiet, convenient place and do all your studying there.

A study of children's learning provides a striking illustration of the benefits of varying conditions of practice. Eight-year-olds and 12-year-olds practiced throwing beanbags at a target on the floor with their vision occluded at the time of each throw. For each age group, half of the children did all their practicing throwing to a target at a fixed distance (for example, 3 feet for the 8-year-olds), while the other half threw to targets that were closer or farther away. After the learning sessions and a delay, all children were tested at the distance used in the fixed-practice condition for their age group (Kerr & Booth, 1978).

Common sense would suggest that the children who practiced at the tested distance would perform better than those who had never practiced at that distance, but the opposite was true for both age groups. The benefits of variation—perhaps learning something about adjusting the parameters of the motor program that corresponded to the throwing motion—outweighed any benefits of being tested at the practiced distance. Many other studies have shown that when testing after training takes place under novel conditions, the benefits of variation during learning are even larger.

Spacing Study or Practice Sessions

The effects of distributed practice on learning are complex. Although massing practice (for example, cramming for exams) supports short-term performance, spacing practice (for example, distributing presentations, study attempts, or training trials) supports long-term retention. The benefits of spacing on long-term retention, called the spacing effect, have been demonstrated for all manner of materials and tasks, types of learners (human and animal), and time scales; it is one of the most general and robust effects from across the entire history of experimental research on learning and memory.

Rather than describing any of the myriad studies that have demonstrated the benefits of spacing, we will simply stress the importance of incorporating spacing and avoiding massing in managing learning. Massing repeated-study activities is often not only convenient, but it can also seem logical from the standpoint of organizing one's learning of different topics, and it frequently results in rapid gains in apparent learning. Good test performance following an all-night cramming session is certainly rewarding, but little of what was recallable on the test will remain recallable over time. In contrast, a study schedule that spaces study sessions on a particular topic can produce *both* good exam performance *and* good long-term retention. Furthermore, because new learning depends on prior learning, spacing study sessions optimally can also enhance transfer of knowledge and provide a foundation for subsequent new learning.

Interleaving versus Blocking Instruction on Separate To-Be-Learned Tasks

Interleaving the practice of separate topics or tasks is an excellent way to introduce spacing and other learning dynamics. In a classic comparison of interleaving and blocking (Shea & Morgan, 1979), participants practiced three different movement patterns, each requiring the participants to knock down three of six hinged barriers rapidly on a pinball-like apparatus in a prescribed order. All participants received 18 trials on each pattern, but in the interleaved condition, practice on a given trial was randomly determined, whereas in the blocked condition, one pattern at a time was practiced.

As you probably suspect, participants given blocked practice improved more rapidly than those given interleaved/random practice. Thus, if the researchers had stopped their study at the end of training, blocking of practice would have seemed the superior learning procedure. But, instead, participants returned 10 days later and were retested under either blocked or interleaved/random conditions. Under interleaved/random testing conditions, participants who had practiced under interleaved conditions performed far better than did the blocked-practice participants, who appeared, when tested under a random schedule, to have learned virtually nothing. Under blocked testing conditions, performance was essentially the same for both groups, but the small difference still favored the interleaved group.

The skills literature includes many replications of the pattern that blocked practice *appears* optimal for learning, but interleaved practice actually results in superior long-term retention and transfer of skills, and research illustrates that learners—as well as instructors—are at risk of being fooled by that pattern. For example, when participants who had learned three different keystroke patterns were asked to predict their performance on a test the next day, those given interleaved practice predicted their performance quite closely, whereas those given blocked practice were markedly overconfident (Simon & Bjork, 2001). In effect, the blocked-practice group misinterpreted their good performance during practice as evidence of long-term learning, rather than a product of the local (that is, blocked) conditions. Said differently, they misinterpreted the retrieval strength of a given keystroke pattern as an index of its storage strength.

Other results illustrate that the benefits of interleaved practice extend beyond the learning of motor skills. For example, when participants were asked to learn formulas for calculating the volumes of different solids, such as a truncated cone, in either a blocked or interleaved manner, interleaved instruction enhanced performance on a delayed test. The size of the long-term advantage of interleaved practice was striking: 63 percent versus 20 percent of new problems worked correctly a week later (Rohrer & Taylor, 2007).

More recently and surprisingly, we have found that interleaving even enhances inductive learning (Kornell & Bjork, 2008). When participants were asked to learn the styles of each of 12 artists based on a sample of 6 paintings by each artist, interleaving a given artist's paintings among the paintings by other artists—versus presenting that artist's paintings one after another (blocking)—enhanced participants' later ability to identify the artist responsible for each of a series of new paintings. This result is surprising because blocking would seem to make it easier to note the commonalities that characterize a particular artist's style. Indeed, as illustrated in Figure 1, the majority of participants—when asked after the test whether interleaving or blocking had helped them learn an artist's style better—definitely had the impression that blocking had been more effective than interleaving, the op-

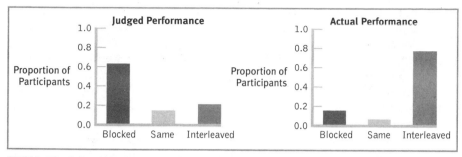

FIGURE 1 The left panel shows the proportion of participants who selected "blocked," "interleaved," or "the same" in response to the question: "Under which condition do you believe you learned better?" The right panel indicates the proportion of participants who actually performed better in the blocked or interleaved conditions or performed the same in the two conditions. (Kornell & Bjork, 2008)

posite of their actual learning. Blocking may indeed have facilitated noticing commonalities, but the final test required distinguishing among the artists, and interleaving may have fostered learning the differences as well as similarities among the styles of different artists.

Why might interleaving enhance long-term retention and transfer? One theory suggests that having to resolve the interference among the different things under study forces learners to notice similarities and differences among them, resulting in the encoding of higher-order representations, which then foster both retention and transfer. Another explanation suggests that interleaving forces learners to reload memories: If required to do A, then B, then C, and then A again, for example, the memory for how to do A must be reloaded a second time, whereas doing A and then A again does not involve the same kind of reloading. Such repeated reloadings are presumed to foster learning and transfer to the reloading that will be required when that knowledge or skill is needed at a later time.

From the standpoint of our theoretical framework (Bjork & Bjork, 1992), learning from reloading is an instance of a broader dynamic in human memory: Namely, that forgetting (losing retrieval strength) creates the opportunity for increasing the storage strength of to-be-learned information or skills. Said differently, when some skill or knowledge is maximally accessible from memory, little or no learning results from additional instruction or practice.

Generation Effects and Using Tests (Rather Than Presentations) as Learning Events

An effect that rivals the spacing effect for its generality and its significance for instruction and learning is the generation effect, which refers to the long-term benefit of generating an answer, solution, or procedure versus being presented that answer, solution, or procedure. Basically, any time that you, as a learner, look up an answer or have somebody tell or show you something that you could, drawing on current cues and your past knowledge, generate instead, you rob yourself of a powerful learning opportunity. Retrieval, in effect, is a powerful "memory modifier" (Bjork, 1975).

Closely related to the generation effect are the benefits that accompany retrieving information studied earlier. Much laboratory research (for example, Landauer & Bjork, 1978; Carrier & Pashler, 1992) has demonstrated the power of tests as learning events, and, in fact, a test or retrieval attempt, even when no corrective feedback is given, can be considerably more effective in the long term than reading material over and over. The reason why rereading is such a typical mode of studying derives, we believe, from a faulty model of how we learn and remember: We tend to think of our memories as working much like an audio/video recorder, so if we read and reread or take verbatim notes, the information will eventually write itself on our memories. Nothing, however, could be further from the way we actually learn and remember.

Unfortunately, the effectiveness of tests as learning events remains largely underappreciated, in part because testing is typically viewed as a vehicle of assessment, not a vehicle of learning. As Henry L. Roediger, Kathleen B. McDermott, and Mark A. McDaniel describe in their essay in this chapter, however, recent research using more educationally realistic materials and retention intervals has clearly demonstrated the pedagogical benefits of tests (for example, Roediger & Karpicke, 2006). Similar to the pattern with variation, spacing, and interleaving, repeated study opportunities appear, in the short term, to be more effective than repeated testing, but testing produces better recall in the long term.

Two other pedagogical benefits of tests must be mentioned: First, tests have metacognitive benefits in terms of indentifying whether information has or has not been understood and/or learned. A student's ability, for example, when going back over a chapter in a textbook, to judge whether information will be recallable on an upcoming examination is severely limited, whereas attempting to answer a fellow student's questions on the chapter can identify what has and has not been learned.

The second, related benefit is that tests can potentiate the effectiveness of subsequent study opportunities even under conditions that insure learners will be incorrect on the test (Kornell, Hays, & Bjork, 2009). Again, the basic message is that we need to spend less time restudying and more time testing ourselves.

Concluding Comments

For those of you who are students, we hope we have convinced you to take a more active role in your learning by introducing desirable difficulties into your own study activities. Above all, try to rid yourself of the idea that memory works like a tape or video recorder and that re-exposing yourself to the same material over and over again will somehow write it onto your memory. Rather, assume that learning requires an active process of interpretation—that is, mapping new things we are trying to learn onto what we already know. (There's a lesson here for those of you who are teachers—or parents—as well: Consider how you might introduce desirable difficulties into the teaching of your students or children.)

Be aware, too, when rereading a chapter or your notes, that prior exposures create a sense of familiarity that can easily be confused with understanding. And perhaps most importantly, keep in mind that retrieval—much more than restudying—acts to modify your memory by making the information you practice retrieving more likely to be recallable again in the future and in different contexts. In short, try to spend less time on the input side and more time on the output side, such as summarizing what you have read from memory or getting together with friends and asking each other questions. Any activities that involve testing yourself—that is, activities that require you to retrieve or generate information, rather than just representing information to yourself—will make your learning both more durable and flexible.

Finally, we cannot overstate the importance of learning how to manage your own learning activities. In a world that is ever more complex and rapidly changing, and in which learning on one's own is becoming ever more important, learning how to learn is the ultimate survival tool.

Suggested Further Reading

Bjork, R. A., & Bjork, E. L. (2006). Optimizing treatment and instruction: Implications of a new theory of disuse. In L-G. Nilsson and N. Ohta (Eds.), *Memory and society: Psychological perspectives* (pp. 109–133). Hove, East Sussex, England, and New York: Psychology Press.

Bjork, R. A. (1999). Assessing our own competence: Heuristics and illusions. In D. Gopher and A. Koriat (Eds.), *Attention and performance XVII: Cognitive regulation of performance: Interaction of theory and application* (pp. 435–459). Cambridge, MA: MIT Press.

References

Bjork, R. A. (1975). Retrieval as a memory modifier. In R. Solso (Ed.), *Information processing and cognition: The Loyola Symposium*, pp. 123–144. Hillsdale, NJ: Erlbaum.

Bjork, R. A. (1994). Memory and metamemory considerations in the training of human beings. In J. Metcalfe and A. Shimamura (Eds.), *Metacognition: Knowing about knowing* (pp. 185–205). Cambridge, MA: MIT Press.

Bjork, R. A., & Bjork, E. L. (1992). A new theory of disuse and an old theory of stimulus fluctuation. In A. Healy, S. Kosslyn, & R. Shiffrin (Eds.), *From learning processes to cognitive processes: Essays in honor of William K. Estes* (Vol. 2, pp. 35–67). Hillsdale, NJ: Erlbaum.

Carrier, M., & Pashler, H. (1992). The influence of retrieval on retention. *Memory & Cognition, 20,* 633–642.

Kerr, R., & Booth, B. (1978). Specific and varied practice of a motor skill. *Perceptual and Motor Skills, 46,* 395–401.

Kornell, N., & Bjork, R. A. (2008). Learning concepts and categories: Is spacing the "enemy of induction"? *Psychological Science, 19,* 585–592.

Kornell, N., Hays, M. J., & Bjork, R. A. (2009). Unsuccessful retrieval attempts enhance subsequent learning. *Journal of Experimental Psychology: Learning, Memory, and Cognition, 35,* 989–998.

Landauer, T. K., & Bjork, R. A. (1978). Optimum rehearsal patterns and name learning. In M. M. Gruneberg, P. E. Morris, & R. N. Sykes (Eds.), *Practical aspects of memory* (pp. 625–632). London: Academic Press.

Roediger, H.L., & Karpicke, J.D. (2006). Test-enhanced learning: Taking memory tests improves long-term retention. *Psychological Science, 17,* 249–255.

Rohrer, D., & Taylor, K. (2007). The shuffling of mathematics practice problems improves learning. *Instructional Science, 35,* 481–498.

Shea, J.B., & Morgan, R.L. (1979). Contextual interference effects on the acquisition, retention, and transfer of a motor skill. *Journal of Experimental Psychology: Human Learning and Memory, 5,* 179–187.

Simon, D., & Bjork, R. A. (2001). Metacognition in motor learning. *Journal of Experimental Psychology: Learning, Memory, and Cognition, 27,* 907–912.

Smith, S. M., Glenberg, A. M., & Bjork, R. A. (1978). Environmental context and human memory. *Memory & Cognition, 6,* 342–353.

Using Testing to Improve Learning and Memory
Henry L. Roediger, III, Kathleen B. McDermott, and Mark A. McDaniel
Washington University in St. Louis

▶ *Please describe your current position and research interests.*

Henry L. Roediger, III: I am the James S. McDonnell Professor in the Department of Psychology, Washington University in St. Louis. All three of us are interested in educational applications of memory research. In addition, I study issues related to arousal of illusory or false memories and implicit (or automatic) uses of memory.

Mark A. McDaniel: I am Professor of Psychology, Washington University in St. Louis. In addition to my work on educational applications of memory research, my research focuses on prospective memory (remembering to do things in the future) as well as aging and memory.

Kathleen B. McDermott: I am Associate Professor of Psychology, Washington University in St. Louis. In addition to our educational applications work, I study illusory memories, the neuroimaging of memory using functional magnetic resonance imaging (fMRI), and episodic future thought (how people use memory to think about possible future events).

▶ *How did you get interested in how testing could be used to enhance learning?*

All three of us had been involved in basic laboratory research on the effects of testing memory. These effects are often powerful and many studies showed that successful retrieval during testing has a greater impact on long-term retention than does repeated studying. A natural next step was to ask if we could improve students' performance in the classroom from our program of test-enhanced learning. Of course, we also encourage students to use self-testing as a study strategy to promote good retention.

▶ *What has been the real-world impact of this work?*

Our work has encouraged teachers at every level from elementary school to college and medical school to begin using more frequent testing in their courses and to tell their students about self-testing as a study strategy. However, we hope to reach a wider audience as our research program matures and we can reach an increasing number of people.

How do you prepare for a test? If you are like most students, rereading your textbook—accompanied by underlining or highlighting—is your preferred study strategy. Perhaps you underline or highlight important points the first time you read a chapter, and maybe you reread critical parts that you marked earlier. Likely you reread your class notes, too. If these study strategies seem familiar, they are not unreasonable. Repetition often aids memory. But, unfortunately, the strategies are not particularly effective. In fact, research shows that rereading has less influence on later memory than you might expect. In some studies, rereading was *no more effective* in improving learning than a single, initial reading (Callender & McDaniel, 2009).

Research by cognitive and educational psychologists has shown that effective study strategies exist, although most require more effort than simple rereading. Relating new information to what we already know, a strategy called elaboration, can make the material meaningful and, therefore, memorable. Similarly, when we outline or take notes, we recode the information—putting it in our own words—and much research shows that such active generation improves retention. Converting verbal information into vivid mental images can also improve learning. Spacing study sessions rather than massing them together also aids long-term retention. Research evidence strongly supports the effectiveness of these and many other active inquiry strategies in mastering information (McDaniel & Callendar, 2008).

Research in our laboratories at Washington University in St. Louis has led us to advocate an additional strategy, which we call test-enhanced learning. As you read text material, make up questions (or use the ones supplied at the end of the chapter) and then later test yourself. If you can retrieve the information from memory, great; having retrieved it once, you will remember it even better. If you can't retrieve the answer, study the material again and retest yourself until you're sure you know it. But even if you are able to retrieve the answer once, don't stop. Test yourself repeatedly and keep retrieving answers. Repeated retrieval is the key to long-term retention (Karpicke & Roediger, 2007).

Our advice regarding test-enhanced learning represents the bottom line of this essay. In the next few pages, we'll describe some evidence that supports our advice (McDaniel, Roediger, & McDermott, 2007; Roediger & Karpicke, 2006a, b).

Test-Enhanced Learning

Most students and teachers think of tests as assessment devices, designed to measure what students have learned and to provide a basis for assigning grades. In many college courses, especially large introductory courses, tests are infrequent, occurring perhaps two or three times a semester. Assessment is a perfectly valid reason for testing, but, as we have said, it can also improve learning.

Consider the powerful testing effect we recently demonstrated in an experiment comparing three groups who were asked to use different methods to study brief prose passages such as what you might encounter in a textbook. All participants read the passage once. Then one group (SSSS) studied the passage three more times; a second group (SSST) studied the passage two more times and then took one test; a third group (STTT) took tests on the passage three successive times after reading it once. When tested, participants simply recalled as much as they could, but because the tests were relatively immediate and the passages were reasonably short, they were able to recall about 70 percent of the information. Importantly, no feedback was given on test results (Roediger & Karpicke, 2006b).

Then participants took a break. For some participants, the break lasted only 5 minutes; others were asked to come back to the laboratory after a week. How did the different study conditions affect later recall? As you can see in Figure 1, when tested after 5 minutes, the more students had studied, the better they did—evidence that cramming just before the exam can actually work! However, after 1 week, the outcome was completely reversed. Now students who had studied only once but recalled the material three times did best; those who had studied it three times and were tested once were next best; and those who had studied material the most but were never tested performed worst. The clear implication is that for long-term retention—the kind educators hope to foster and students seek—repeated retrieval of material is better than reading it over and over.

The finding that the act of taking a test can enhance learning may seem surprising, but convincing supporting evidence has been reported in many different experiments over the years (see Roediger & Karpicke, 2006a, for a review of the literature). In fact, you can probably find confirmation in your own elementary school experience. Think back: What strategies were suggested for learning multiplication tables, foreign language vocabulary, or other systems of material? You probably used some type of flash card with the problem or word visible and the answer hidden. Did you practice over and over until the information was so well learned that answers would immediately spring to mind? Such self-testing can be adopted for almost any type of material and can create effective means for learning large amounts of information and retaining it for long periods of time.

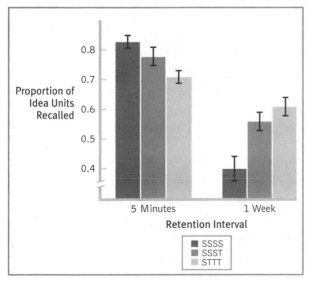

FIGURE 1 Proportion of ideas recalled after 5 minutes and after 1 week as a function of three experimental conditions. The data on the left side show recall on the final test given after 5 minutes; the data on the right, results after 1 week. (Roediger & Karpicke, 2006b)

The Importance of Feedback

Participants in the test-enhanced learning experiment did not receive feedback after taking the test. As we noted, however, the first tests were given under conditions in which memory performance was reasonably good. Thus, we wondered whether the testing effect would occur under conditions where memory performance is mediocre or poor. Interestingly, the answer is *no*, or at least *not always*. If students are given a test on a large amount of material or if they are given a test long after the material has been studied, the testing effect disappears (Kang, McDermott, & Roediger, 2007). In fact, if performance on the test is very poor, the test offers no benefit at all.

Suppose a test, given under conditions of poor recall, is followed by feedback (that is, correct answers). How will performance on a retest compare with a condition in which untested participants simply read correct answers in advance? To answer that question, we asked students to read four brief articles about topics in psychology. Each article had a different follow-up: a multiple-choice test, a short-answer test, a reading task involving the material that was tested in other conditions, or no activity (the control condition). The design of the study is shown in Figure 2. Because they were unaware there would be follow-up, all participants were presumed to have studied the articles in the same way (Kang et al., 2007, Experiment 2). To further account for unexpected influences, information in the questions was carefully controlled. For example, one short-answer question was, "What is hostile media bias?" The multiple-choice question was the same, but four possible answers were provided. The reread-condition statement was, "Hostile media bias refers to the phenomenon in which people on both sides of a controversy perceive the media as being hostile to their group." Students who took the short-answer or multiple-choice test received feedback that consisted of statements like those presented in the reread condition. Students in the reread condition read statements for a third time to equalize exposure to

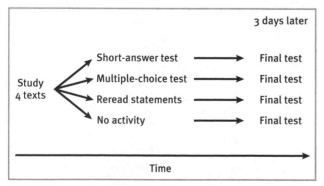

FIGURE 2 The design of the Kang, McDermott, and Roediger (2007) experiment. Students studied a passage and then either took a short-answer test, took a multiple-choice test, reread certain facts, or had no activity related to the passage. They took a final test 3 days later.

the material. All participants took a final short-answer test (sort of like a final exam) 3 days later.

As you can see in Figure 3, a short-answer test resulted in the best performance on the final test, with the multiple-choice test next best, although the difference between simply reading statements and taking a multiple-choice test was not very great. Not surprisingly, the no-review condition resulted in the worst performance. However, the relatively good performance in the rereading condition may reflect a flaw in the comparison condition: Participants read only statements that would later appear on the test—as if, for example, they had gotten hold of a copy of the final exam. Nevertheless, after a delay, testing still led to better performance than rereading, just as it had before. Performance on the final test was better in the short-answer test-with-feedback condition than in the multiple-choice test-with-feedback condition, perhaps because of the extra effort involved in generating answers.

You may be thinking, "But wait! Maybe if a multiple-choice test had been the final test, then taking a prior multiple-choice test would have produced better performance than taking a short-answer test." We thought of that too, and so we included in our experiment conditions in which multiple-choice items made up the final test. We found that an intervening short-answer test still produced the best performance (Kang et al., 2007). The greater retrieval effort required to produce information on a short-answer test (relative to recognizing it on a multiple-choice test) probably confers the greater benefit.

In other studies, we showed that delaying feedback a bit after a question is more effective than giving it immediately (Butler, Karpicke, & Roediger, 2008). Most teachers who provide feedback probably do this anyway.

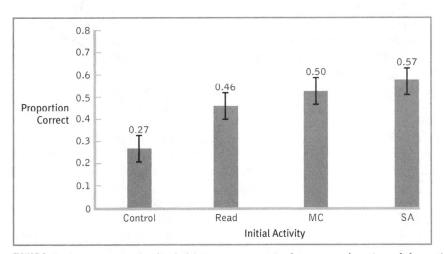

FIGURE 3 Performance on the final short-answer test is shown as a function of the activity that participants performed after reading. The immediate short-answer test with feedback produced the best performance on the final test. Data are from Kang, McDermott, and Roediger (2007).

Quizzing can also improve retention of related but untested information (Chan, McDermott, & Roediger, 2006). If verified, this finding has important implications for learning: Because only a small amount of material can be quizzed, a large part of the content of college courses is not tested. The possibility that self-testing might aid in the retention of material that instructors don't get around to quizzing is a comforting notion.

Does Testing Work in the Classroom?

You may be wondering whether our laboratory research evidence has real-world relevance. After all, college students study for varying amounts of time and in different ways, and the time between classroom quizzes and a final test are much longer than they are in typical lab studies. We wondered about that, too. And the answer is *yes*, at least in the first studies that have asked this question.

A Web-based course on brain and behavior at the University of New Mexico was the site of one of these experiments (McDaniel et al., 2007). Students in the course, who were assumed to have completed 40-page weekly reading assignments, were assigned to the now-familiar four conditions: short-answer quizzes, multiple-choice quizzes, the opportunity to reread, and no intervention at all (control condition). Because this was a real class, of course, some students may have read the assignment multiple times, some once, and some not at all. Feedback was given after the quizzes and again for the third (read facts) condition in which students read the facts a second time to equate for exposure.

After three assignments had been completed, students took a multiple-choice unit test. The content was the same but the wording of the questions was changed, thus requiring different answers. For example, in the multiple-choice quiz, students were asked, "All preganglionic axons, whether sympathetic or parasympathetic, release _____ as a neurotransmitter." (The correct answer is acetylcholine.) On the unit exam, the question was "All _____ axons, whether sympathetic or parasympathetic, release acetylcholine as a neurotransmitter." Thus, students could not memorize answers from the quiz, but had to know the whole fact. Students in the two groups that had been quizzed did better on the unit exams (54 percent correct) than those in the other two groups (46 percent correct). Again, the short-answer format offered a better opportunity for retention than did the multiple-choice format, with the latter format leading to only slightly better retention than rereading, and rereading proving superior to no re-exposure at all. In short, the results of the classroom study agree remarkably well with those of the laboratory study, as well as with other laboratory results (see, for example, Butler & Roediger, 2007). Keep in mind that the lab experiment used short-answer items as the final test, whereas the classroom experiment used multiple-choice questions. We find it reassuring that the same pattern of results holds with both types of test.

In current research in three middle-school classrooms, we have also found strong testing effects. Students in social studies, for example, achieved scores about 10 points higher on material on which they had been quizzed than on material that was not quizzed (Roediger et al., 2007). Quizzing helped raise grades a letter, from B- to A- levels.

Practical Implications for How to Study

One of us (KBM) teaches an undergraduate course on human memory, which meets twice a week for an hour and a half. As in most classes, readings are assigned for that day, and the lecture builds on and supplements the readings. However, unlike most classes, the last 5 to 10 minutes of the class are devoted to a quiz, with questions drawn from everything assigned as a reading for that day and from the lecture. Students also take three regular tests and a final exam. The news about the quiz schedule always leads a few faint-hearted students to drop the course. However, by the end of the semester, students' reactions are mostly quite positive.

Of course, as a student, you are in no position to tell the instructor how many tests to give, and it would take an unusually brave student to even broach the idea of an instructor giving more tests. How can you use the information we have provided to craft more effective study strategies for yourself? In providing advice, we draw on research not discussed in this essay (see McDaniel & Callender, 2008, for a summary) to provide advice on how to read your textbook and get the most from it, how to best use lectures and lecture notes, and how to review prior to tests.

Reading a textbook may seem obvious and easy, but effective reading requires a strategy sometimes called the PQ4R technique: *Preview, Question, Read, Reflect, Recite, Review.*

- *Preview.* Skim through the chapter, looking at the headings and the figures to see what topics will be covered. If there are summaries, read them first to see where you will be heading. Also, see if there is a set of key terms and review questions at the end of the chapter, and possibly other study aids.

- *Question, Read.* If there were no key terms and no questions, make them up as you go along. List the important terms and write the definitions.

- *Reflect.* Read with an inquiring mind: Try to convert headings into questions that will be answered. So, if one heading is "Classical conditioning" ask yourself, "What is classical conditioning?" and your reading will answer that question. Jot down these questions to help you with later study and review. Some students find it worthwhile to outline chapters as they are reading, which forces them to think hard about the relationship among sections of a chapter and produce it in their own words.

- *Recite, Review.* Reading carefully takes longer than simply blasting through the chapter with a highlighter, but studies show that students remember the material much better when they have carefully considered it this way. At the end of the chapter, review the key terms (either provided in the book or collected by you). Look up and restudy any terms about which you are shaky. If you can't remember it just after you have read it, what chance will you have on a test later? Similarly, review the study questions and try to answer them. Again, review (or give yourself feedback) on questions you cannot answer.

Paying careful attention and taking good notes in class is an art that some students master and others do not. We suggest regular class attendance, focused listening, copious note taking, and careful attention to the instructor's suggestions. These steps may seem obvious, but, surprisingly, many students view them as optional. After a class, read over your notes carefully. You were writing fast, at least some of the time, so you should go over the notes while the lecture is still fresh in your mind and flesh them out. Or, if you were taking notes on your laptop, you may need to edit them to extract key points.

Treat your notes the same way that you read the text: Cull out key terms and think of possible review questions. What the teacher covers in class is often what she or he considers most important and is therefore likely to include on the test. For some parts of the lecture that you might have found confusing, consult your notes, the Internet, or your instructor during office hours.

If you have thoughtfully studied your text and class notes, preparing for exams should be relatively easy. But, as should be clear by now, repeatedly rereading your text and notes is not a particularly effective strategy. Pre-exam time is the moment to put into practice our test-enhanced learning method. Test yourself on key terms and definitions. Examine the review questions in the book or the ones you created. If you are unsure of the meaning of a term or can't answer a question, review the book, your lecture notes, or both. Keep questioning yourself until you have the information down. By testing yourself, you can help gauge whether or not you know the material.

Repeated rereading can make information seem quite familiar without making it easy to retrieve when you need it—on the test. Repeated retrieval is the key to long-term retention (Karpicke & Roediger, 2007). So, even if you think you know the answers to questions, if you keep practicing retrieving them at spaced intervals, you will remember them better over the long term. Self-testing not only aids learning, but it also lets you know what you do not know and where you need to focus your efforts.

Conclusion

Repeated retrieval makes information more likely to be accessible in the future. Testing in the classroom accomplishes this goal, but so does studying by self-test. As William James wrote (1890, p. 646), "A curious peculiarity of our memory is that things are impressed better by active than by passive repetition. I mean that in learning (by heart, for example), when we almost know the piece, it pays better to wait and recollect by an effort from within, than to look at the book again. If we recover the words in the former way, we shall probably know them the next time; if in the latter way, we shall very likely need the book once more."

Acknowledgements

The research reported here was supported by a James S. McDonnell Foundation 21st Century Science Initiative in Bridging Brain, Mind and Behavior/Collaborative Award and by the Institute of Education Sciences, U.S. Department of Education, through Grant #305H060080 to Washington University in St. Louis. The opinions expressed are those of the authors and do not represent views of the Institute or the U.S. Department of Education.

Suggested Further Reading

McDaniel, M. A., & Callender, A. A. (2008). Cognition, memory, and education. In J. H. Byrne (Series Ed.) & H. L. Roediger (Vol. Ed.), *Learning and memory: A comprehensive reference: Vol. 2. Cognitive psychology of memory* (pp. 819–843). Oxford: Elsevier.

McDaniel, M. A., Roediger, H. L., & McDermott, K. B. (2007). Generalizing test-enhanced learning from the laboratory to the classroom. *Psychonomic Bulletin & Review, 14,* 200–206.

References

Butler, A. C., & Roediger, H. L. (2007). Testing improves long-term retention in a simulated classroom setting. *European Journal of Cognitive Psychology, 19,* 514–527.

Butler, A. C., Karpicke, J. D., & Roediger, H. L. (2008). The effect of type and timing of feedback on learning from multiple-choice tests. *Journal of Experimental Psychology: Applied, 13,* 273–281.

Callender A. A., & McDaniel M. A. (2009). The limited benefits of rereading educational texts. *Contemporary Educational Psychology, 34,* 30–41.

Chan, C. K., McDermott, K. B., & Roediger, H. L. (2006). Retrieval induced facilitation: Initially nontested material can benefit from prior testing. *Journal of Experimental Psychology: General, 135,* 533–571.

James, W. (1890). *The principles of psychology.* New York: Holt.

Kang, S., McDermott, K. B., & Roediger, H. L. (2007). Test format and corrective feedback modulate the effect of testing on memory retention. *European Journal of Cognitive Psychology, 19,* 528–558.

Karpicke, J. D., & Roediger, H. L. (2007). Repeated retrieval during learning is the key to long-term retention. *Journal of Memory and Language, 57,* 151–162.

McDaniel, M. A., Anderson, J. L., Derbish, M. H., & Morrisette, N. (2007). Testing the testing effect in the classroom. *European Journal of Cognitive Psychology, 19,* 494–513.

McDaniel, M. A., & Callender, A. A. (2008). Cognition, memory, and education. In J. H. Byrne (Series Ed.) & H. L. Roediger (Vol. Ed.), *Learning and memory: A comprehensive reference: Vol. 2. Cognitive psychology of memory* (pp. 819–843). Oxford: Elsevier.

McDaniel, M. A., Roediger, H. L., & McDermott, K. B. (2007). Generalizing test-enhanced learning from the laboratory to the classroom. *Psychonomic Bulletin & Review, 14,* 200–206.

Roediger, H. L., & Karpicke, J. D. (2006a). The power of testing memory: Basic research and implications for educational practice. *Perspectives on Psychological Science, 1,* 181–210.

Roediger, H. L., & Karpicke, J. D. (2006b). Test-enhanced learning: Taking memory tests improves long-term retention. *Psychological Science, 17,* 249–255.

Roediger, H. L., McDaniel, M. A., McDermott, K. B., & Agarwal, P. K. (2007, November). Testing-enhanced learning in the classroom: The Columbia Middle School project. Poster presented at the Psychonomic Society meeting, Long Beach, CA.

Memory

Fergus I. M. Craik
Levels of Processing in Human Memory

Elizabeth F. Loftus
Crimes of Memory: False Memories and Societal Justice

Levels of Processing in Human Memory
Fergus I. M. Craik
Rotman Research Institute, Toronto

▶ *Please tell us about your current position and research interests.*
I am a senior scientist at the Rotman Research Institute in Toronto. My research interests focus on theoretical and experimental studies of human memory, using mostly behavioral techniques but also involving some neuroimaging. A second interest is in age-related changes in attention and memory.

▶ *What got you interested in studying the effect of the type of processing on memory performance?*
As a graduate student, I became interested in how attention, perception, and memory are interrelated, and this interest led to the development of the "levels-of-processing" ideas.

▶ *What has been the real-world impact of this work?*
These ideas have practical implications for investigations of "the memory trace." Such investigations will take a different form if remembering reflects a dynamic pattern of cortical activity as opposed to the revival of a specific modular unit. The levels-of-processing ideas also have implications for education (how best to teach and learn) and for presurgical planning; for example, locating language areas by asking patients to carry out verbal processing tasks in an fMRI scanner.

How do you make a good memory? More technically, what is the best way to process information about an event if you wish to remember that event at a later date? Psychologists refer to the learning or acquisition stage of the memory process as encoding—the manner in which information is treated by the brain to form a stable representation that can be brought back to mind at a later time—and the remembering stage as retrieval. One central question about memory concerns the relations between encoding and retrieval processes. My research with colleagues in Toronto and elsewhere has focused substantially on the nature of memory-encoding processes, how they relate to retrieval processes, and, indeed, how they relate to other cognitive activities such as perception, attention, learning, and thinking.

When I was a graduate student and young faculty member in Britain in the 1960s, ideas about memory encoding were changing from the belief that the formation of associations between two mental events was key, to concepts derived from information-processing theory. Models of this latter type focused on a series of memory stores—sensory memory, short-term and long-term memory—with the idea that incoming sensory information was first passed to short-term memory by the processes of attention, and then transferred to a more permanent long-term memory store by repetition and rehearsal (Atkinson & Shiffrin, 1968, 1971).

This scheme was not without problems, however. Researchers talked about the capacity of the various stores, but the capacity of sensory buffers is difficult to assess, the capacity of the short-term store appears to vary substantially depending on the type of material being held, and the capacity of long-term memory has no apparent limits. As one example, the short-term store can hold only 4 to 5 unrelated words, but if the words form a sentence, it is relatively easy to reproduce strings of 20 to 25 words. Another problem arose when trying to determine the qualitative manner in which items are encoded in the short-term store. Work by Alan Baddeley and other British researchers had shown that short-term codes are auditory or phonological. (Letter strings such as PVGDCET are more difficult to remember than acoustically distinct strings such as APXIOQR.) However, other studies showed that codes could be visual or even semantic. Again, there seemed to be no one answer.

Treisman's Model of Attention

Much of the research in British experimental psychology around that time was concerned with the mechanisms of attention—how we are able to pay attention to one conversation in a room full of noisy conversations, for example. The eminent psychologist Donald Broadbent (1926–1993) had proposed a model involving an all-or-none selection device that could be tuned to accept messages of a particular type and reject others. This model was extended by his colleague Anne Treisman from results she had obtained using the dichotic listening paradigm. In these experiments, participants wore headphones, and different messages were played to the two ears; the participant's task was to attend to one message and to repeat it back out loud, a method known as shadowing. Treisman found that when participants were shadowing continuous passages of prose, they could tell very little about the message being played to their unattended ear. They did not even realize that this message sometimes changed to a different language!

Participants in Treisman's studies could easily tell if the voice in the unattended ear switched from a male to a female speaker, leading her to theorize that sensory aspects of incoming signals are analyzed automatically, whereas the analysis of meaning requires attention. Accordingly, she proposed a model of selective attention in which incoming information is processed through a series of tests, or levels of analysis, in which the early levels were concerned with such sensory qualities as loudness, brightness, and pitch; later levels with detection of phonemes, syllables, or visual shapes; and the latest or deepest with meaning and implication (Treisman, 1964).

Treisman suggested that each successive level of analysis acts as a sort of pass-fail exam; only those messages that "pass the test" at any one level are sent on to be analyzed at the next deeper level. In school exams of this pass-fail type, two main factors determine whether a person passes or fails—how bright the student is and where the pass mark is set. A really bright student will pass the test even if the pass mark is set at 80 percent, but, of course, many students will fail. If the pass mark is set at 30 percent, on the other hand, virtually everyone will proceed to the next level. In her model, Treisman proposed that the bright-student factor is signal strength, so a loud or bright signal will pass many tests and be perceived regardless of attention. The pass-mark factor, on the other hand, is set from the *inside*, and reflects how probable or expected a particular signal is. Your own name is always important to you, for example, so the relevant tests are always set with a low criterion (pass mark), explaining why you hear your own name in noisy surroundings even when you can make out little else.

One intriguing result emerged from an experiment in which participants were shadowing a prose passage in one ear while, unknown to them, the *same* passage was played into the unattended ear, but staggered in time so that corresponding parts of the message were 10 seconds or more apart. The procedure could be modified so that the unattended message was gradually brought closer in time to the attended version until the participant realized "Hey, the same message is playing in my other ear!" Treisman's question was: How close in time must the unattended message be for that realization to occur? And the answer was: It depends on whether the unattended message precedes or follows the shadowed message. If the unattended message came *after* the version that had just been shadowed, participants detected the similarity when the messages were 5 seconds apart, but when the unattended message came first, it had to be moved to within 1½ seconds of the attended version before participants realized that the messages were the same. Put another way, if the passage has just been attended to, analyzed, and understood, the following unattended message is also easily analyzed, and this facilitation lasts for at least 5 seconds. If the unattended message comes first, however, only its sensory aspects are analyzed, and the products of such analyses apparently disappear very quickly.

Our Levels-of-Processing Model of Memory

When I read Treisman's work in London in the early 1970s, it occurred to me that memory could be described in the same terms as her levels-of-analysis model of attention. Perhaps we don't have any "memory stores" as such, but memory may depend on how fully incoming information is attended to and how deeply it is processed on a continuum running from "shallow" sensory analyses through to the "deeper" analyses concerned with meaning and implication. About that time I moved from London to the University of Toronto and found that my Australian friend Bob Lockhart, who was already at Toronto, had been thinking about memory in very similar ways. Endel Tulving was the editor of the *Journal of Verbal Learning and Verbal Behavior* at that time; he liked the ideas and encouraged us to write them up for the journal in the summer of 1972. We did just that, with a lot of editorial help from Endel, and the article entitled "Levels of processing: A framework for memory research" (Craik & Lockhart, 1972) duly appeared at the end of that year.

The main points of the article included the idea, endorsed by many previous writers, that information processing consists of a hierarchy of processing stages, running from early sensory analyses, through more full-fledged perceptual analyses, to deeper conceptual analyses of meaning and implication. The other central notion was that the memory record was essentially a by-product of whatever perceptual/conceptual analyses had been carried out, with longer-lasting memory traces being associated with deeper levels of analysis. We assumed that processing could be extended or elaborated at any level but that the strength and persistence of the memory record reflected the greatest depth to which the stimulus or event had been processed. This scheme was applied to verbal materials (for example, phonological analysis, word identification, sentence comprehension, preparation for appropriate actions) but not *only* to verbal materials; the notion of levels or processing could also be applied to the perception and comprehension of pictures, faces, environmental sounds, tastes, and smells. In all these cases, the idea was that the quality and "strength" of a memory can be understood in terms of the specific analyses that have been carried out.

Our article made some further points also. One that became important later is the notion that memory performance would reflect the *amount* of processing at any level as well as the qualitative depth. We said, "After the stimulus has been recognized, it may undergo further processing by enrichment or elaboration" (p. 675). One example of this is the difference between proofreading and reading for gist—the former involves quite elaborate processing at the level of letters and words, whereas the latter involves relatively little processing at that level but much more at the level of meaning and implication. So, processing is flexible and guided by purposes and goals, but in all cases the memory record will reflect the operations that were carried out.

Another point concerned the sequence of processing operations within the analytic hierarchy. We discussed evidence suggesting that deeper analyses might sometimes precede analyses that are logically prior—for example, highly meaningful or expected events (say, simple pictures or highly probable words) may be processed rapidly to a deep level, with relatively slight amounts of sensory analysis. We commented that such stimuli "will be processed to a deep level more rapidly than less meaningful stimuli and will be well retained. Thus, speed of analysis does not necessarily predict retention" (p. 676). In fact, because of this "expectedness" or "meaningfulness" factor, neither processing time nor the amount of attention necessary for processing will serve as a reliable index of depth. This inconvenient truth got us into trouble later on with critics who (reasonably enough) wanted to see some objective index of processing depth.

A third point dealt with the concept of short-term memory. Despite what some textbooks tell you, the Craik and Lockhart article did *not* seek to abolish the distinction between short-term and long-term memory! In fact, we accepted the idea that information can be held in two different ways, but rejected the notion that short-term maintenance depended on a separate store. On page 676, we suggested that in addition to the memories formed as a consequence of processing to various levels, "there is a second way in which stimuli can be retained—by recirculating information at one level of processing." In our view, maintaining information at one level is equivalent to continued attention to some aspects of the processed stimulus. In keeping with historical precedent, we termed this maintenance process *primary memory*, which in our case meant continued attention to such features as phonological properties of words, visual aspects of pictures, or even conceptual aspects of stimuli. So, rather than envisaging short-term memory as a store in which various types of items are held, we suggested that information can be retained temporarily in conscious awareness by the flexible allocation of attention to a variety of different analyzed features.

While writing the article, Lockhart and I alternated between feeling that we were really onto something, and feeling that the "something" was maybe rather trivial—a dichotomy later echoed by our fans and critics! One flash-bulb memory: Our fellow memory researcher Bennet Murdock came into our office late one evening and threw a book on the table with the words, "You fellows should be interested in this!" The book was *Human memory: Research and theory* by Laird Cermak, a Boston researcher, and in it Cermak laid out a scheme quite similar to ours. We joined forces later by organizing a conference on levels of processing in 1977, and the conference papers subsequently appeared as a book (Cermak & Craik, 1979).

Testing the Model

Meanwhile, I had been working in the lab to develop some empirical support for the levels framework. If the basic idea is correct, I reasoned, it should be possible to induce different levels of processing by asking different questions about the same stimulus. For example, if the stimulus word is TABLE, we can ask "Is the word printed in capital letters?" or "Does the word rhyme with fable?" or "Is the word a piece of furniture?" In our first experiments, we asked such questions before the word was presented briefly (for 200 milliseconds). Participants were told that we sought information on word processing and that they should answer each question as rapidly as possible after the following word appeared. They were *not* told anything about memory, so the instruction to recall or recognize as many words as possible after the list had been shown came as a surprise. This technique, known as incidental learning, ensured that participants would carry out only the type of processing induced by the question. Each word was presented very briefly to discourage further processing (although that turned out not to matter). The design crossed three levels (or types) of processing—case, rhyme, and semantic questions—with questions that led either to a "yes" response ("furniture?"—TABLE) or a "no" response ("written in small print?"—LION).

The results of this experiment are shown in Table 1a. The probability of recognizing a word correctly runs from 0.14 to 0.93—a factor of 6!—despite the fact that all words were shown for the same length of time, were ordinary nouns, and, in fact, were the *same words* across conditions because each participant was presented with words under different encoding instructions. Table 1b shows a replication of the study using sentence frames for the semantic condition. Participants were shown a sentence with a blank space before each word was shown, and had to decide weather the word was a meaningful fit. (For example, if the sentence was "The girl placed the __ on the table," the word *BOOK* would yield a positive response, whereas the response to the word *CLOUD* would be negative.) In

TABLE 1	Proportions of words recognized correctly as a function of the initial encoding task		
(a) Encoding question:	Case	Rhyme	Category
"Yes" responses	0.18	0.78	0.93
"No" responses	0.14	0.36	0.63
(b) Encoding question:	Case	Rhyme	Sentence
"Yes" responses	0.15	0.48	0.81
"No" responses	0.19	0.27	0.49
(c) Encoding question:	Case	Rhyme	Category
"Yes" responses	0.23	0.59	0.81
"No" responses	0.28	0.33	0.62

Note: The figures in the table are probabilities of correct recognition following three types of encoding. In sections (a) and (b), words were initially shown for 200 milliseconds, with each word preceded by a question concerning either its visual appearance (case), sound (rhyme), or meaning (category or sentence frame). The questions led to either a positive (yes) or negative (no) response. In section (c), the words were initially shown for 6 seconds each. The results show that later recognition memory for words is greatly affected by the type of initial encoding, with deep levels of processing (semantic decisions) resulting in higher recognition levels than processing of sound or appearance. (Data from Craik & Tulving, 1975)

this condition, recognition rates varied from 0.15 to 0.81; again a very large difference.

Endel Tulving became interested in these studies and persuaded me that the 200-millisecond exposure was unnecessary. He predicted that he would obtain the same pattern if the target words were displayed for 6 seconds rather than 200 milliseconds, and even if the participants knew there would be a later memory test. Endel phoned me at home when the results were obtained (Table 1c) and I have another flashbulb memory of the event, the data seemed so amazing! The words and questions we used are given in the paper we subsequently published (Craik & Tulving, 1975). Try running the experiment on some friends; the levels-of-processing effect comes with a cast-iron guarantee!

One unexpected result was that the words associated with "yes" responses were much better recognized than those associated with "no" responses— for rhyme and semantic judgments at least. Our conjecture is that in the positive cases the word can be integrated with the preceding question, and perhaps elaborated by it, thereby forming a qualitatively richer record that is particularly well recognized.

The first reaction of the experimental psychology community to these results was that they must reflect something else than the vaguely defined levels-of-processing model—maybe deeper processing simply takes longer to achieve? The theoretical ideas in the Craik and Lockhart article were also met skeptically by some critics; many of them were British friends of mine, which pained me slightly. After all, the ideas stemmed from such eminent British psychologists as Sir Frederic Bartlett, Donald Broadbent, and Anne Treisman! Probably the best critical paper is by Alan Baddeley (1978), and we set out some answers to the criticisms in Lockhart and Craik (1990) and Craik (2002). But the ideas were welcomed for the most part, and it is interesting to note that the Craik and Lockhart article is still reasonably well cited—over 100 citations in 2008—36 years after publication!

It was exciting to work through the theoretical ideas and fun to devise experiments to test them. A research project is a bit like a detective mystery; the researcher hunts for clues that nature provides, pieces the fragments together to form a plausible story, and then confronts the suspect with a series of experiments. If you get it right, Mother Nature owns up with a smile, and the detective-researcher can file the story with satisfaction—and move on to the next case!

Suggested Further Reading

Craik, F. I. M. (2002). Levels of processing: Past, present . . . and future? *Memory, 10,* 305–318.

Craik, F. I. M., & Lockhart, R. S. (1972). Levels of processing: A framework for memory research. *Journal of Verbal Learning and Verbal Behavior, 11,* 671–684.

References

Atkinson, R. C., & Shiffrin, R. M. (1968). Human memory: A proposed system and its control processes. In K. W. Spence and J. T. Spence (Eds.), *The psychology of learning and motivation: Advances in research and theory, Vol II* (pp. 89–195). New York: Academic Press.

Atkinson, R. C., & Shiffrin, R. M. (1971). The control of short-term memory. *Scientific American, 225,* 82–90.

Baddeley, A. D. (1978). The trouble with levels: A re-examination of Craik and Lockhart's framework for memory research. *Psychological Review, 85,* 139–152.

Cermak, L. S., & Craik, F. I. M. (Eds.). (1979). *Levels of processing in human memory.* Hillsdale, NJ: Lawrence Erlbaum Associates.

Craik, F. I. M. (2002). Levels of processing: Past, present . . . and future? *Memory, 10,* 305–318.

Craik, F. I. M., & Lockhart, R. S. (1972). Levels of processing: A framework for memory research. *Journal of Verbal Learning and Verbal Behavior, 11,* 671–684.

Craik, F. I. M., & Tulving, E. (1975). Depth of processing and the retention of words in episodic memory. *Journal of Experimental Psychology: General, 104,* 268–294.

Lockhart, R. S., & Craik, F. I. M. (1990). Levels of processing: A retrospective commentary on a framework for memory research. *Canadian Journal of Psychology, 44,* 87–112.

Treisman, A. (1964). Selective attention in man. *British Medical Bulletin, 20,* 12–16.

Crimes of Memory: False Memories and Societal Justice

Elizabeth F. Loftus
University of California, Irvine

▶ *Please tell us about your current position and research interests.*
I'm currently Distinguished Professor at the University of California, Irvine.
I hold positions in Psychology and Social Behavior and in Criminology,
Law and Society. And I'm Professor of Law.

▶ *What got you interested in studying the effect of leading questions on memory?*
I wanted to study a psychological problem that would have real-world applications. The problem of leading questions was obviously applicable to real court cases involving crimes, accidents, and other important events.

▶ *What has been the real-world impact of this work?*
Based not only on my work, but the work of many others in this field, the legal system has made changes. There are guidelines for how witnesses should be interviewed and handled in the legal system. There are courts that have decided that jurors should hear expert testimony from psychologists on the science of eyewitness testimony.

Memory. It's a paradox. Memory is the bedrock of who we are. Without memory, life would not have the sense of continuity that it does. It would consist only of momentary experiences that don't relate to each other. Without memory we could not remember what we want to say. Nor would we have the sense of continuity to know who we are. At the same time, as my scientific research over the last 30 years has shown, memory is utterly malleable, selective, and changing. The malleable nature of memory doesn't matter when the changes are small and insignificant—as when I tell my friend I ate chicken last night when I really had beef. But sometimes the changes are so significant that they lead to ruined lives.

Each year my work brings me face to face with an important group of people—individuals falsely accused of crimes that someone else committed. Sometimes I meet people who are accused of crimes that never even happened. And when I learn more about the cases, I usually discover that faulty human memory is the major cause of these human tragedies. To put faces on some of these wrongfully convicted people, one need only visit the Web site of the Innocence Project (http://www.innocenceproject.org).

The project, initiated by lawyers Barry Scheck and Peter Neufeld, brings together lawyers, journalists, and institutions to tackle claims of innocence that can be proven (for example, by DNA evidence.) On the Innocence Project Web site, you can see the faces of actual innocence. One of the most famous, Ronald Cotton, had been identified by Jennifer Thompson, an attractive college student, as the man who raped her. Cotton served more than 10 years of a life sentence before he was exonerated based on DNA evidence. Unlike many cases, the real perpetrator was found. To her credit, Jennifer accepted her mistake and used her newfound knowledge of faulty memory to crusade for the victims of mistaken memory—the wrongfully accused. Eventually Jennifer Thompson, a true victim, and Ronald Cotton, a different kind of victim, came together for a meeting. She apologized. He forgave her.

The Science of Memory Distortion

It was my scientific work on memory distortion that brought me face to face with the falsely accused. In the initial studies, conducted in the 1970s, I showed what can happen when a person sees a crime or an accident and is later questioned about the incident in a biased way. In one study, people who had seen simulated car accidents were asked, "How fast were the cars going when they smashed into each other?" This leading question led them to estimates of speed that were higher than those of people asked the more neutral question: "How fast were the cars going when they hit each other?" Moreover, the leading "smashed" question led more witnesses to later falsely remember that they had seen broken glass at the scene, when there was no broken glass at all (see Figure 1).

In another study, a simple question that referred to a stop sign (when it was actually a yield sign) led many people to believe they had seen a stop sign. In yet another study, we created a false memory for something as large and conspicuous as a barn. We asked some witnesses to a simulated accident a leading question that made reference to a barn. Some of those witnesses later claimed to have seen a barn in the country landscape that contained no buildings at all. (See Loftus, 1979/1996, for a review of these early studies.)

In the years since my initial work, hundreds of studies have documented the ways in which exposure to misinformation can supplement, contaminate, or distort our memories. We pick up misinformation not only from biased and leading questions, but also when we talk with other people who (consciously or inadvertently) give an erroneous version of a past event (Loftus, 2005). Inaccuracy in memory caused by erroneous information provided after an event is known in psychology as the misinformation effect.

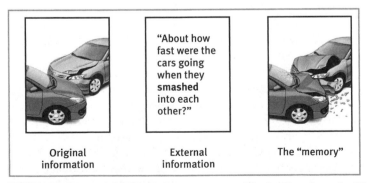

FIGURE 1 Two types of information in memory. The leading "smashed" question led more witnesses to later falsely remember that they had seen broken glass at the scene, when there was no broken glass at all. (From Loftus, 1979/1996.)

Based on this research, we know that the timing of misinformation is important. For example, if the original memory has a chance to fade, it becomes more prone to being altered by misinformation. Young children are especially susceptible to having their memories modified by misinformation. Once the modified version takes hold, people can be very confident about their misinformed memories, even though they may be totally wrong.

Eyewitness Identifications of People

It's not just memory for event details that can be changed, but so can memory for people we have seen before. Every day in the United States alone, more than 200 people are estimated to become defendants in criminal cases after having been identified by a witness from a lineup or photo spread (see Wells et al., 2000). Thousands of studies have shown that certain conditions increase the chances that someone will be mistakenly identified (Cutler & Penrod, 1995). Some factors we simply have to live with because the justice system can't change them—for example, the comparatively low reliability of cross-racial identifications. But the justice system can change other factors, such as the instructions that are given to a witness before viewing a lineup.

Concerned about the growing number of proven cases of wrongful conviction based on faulty memory, the U.S. Department of Justice released a national guide for collecting and preserving eyewitness evidence (Technical Working Group for Eyewitness Evidence, 1999). The authors of the guide relied on findings from scientific memory research to shape their recommendations. The guide, for example, instructs investigators to use open-ended questions ("What can you tell me about the car?"), augmented by more specific ones ("What color was the car?"), rather than leading questions ("Was the car red?"). The guide offers advice about what instructions to give witnesses before they view lineups, how many fillers should be in the lineup, and how those fillers should be selected. Although at times arduous, the process of eliciting agreement amongst prosecutors, defense attorneys, police, and scientists ultimately resulted in a landmark product that surely is a major step toward reducing the chances of wrongful convictions (Doyle, 2005).

Planting Wholly False Memories

In the early 1990s, North America began to see an altogether more extreme sort of memory phenomenon. Some individuals were going into therapy with one kind of problem, like depression or anxiety, and leaving with another problem—"memory" of horrific abuse, perpetrated against them by loved ones, often involving satanic rituals that included bizarre and sometimes impossible elements. One woman recalled being impregnated by her father even though she was ultimately shown to be a virgin and he was sterile. Hundreds of the accused found themselves being prosecuted or sued civilly, based on these suspect memories. Hundreds of the accusers would eventually retract their memories, and some of them sued their former therapists for malpractice, charging that they had planted false memories. Monetary settlements for the retractors were often high, topping $10 million in one case.

Where could these bizarre "memories" have come from? Highly suggestive therapy procedures, such as guided imagination, dream interpretation, hypnosis, and exposure to false information, became the suspects.

To explore whether such techniques could in fact lead to rich false memories, researchers developed procedures that were inspired by some of the problematic therapies. Using suggestion, my colleagues and I initially got people to believe that when they were children they had been lost in a shopping mall for an extended time. The lost-in-the-mall technique used information obtained from their mothers and fathers to help create scenarios that described some true events and also the false event about getting lost. The scenarios were then fed to the participants as if they were entirely true. In that initial work, about a quarter of participants fell sway to the misinformation and claimed to have gotten lost in the suggested fashion.

Later research using the lost-in-the-mall technique showed that people would also accept suggestions that they experienced events that were more bizarre and upsetting. In one Tennessee study, about a third of participants were persuaded that as children, they had nearly drowned and had to be rescued by a lifeguard. In a study done in Canada, researchers succeeded in convincing half of participants that something as horrible as being a victim of a vicious animal attack had occurred in their childhood (see Loftus, 2003, for a review of this work).

Telling people that their parents are the source of biographical information is a strong form of suggestion, no doubt about it. But subsequent work showed that comparatively subtle suggestions can also lead people to develop false beliefs and memories. One such technique, common in some psychotherapy offices, is guided imagination, in which a therapist says something like, "You don't remember your abuse, but you have all the symptoms. Why don't you just close your eyes and try to imagine who might have done it?" The guided imagination technique persists despite good evidence that imagining an event that didn't happen (like breaking a window with your hand) can lead people to think that it did happen. Researchers call this phenomenon imagination inflation.

Who is susceptible to inflation by manipulation? Probably we are all susceptible to some degree. But some individuals are somewhat more susceptible than others—for example, people who tend to have lapses in memory and attention and people who have vivid visual imagery. The implications for clinical practice are obvious: Professional therapists who use techniques involving any form of imagination need to better appreciate its capacity for distorting memory.

A common complaint about the false memory research is that the suggestion may be reviving a true memory rather than planting a false one. Perhaps the individual really did break a window, forgot it, and the imagination exercise revived it. Perhaps the individual really did get attacked by an animal, forgot it, and the strong suggestion revived the memory. To address this concern, researchers sought to plant implausible or even impossible memories. In one set of studies, people were led to believe that they had witnessed a person being demonically possessed as a child. Even though subjects entered the experiment thinking this was not very plausible, many of them ended up, after strong suggestion, with increased confidence that this had occurred to them before the age of 3. In another set of studies, many people were led to believe that as children they had met and shaken hands with Bugs Bunny on a trip to a Disney resort. This event is impossible because Bugs Bunny is a Warner Brothers character and would not be seen at a Disney resort. Nevertheless, some participants even embellished their "memories" with unique sensory details, such as remembering that they hugged Bugs, or touched his tail, or heard him say, "What's up, Doc?"

The sensory details are especially important to memory scientists because people typically use sensory detail to assist in distinguishing between our true memories and those that are products of imagination, dreams, or some other process. And when we listen to the stories of others, which we do as therapists, or police officers, or jurors, or as friends, we use sensory detail as a cue to tell us that we are hearing a report that is based on authentic memory. But these studies are showing that false memories can be detailed. In fact, false memories can be not only detailed, but they can be held with confidence, and expressed with emotion—other cues that usually make us think that memory reports are true.

False Memories Have Consequences

People who have developed false beliefs about relatives brutalizing them in childhood often act on those beliefs. They sever ties with their family members. They sometimes initiate criminal prosecutions or civil litigation against those whom they have accused. They frequently fail to get the kind of professional help that might restore their health (McNally, 2003).

Although ethical barriers prevent researchers from experimentally producing such dire consequences, they have devised harmless ways of collecting evidence about the consequences of false beliefs. In one set of studies, researchers planted a false belief that as children, participants had gotten sick eating dill pickles, hard-boiled eggs, strawberry ice cream, and other foods (Bernstein et al., 2005). Not only were researchers successful at planting these beliefs in a significant minority of subjects (sometimes as many as 40 percent), but those who fell for the suggestion later reported a decreased interest in the specified foods. This particular line of research has unique implications for nutritional selection and, perhaps, the obesity problem facing our society, demonstrating as it does that false beliefs affect later thoughts, intentions, and behaviors.

False Memories and Society

The Science of False Memory is the title of a 557-page tome published by Oxford University Press (Brainerd & Reyna, 2005). Thousands of researchers have contributed to the solid science it reports. Despite more than a quarter century of investigation, however, false memories remain a problem for society. Hundreds of individuals—most of whom landed in hot water because of someone's faulty memory—have been wrongly convicted of crimes. While they were imprisoned, the real culprit was free—often committing further crimes.

Hundreds, if not thousands, of fathers and mothers and uncles and grandparents and neighbors have been accused of crimes that may not have occurred at all. Some of the accused remain in prison. False memory is the root cause.

The science of false memory teaches us much about innovations that can reduce these tragedies, and police, mental health professionals, and others are already implementing some of the changes. Communicating what we have learned to the broader public will go a long way toward minimizing the damage that false memories can cause. If there is one lesson to be learned from our findings, it is this: Just because a memory is expressed with confidence, just because it contains detail, just because it is expressed with emotion, doesn't mean it really happened. We can't yet reliably discriminate true memories from false ones; we still need independent corroboration. Advances in neuroimaging and other techniques may some day aid in this endeavor. But in the meantime, we as a society would do well to continually keep in mind that memory—like liberty—is fragile.

Acknowledgements

Funding for much of the underlying research described was provided by the U.S. National Science Foundation, the U.S. National Institute of Mental Health, the University of California–Irvine, and the Grawemeyer Prize in Psychology awarded to Elizabeth Loftus.

Suggested Further Reading

Doyle, J. M. (2005). *True witness*. New York: Palgrave MacMillan.

Loftus, E. F. (2003). Make-believe memories. *American Psychologist, 58*, 864–873.

References

Bernstein, D. M., Laney, C., Morris, E. K., & Loftus, E. F. (2005). False beliefs about fattening foods can have healthy consequences. *Proceedings of the National Academy of Sciences, 102*, 13724–13731.

Brainerd, C. J. & Reyna, V. F. (2005). *The science of false memory*. New York: Oxford University Press.

Cutler, B. L., & Penrod, S. D. (1995). *Mistaken identification*. Cambridge: Cambridge University Press.

Doyle, J. M. (2005). *True witness*. New York: Palgrave MacMillan.

Loftus, E. F. (1979/1996). *Eyewitness testimony*. Cambridge, MA: Harvard University Press.

Loftus, E. F. (2003). Make-believe memories. *American Psychologist, 58*, 864–873.

Loftus, E. F. (2005). A 30-year investigation of the malleability of memory. *Learning and Memory, 12*, 361–366.

McNally, R. J. (2003). *Remembering trauma*. Cambridge, MA: Harvard University Press.

Technical Working Group for Eyewitness Evidence. (1999). Eyewitness evidence: A guide for law enforcement [Booklet]. Washington, DC: U.S. Department of Justice, Office of Justice Programs.

Wells, G. L., Malpass, R. S., Lindsay, R. C. L., Fisher, R. P., Turtle, J. W., & Fulero, S. M. (2000). From the lab to the police station: A successful application of eyewitness research. *American Psychologist, 55*, 581–598.

Language and Thought

Susan Goldin-Meadow
Creating and Learning Language by Hand

Herbert S. Terrace
Thinking Without Language

Creating and Learning Language by Hand

Susan Goldin-Meadow

University of Chicago

▶ *Please tell us about your current position and research interests.*

I am the Beardsley Ruml Distinguished Service Professor in the Departments of Psychology and Comparative Human Development at the University of Chicago. In my current research, I am exploring three questions: (1) In rural Nicaragua, where the absence of oral schools for deaf children means that hearing parents provide a different kind of gestural model than do hearing parents of deaf children in the United States, I am asking whether this model makes a difference in the children's homesign systems; (2) In my continuing observation of the gestures that hearing children produce as they learn language, my goal is to figure out the moment when gesture no longer replaces single words but begins to convey larger propositions and thus looks more adult-like; and (3) In studies of whether gesturing plays a role in learning by encouraging children to either gesture or act during instruction, my hypothesis is that because gesture grounds thought in action, it is at least as effective as action (and maybe even more effective) in bringing learning about.

▶ *What got you interested in studying deaf children's spontaneous sign systems?*

I was interested in where language comes from and whether not having a language would affect the way a person thinks. I therefore wanted to study children who had not been exposed to language, and had heard that deaf children who were orally trained nevertheless used their hands to communicate. This seemed an ideal situation to explore the roots of language. But to explore the effect of language on thinking, I needed to first describe how much of language these deaf children could and could not invent.

▶ *What has been the real-world impact of this work?*

My studies of gesture in deaf children suggest that children are likely to be expressing themselves in structured ways even if they are not using the language of the community. Clinicians and teachers can use the deaf children's gestures as a starting point for teaching them conventional language, either signed or spoken. More generally, because hearing children often express thoughts in gesture, teachers and parents can use their gestures to find out more about what's on their minds. Because gesturing may itself promote learning, adults can encourage children to gesture in learning situations. At the least, these gestures will give the adults an additional window onto what the children are thinking—and the act of gesturing may itself change the way the children think.

Imagine what it would be like if you had no exposure to language and you wanted to make your desires and thoughts known to another person. How would you get someone to do something as simple as help you open a jar?

You might instinctively turn to your hands—perhaps pointing to the jar and twisting your hand in the air. That is, in fact, the strategy adopted by children who cannot learn the language of their community.

Although many profoundly deaf children are exposed at an early age to a conventional sign language, some are not. These children lack a usable model for language: They can't hear the oral language that their hearing parents are using, and they don't have access to a manual language like American Sign Language. You might guess that, under circumstances such as these, a child would not try to communicate at all. But this guess would be wrong. The child will indeed try to communicate and will use one or both hands to do so. The child will gesture.

What's interesting about this finding, however, is not that deaf children gesture (everyone gestures), but that their gestures have properties in common with natural languages handed down from generation to generation. Indeed, the deaf children's spontaneously invented gestures are similar enough in structure to signed and spoken languages to have earned the label *homesign*. Homesign tells us just how resilient language is in humans.

Using the Hands to Create Language

When deaf children are exposed to sign language from birth, they learn that language as naturally as hearing children learn spoken language. However, 90 percent of deaf children are not born to deaf parents who could provide early access to sign language. Instead, they are born to hearing parents, some of whom choose to expose their children solely to speech. Unfortunately, deaf children with profound hearing losses are unlikely to acquire spoken language, even with specialized instruction.

My colleagues and I have studied 10 profoundly deaf, young homesigners in the United States and 4 in Taiwan (Goldin-Meadow, 2003a), and we're now studying 6 deaf children in Turkey. These children's hearing parents chose to educate them in oral schools where sign language was neither taught nor encouraged, and they had made little progress in oral language. With no exposure to sign language, they knew neither sign nor speech.

Interestingly, homesigners use gesture not only to get others to do things for them (to ask someone to open a jar), but also to share ideas and solicit information (to tell someone about a trip to the zoo or to inquire why a toy isn't working). These children even use their gestures to serve some of the relatively sophisticated functions of language—to tell stories, to comment on their own and others' gestures, and to talk to themselves. In this sense, the children's communications are qualitatively different from those produced by nonhuman primates: Language-trained apes use the signs and symbols they are able to develop only to change people's behavior and not to change their ideas.

In Taiwan, we observed Qing, a deaf child of hearing parents, use her gestures to make a generic statement about swordfish. While looking at a picture of a swordfish, she produced five distinct gestures, illustrated in Figure 1, to make four general propositions about swordfish: They can poke people in the chest (proposition 1) and the people then become dead (proposition 2—the bent index finger is a stylized gesture used by hearing speakers in

FIGURE 1 A Chinese homesigner gesturing about swordfish. The child produces five gestures in response to a picture of a harmless swordfish, who is, in fact, playing a xylophone in the picture (not spearing people): She points at the picture of a swordfish (= *swordfish*). She jabs at her own chest as though piercing her heart (= *poke-in-chest*). She crooks her index finger and wiggles it in the air (this is a stylized gesture in Taiwan that hearing speakers use to mean *dead*). She holds her index finger on her nose and extends it outward (= *long-straight-nose*). She wiggles her palm back and forth (= *swim*). Reprinted from Goldin-Meadow (2003a).

Taiwan to mean *dead*); they have long, straight noses (proposition 3); they swim (proposition 4). After gesturing about swordfish in general, Qing went on to invent a fantasy, motivated perhaps by sibling rivalry. She produced the *poke* gesture again, but this time aimed toward her hearing sister's chest rather than her own, and then gestured *dead*.

This example nicely illustrates two of the many properties of natural language found in homesign: *recursion* (the child has expressed several propositions, each about swordfish, within a single gesture sentence) and *displaced communication* (the child has described events that are not taking place in the here and now).

When attempting to determine which properties of language are found in each deaf child's homesign system, we first describe all of the gestures that the child produces, using a system developed to code the forms of signs in languages like American Sign Language. We then use the form of the gesture and the context in which it's produced to assign a meaning. For example, if a child produces a twisting motion in the air after trying unsuccessfully to open a jar of bubbles, we assign the meaning "twist" to the gesture. If the child relaxes her hand or pauses before producing another gesture, we consider the twist gesture to be a "one-gesture" utterance. If, however, the child does not relax her hand but moves seamlessly into the next gesture, we consider the gestures to be a "two-gesture" string. We thus consider a string of gestures to be a single sentence-like unit if the child does not pause or relax her hand between gestures.

Using this system, we find that the deaf homesigners use their gestures to refer to the same range of objects, people, and places as do (1) young hearing children using words and (2) young, sign language–exposed deaf children using signs—and in the same distribution. They refer most often to inanimate objects, followed by people and animals. They also refer to body parts, food, clothing, vehicles, furniture, and places, but less frequently.

We also find that homesigners frequently combine their gestures with other gestures. They use their gesture strings to convey sentence meanings that are the same as those of hearing children acquiring spoken language from their hearing parents (Brown, 1973) and as those of deaf children acquiring sign language from their deaf parents (Newport & Meier, 1985).

Even though homesigners do not have an explicit model to guide them in constructing their gesture systems, they produce gesture strings that are structured in sentence-like ways. For example, their gesture sentences are consistently ordered—when gesturing about beating a drum, the gesture for the object-acted-upon, the *drum*, will typically precede the gesture for the action, *beat*. In addition (as illustrated in Figure 1), the gesture sentences can be complex, containing several propositions. As another example, we observed a child produce the gesture sentence, *drum beat straw sip*, to describe a scene in which a soldier was beating a drum (proposition 1) and a cowboy was sipping from a straw (proposition 2).

Although they had not observed people signing, the deaf children in our studies were exposed to the gestures that their hearing parents—like all hearing speakers—produce as they talk. These gestures could have served as a model for the structure in the children's gesture systems. To explore this possibility, we analyzed videotapes of the gestures that the hearing mothers of our deaf children produced when talking to the children. However, we looked at them not as they were meant to be experienced (that is, with speech) but with the sound turned off, as the deaf child would see them. Using the analytic tools that we had used to describe the children's gestures, we found that the hearing mothers' gestures did *not* have language-like structure (see, for example, Goldin-Meadow & Mylander, 1998).

In sum, the children received as *input* speech-accompanying gestures that were not language-like in form, but they produced as *output* gestures that resembled language.

Using the Hands to Learn Language

The deaf children in our studies were in a unique situation—most children *are* exposed to a usable model for language from birth and have no trouble acquiring that language. But even children who are acquiring a spoken language like English use gesture and, in fact, many produce gestures several months before they produce their first words. The interesting finding is that hearing children seem to be using their hands to help them learn their language.

The early gestures that children produce not only predate their words, they predict them. For example, the words that will eventually appear in a child's spoken vocabulary can be predicted by looking at that child's earlier pointing gestures (Iverson & Goldin-Meadow, 2005). In fact, one of the best ways to predict the size of a child's spoken vocabulary at 42 months is to look at the number of different meanings the child conveys via gesture at 14 months.

In addition to presaging the shape of children's eventual spoken vocabularies, gesture also paves the way for early sentences. Children combine gestures with words to express sentence-like meanings (*eat* + point at cookie) months before they can express these same meanings in a word + word combination (*eat cookie*). Importantly, we can predict when a child will first produce a two-word utterance like *eat cookie* just from knowing the age at which that child first produced a gesture + speech combination like *eat* + point at cookie (Iverson & Goldin-Meadow, 2005). Gesture thus serves as a signal that a child will soon be ready to begin producing multi-word sentences.

Moreover, the types of gesture + speech combinations children produce change over time and presage changes in their speech. For example, children produce gesture + speech combinations conveying more than one proposition (akin to a complex sentence, for example, "I like it" + eat gesture) several months before producing a complex sentence entirely in speech ("I like to eat it") (Ozcaliskan & Goldin-Meadow, 2005). Gesture thus continues to be at the cutting edge of early language development, providing stepping-stones to increasingly complex linguistic constructions.

Finding that gesture predicts the child's initial steps into language learning raises the possibility that gesture could help bring that learning about. Gesture has the potential to play a causal role in language learning in at least two ways.

First, children's gestures could elicit from their parents the kinds of words and sentences that the children need to hear in order to take their next linguistic steps. For example, a child who does not yet know the word "dog" might refer to the animal by pointing at it. His obliging mother might say in response to the point, "Yes, that's a dog," thus supplying him with just the word he is looking for.

Or a child in the one-word stage might point at her father while saying "sock." Her mother replies, "That's daddy's sock," thus translating the child's gesture + word combination into a simple (and relevant) sentence. It turns out that mothers often "translate" their children's gestures into words, thus providing timely models for how one- and two-word ideas can be expressed in English (Goldin-Meadow et al., 2007). Gesture thus offers a mechanism by which children can point out their thoughts to others, who then calibrate their speech to those thoughts and potentially facilitate language learning.

The second way in which gesture could play a causal role in language learning is through its cognitive effects (Goldin-Meadow & Wagner, 2005). In studies of older school-aged children solving math problems, we have found that encouraging children to gesture while explaining how they (incorrectly) solved a math problem increases the likelihood that those children will end up learning how to solve the problem correctly. For example, a child who puts 11 in the blank of the problem $5 + 4 + 2 = \_ + 2$ is more likely to learn that 9 is the correct answer if he is told to move his left hand back and forth under the $5 + 4 + 2$ and his right hand back and forth under the $\_ + 2$ than if he is told to produce the verbal equivalent of these gestures: "To solve the problem, I need to make one side equal to the other side" (Cook, Mitchell, & Goldin-Meadow, 2008).

These findings suggest that the act of gesturing can itself promote learning. Extrapolating from these findings, we might predict that, for children in the early stages of language learning, the act of pointing to an object will increase the likelihood that the pointer will learn a word for that object. Our future work will explore whether gesture can promote language learning not only by allowing children to elicit timely input from their communication partners, but also by directly influencing their own cognitive state.

The Hands Can Provide the First Sign of Developmental Trouble

Because gesture and speech are so tightly intertwined, changes in gesture can predict, and may even help bring about, changes in speech. But what if a child is not following a typical language-learning path? Many, but not all children with pre- or perinatal unilateral brain lesions have early language delays. These early delays are transient for some children but persistent for others. Can we use gesture to predict which children will sustain persistent delays and which children will not?

To find out, we calculated the number of different gestures and words children with brain injury produced during naturalistic interactions with their parents at 18 months, and we then assessed the children's spoken vocabulary on a standardized test at 30 months. Gesture use was highly variable in these children and, importantly, this variability predicted later spoken vocabulary: Children who produced few gesture types at 18 months exhibited delays in vocabulary comprehension 1 year later. Children who produced many gesture types did not (Sauer, Levine, & Goldin-Meadow, 2008).

These findings have both theoretical and practical implications. Theoretically, the fact that gesture and speech remain linked even when different brain structures underlie language functions suggests that early gesture may be inextricably linked to language learning. In terms of practice, the findings suggest that early delays in gesture production can be used to identify children whose language learning is likely to go awry in the future. If so, clinicians can use early gesture diagnostically to identify children likely to have persistent language difficulties well before those difficulties appear in speech. We may therefore be able to offer these children early interventions (perhaps in the form of more intensive gesture instruction).

What Do the Hands Do Once Language Is Learned?

We have seen that children at the earliest stages of learning a spoken language use gestures to stand in for words—a gesture can take the place of a word that a child does not yet have in her spoken vocabulary, and combining gestures with words gives the child a way to express sentence-like meanings before those meanings can be expressed entirely in speech. Importantly, these early uses of gesture predict the entry of particular words into the child's spoken vocabulary and predict the onset of the child's earliest sentences. At the least, early child gesture reflects the child's readiness for learning language. At most, gesture plays a role in the learning process itself, either by eliciting targeted responses from the child's communication partner or by altering the child's own cognitive state.

We have also seen that gesture can function like words for deaf children who have not been exposed to a usable model for language and must invent their own. Gestures act like object-referring words in the homesign systems these deaf children create, and gestures are combined with each other to convey sentence-like meanings in structured ways. But because their gestures must carry the full burden of communication, the homesigning deaf children need to continue to develop their gesture systems—and they do, building more and more linguistic properties into their gesture systems over time (Goldin-Meadow, 2003a).

Hearing children, in contrast, are learning the spoken language that surrounds them. Eventually, they will become proficient language users and will no longer need to substitute gestures for words. But they will continue to gesture. The question is—what form will those gestures take?

Speakers of all ages gesture when they speak, and those gestures are integrated both temporally and semantically with the speech they accompany (McNeill, 1992; Kendon, 1980). The gestures produced by proficient spoken-language users are comparable to those of children on the cusp of spoken language in that, at times, they convey information that is different from that conveyed in speech. Interestingly, the occurrence of such gestures is similar in both groups: They are used most frequently when describing things that the speaker is on the verge of learning (Goldin-Meadow, 2003b).

Note, however, that the task facing the young, hearing language-learner is spoken language itself. Thus, in these early stages, the gesture is used as an assist into the linguistic system, substituting for spoken words that the child has not yet acquired. But once the basics of spoken language have been mastered, gesture is freed up for other purposes—for example, to frame the discourse (McNeill, 1992) or to help speakers grapple with ideas that they are having difficulty expressing in speech, ideas that rarely translate into a single word (see, for example, the math task described earlier). As a result, we see a change in the kinds of ideas expressed in gesture as children become proficient users of spoken language. But at every stage, the gestures that accompany speech serve to enrich the ideas that speakers express.

To summarize, when young children do not have a model for language, they use gesture to fill the void. Even when children do have a model for language, they use gesture to help them take steps into language that they cannot yet take in speech. Indeed, gesturing may actually facilitate children's transition to language. The hands thus set the stage for language, be it created or learned.

Acknowledgements

This work was supported by grants from the National Institute on Deafness and Other Communication Disorders (R01 DC00491) and the National Institute of Child Health and Human Development (R01 HD47450 and P01 HD40605). I thank the many colleagues and students without whom this research would not have happened: Lila Gleitman, Heidi Feldman, Carolyn Mylander, Cindy Butcher, Jana Iverson, Seyda

Ozcaliskan, Meredith Rowe, Whitney Goodrich, Eve Sauer, Susan Levine, Martha Alibali, Breckie Church, Michelle Perry, and Susan Wagner Cook.

Suggested Further Reading

Goldin-Meadow, S. (2003). *Hearing gesture: How our hands help us think*. Cambridge, MA: Harvard University Press.

Goldin-Meadow, S. (2003). *The resilience of language: What gesture creation in deaf children can tell us about how all children learn language*. New York: Psychology Press.

References

Brown, R. (1973). *A first language*. Cambridge, MA: Harvard University Press.

Cook, S. W., Mitchell, Z., & Goldin-Meadow, S. (2008). Gesturing makes learning last. *Cognition, 106,* 1047–1058.

Goldin-Meadow, S. (2003a). *The resilience of language: What gesture creation in deaf children can tell us about how all children learn language*. New York: Psychology Press.

Goldin-Meadow, S. (2003b). *Hearing gesture: How our hands help us think*. Cambridge, MA: Harvard University Press.

Goldin-Meadow, S., Goodrich, W., Sauer, E., & Iverson, J. (2007). Young children use their hands to tell their mothers what to say. *Developmental Science, 10,* 778–785.

Goldin-Meadow, S., & Mylander, C. (1998). Spontaneous sign systems created by deaf children in two cultures. *Nature, 91,* 279–281.

Goldin-Meadow, S., & Wagner, S. M. (2005). How our hands help us learn. *Trends in Cognitive Science, 2005, 9,* 234–241.

Iverson, J.M., & Goldin-Meadow, S. (2005). Gesture paves the way for language development. *Psychological Science, 16,* 368–371.

Kendon, A. (1980). Gesticulation and speech: Two aspects of the process of utterance. In M. R. Key (Ed.), *Relationship of verbal and nonverbal communication* (pp. 207–228). The Hague: Mouton.

McNeill, D. (1992). *Hand and mind: What gestures reveal about thought*. Chicago, IL: University of Chicago Press.

Newport, E. L., & Meier, R. P. (1985). The acquisition of American Sign Language. In D. I. Slobin (Ed.), *The cross-linguistic study of language acquisition, Vol. 1: The data*. Hillsdale, NJ: Erlbaum.

Ozcaliskan, S., & Goldin-Meadow, S. (2005). Gesture is at the cutting edge of early language development. *Cognition, 96,* B01–113.

Sauer, E., Levine, S. C., & Goldin-Meadow, S. (2008). Early gesture predicts language delay in children with pre- or perinatal brain lesions. *Child Development,* revision under review.

Thinking Without Language
Herbert S. Terrace
Columbia University

▶ *Please tell us about your current position and research interests.*
I am Professor of Psychology and Psychiatry at Columbia University and the New York Psychiatric Institute. My colleagues and I at Columbia's Primate Cognition Laboratory focus on the cognitive abilities of nonhuman primates: their ability to learn lists of pictures and numerical stimuli and to evaluate their own performance on various tasks.

▶ *What got you interested in the intellectual abilities of nonhuman primates?*
I've always been interested in the evolution of language. Recently, my focus has been on the cognitive and social precursors of language.

▶ *What has been the real-world impact of this work?*
Our findings offer the beginnings of understanding of the evolution of human cognition and its prelinguistic origins.

> *It is a very remarkable fact that there are none so depraved and stupid, without even excepting idiots, that they cannot arrange different words together, forming of them a statement by which they make known their thought; while, on the other hand, there is no other animal, however perfect and fortunately circumstanced it may be, which can do the same.*
>
> **Descartes (1637)**

Psychological science is the only life science that has not fully assimilated the theory of evolution. The main obstacle is the human mind—language, in particular. Many people are willing to accept the argument that nonhumans evolved according to the Darwinian principles of "descent with modification" as honed by "natural selection," but they balk at applying those principles to something as complex as the human mind.

The human mind and language seem inseparable, and with good reason. Most people can't imagine how thinking can occur without language. During the last 50 years, however, many psychologists have begun research programs on animal cognition to obtain evidence that nonhuman animals can think without language. And, since the 1970s, another line of research has focused on whether nonhuman animals can learn language. The consensus is that they cannot. That leaves us with the question: How do animals think without language? I have conducted research programs on both issues.

Project Nim

The goal of Project Nim was to teach a young chimpanzee American Sign Language (ASL), a complex, natural language used by thousands of deaf, English-speaking North Americans. Why sign rather than vocal language?

The human and chimpanzee vocal apparatuses differ significantly, and chimpanzees' inability to articulate human sounds seemed to explain earlier, failed attempts to teach chimpanzees English or Russian by imitation (Terrace, 1979). The idea was to use a human language that didn't depend on the vocal apparatus.

In December 1973, I acquired a 2-week-old infant chimpanzee from a chimpanzee colony in Oklahoma. I named him Nim Chimpsky, flew with him to New York, and then, with the help of a family who lived on the Upper West Side of Manhattan, raised him in an environment in which he was taught to use ASL. My project was modeled after one started by Beatrice and Allen Gardner (Gardner & Gardner, 1969) with a chimpanzee named Washoe.

My interest in the Gardners' project was based on their claim that Washoe was producing sentences in ASL. That claim was significant for two reasons: Descartes and other philosophers have argued that language is exclusively human. More recently, Noam Chomsky (1968), who is arguably the greatest linguist of the twentieth century, developed descriptive grammars that made explicit what counts as human language. As opposed to a formal, prescriptive grammar that students learn in elementary school (and that tells them the proper way to speak), a descriptive grammar is an objective, nonjudgmental description of the rules for generating sentences; it shows how words, proper or not, relate to other words in a sentence.

I shared with the Gardners the goal of training a chimpanzee to learn a large vocabulary of signs and then determining whether it could combine those signs to generate different meanings. That approach was consistent with the general view of psycholinguists that human language makes use of two levels of structure: the word and the sentence. In contrast to the fixed character of various forms of animal communication (for example, bird songs that function as mating or "stay-out-of-my-territory" calls or bee "dances" that specify the location of a food source with respect to the hive), the meaning of a word is arbitrary. A bird cannot learn new mating or "stay-out-of-my-territory" calls, nor can bees learn new dances to communicate the distance and the direction that other bees have to fly in order to obtain food.

No such restrictions limit human speakers: It matters not if you refer to a particular color as *red, rouge, roit,* or any of the thousands of equivalents that can be found in other languages. However, the range of meanings of individual words pales in comparison to the essentially innumerable meanings that can be created by combining words. That chimpanzees and other animals to some extent share with humans the ability to learn individual "words" was clear. But humans can produce and understand sentences—an ability that requires knowledge of a grammar, a second level of structure that specifies the rules for combining words to create particular meanings. Chomsky and others argued that that knowledge separates human and animal communication.

In an early diary report, the Gardners noted that Washoe combined signs to create particular meanings. For example, when her trainer, Roger Fouts, asked her "What's that?" in the presence of a swan, Washoe reportedly signed "Water bird." That report prompted Roger Brown (1925–1997), a highly respected psycholinguist, to comment, "It was rather as if a seismometer left on the moon had started to tap out 'S-O-S.'"

I was also surprised when I read the Gardners' report, but I felt skeptical. I thought that any of following three simpler interpretations of *water bird* could apply: Washoe may have been prompted by Fouts to sign *water bird*; Washoe may have signed *bird water*, but Fouts may have recorded Washoe's utterance in the order we naturally speak; or Washoe may have signed *water* and *bird* as two separate utterances. I decided that the only way to eliminate my doubts was to run a project on which a chimp's signs and their contexts were recorded in diaries made by independent observers and then compared for reliability. To obtain an accurate corpus of a young chimp's utterances was the main goal of Project Nim.

At about the same time, other efforts were underway to teach chimpanzees to use a language, but those researchers represented words with artificial external stimuli. David Premack (1976) used plastic chips of different shapes, colors, and sizes in training a chimpanzee he called Sarah. For example, if Sarah wanted a piece of apple, as opposed to a piece of bread, she would have to give her trainer a blue triangle rather than the symbol for bread, a tan rectangle with a jagged edge. Sue Savage-Rumbaugh and Duane Rumbaugh (Rumbaugh, 1977) used "lexigrams" composed of abstract geometric shapes that were imposed on backgrounds of different colors to teach "words" to a chimpanzee they called Lana. The icons were displayed on a large panel in front of a computer that recorded Lana's "word" use during her training sessions.

Once Sarah and Lana acquired a basic vocabulary of about 30 words, they were trained to make various requests by combining two words—for example, *give apple*. Eventually both learned to make 4-item sequences—for example, Sarah: *Mary → give → apple → Sarah*, or Lana: *Please → machine → give → drink*. As compared to the free-flowing nature of Projects Washoe and Nim, the rigid nature of Premack's and the Rumbaughs' projects allowed both to keep comprehensive records of the sequences their chimps produced.

By the late 1970s, much evidence had accumulated purporting to show that apes could create sentences—specifically, that an ape could create new meanings by combining words according to grammatical rules. However, the "sentences" could be explained without reference to grammatical competence. My associates and I analyzed 20,000 of Nim's combinations of two or more signs. Superficially, many of Nim's combinations appeared to be generated by the rules of a simple finite-state grammar—for example, *More + x*; *transitive verb + me* or *Nim*, etc. Taken by themselves, such combinations provided the strongest evidence that apes could create a sentence. Indeed, many of Nim's multisign utterances resembled a child's initial multiword utterances (Nelson, 1981).

A frame-by-frame analysis of videotapes of his signing, however, revealed that Nim responded mainly to the urgings of his teacher and that most of what he signed was a full or partial imitation of his teacher's prior utterance(s). Although young children also imitate many of their parents' utterances, the relative frequency of imitated utterances is substantially lower than Nim's. Also, Nim never moved beyond the imitative phase of language development (Terrace et al., 1979). Analysis of the available films of other signing apes showed that the patterns of their signing were similar to Nim's; specifically, that their signs were highly imitative.

The conclusions of Project Nim were criticized on various methodological grounds by other investigators attempting to teach an ape to use sign language. Importantly, however, my conclusions did not depend on the data collected from Nim. I could have reached the same conclusions by looking at videotapes of other chimps using ASL. And they could have refuted my conclusions by providing lengthy unedited videotapes of a chimpanzee signing with a human companion. However, during the almost 40 years that have elapsed since I published my conclusions, there hasn't been a single videotape bearing evidence that challenged them.

Different considerations lead to a rejection of the view that Sarah's and Lana's sequences were sentences. In one analysis of a corpus of approximately 14,000 of Lana's combinations collected by a computer, researchers concluded that those combinations could be accounted for almost entirely as conditional discriminations (Thompson & Church, 1980). First, Lana learned by rote to use "lexigrams" such as *apple, music, banana,* and *chocolate* in sequences like *Please machine give X.* If there was no incentive in view, the appropriate sequence would be *Please put into machine X.* Typically, the symbol for a particular reward was inserted into the last position of the stock sentence. Although Lana clearly understood the meanings of the lexigrams that referred to a particular reward (in the sense that she could use them contrastively to make specific requests), there is no evidence that she understood the meanings of the other lexigrams that composed the stock sequences she learned to produce (for example, *Please, machine, give, put,* or *piece of*).

Moving on to Monkeys

I developed circumstantial evidence that Lana's and Sarah's sequences were not sentences by creating studies demonstrating that monkeys can learn sequences composed of four arbitrarily selected photos to which they have to respond in a particular order (Terrace, 2002). Thus, one list might consist of the items fish → tree → mountain → person; another, the items flower → bird → rodent → beach; and so forth. Because the selection of the photos was completely arbitrary, as was the order of a particular sequence, any of these sequences could "mean," say, *please machine give Coke.* We used rhesus macaques in these experiments because they were less expensive than chimpanzees and because they did not require extensive socialization. The most widely used monkeys in experiments on cognition, rhesus macaques are also considered to be the brightest species of monkey.

The photographs that we used in these experiments were presented simultaneously on a touch-sensitive video monitor in configurations that varied from trial to trial to insure that the sequence could not be learned as a motor sequence. Because no differential feedback was provided as the monkey moved from one photo to the next, its performance on such *simultaneous chains* couldn't be explained by traditional *chaining theory*, which posits that a sequence is composed of items that are independent of each other. Thus, when

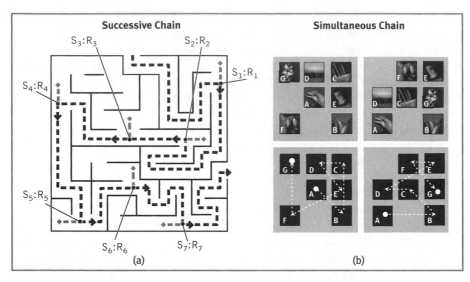

FIGURE 1A What a subject learns in a maze with n choice points. According to chaining theory, a subject learns n discrete stimulus–response (S–R) associations. In the maze shown here, learning 7 associations allows the subject to arrive at the goal by executing the following successive chain: $S_1:R_1 \to S_2:R_2 \to S_3 \ldots S_7:R_7 \to$ SR. Crucially, this knowledge also insures that (1) having responded correctly to S_n, that stimulus disappears and (2) encounter S_{n+1}, and only S_{n+1}, will be encountered at the next choice point. Thus, when the subject is at, say, S_3, cues from the other choice points cannot compete for attention.

FIGURE 1B Two paths to responding correctly on trials of a 7-item simultaneous chain. In a typical trial, the 7 stimuli are presented until the subject either makes an error or earns a reward by responding to those stimuli in the correct order. Because the spatial configuration of choice points changes randomly from trial to trial, subjects cannot learn the required sequence as a fixed set of motor responses. (Terrace, 2005)

a rat is trained to run a maze, it can't respond to choice point C when it is responding to choice point B. A typical successive maze is shown in Figure 1a.

Starting with the ideas of Hermann Ebbinghaus (1850–1909), various forms of chaining theory have assumed that an understanding of learned sequences in animals and humans would follow directly from an understanding of how particular stimuli become associated with particular responses. In this view, all instances of serially organized behavior are reducible to discrete stimulus-response units, each unit linked to the next by virtue of extensive practice. It matters not whether the sequence in question was a sentence or tying a shoelace.

In one of the most influential articles in modern psychology, Karl Lashley (1890–1958) challenged chaining theory on the grounds that it cannot explain a person's knowledge of relationships between items that are not adjacent to one another—for example, between words from different parts of a sentence (Lashley, 1951). Because Lashley's arguments were based on examples of human behavior, his critique had less influence on ideas about animal cognition than it had on human cognitive theory and research. Indeed, critics have argued that Lashley's ideas do not apply to animals because their learned behavior does not approach the complexity of human skills and their communication is simpler and less arbitrary than human language. That view is no longer tenable. Recent advances in our understanding of serially organized behavior in animals have confirmed that Lashley's criticisms of chaining theory apply with the same force to animal behavior as they do to human behavior.

Ironically, the main impetus for my interest in serially organized behavior in animals was the now discredited claim that apes (mainly chimpanzees) could create grammatical sequences and by the success of a new paradigm for training monkeys to produce complex sequences without the benefit of any "linguistic" training (Terrace, 2002). Those sequences differed in many respects from the kind of sequences on which animals have been traditionally trained. To highlight those differences, I have referred to the former as simultaneous chains and to the latter as successive chains (Terrace, 2005). On *successive chains*—for example, a rat running through a maze—the choice points are spatially and temporally isolated from one another. A subject need only attend to the choice point on hand. On *simultaneous chains*, all of the choice points are presented simultaneously, and an error is possible at any point of the sequence. A 7-item simultaneous chain is shown in Figure 1b.

Thinking Without Language

On the one hand, my negative conclusions about the linguistic abilities of chimpanzees support Descartes' view that animals are incapable of communicating with language. On the other hand, the ability of monkeys to recall difficult sequences challenges Descartes' view that because animals cannot use language, they are incapable of thinking. In the remainder of this essay, I will describe some of the serial learning experiments I performed that provide unequivocal evidence that animals can think without language. In one experiment, for example, four monkeys had to learn by trial and error the correct order in which to respond to four different lists, each composed of seven arbitrarily selected photographs. Each list was composed of novel photos. The monkeys had to guess the correct order in which to respond to the items of each list. The probability of guessing the correct sequence on a 7-item list was 1/5040 (Terrace, Son, & Brannon, 2003).

A Thought Experiment

To appreciate the difficulty of learning a single 7-item list, imagine trying to enter your 7-digit personal identification number (PIN), say *9-2-1-5-8-4-7*, at a cash machine on which the positions of the numbers were changed each time you tried to operate it. You could not enter your PIN by executing a sequence of distinctive motor movements. Instead, you would have to locate each number on the number pad and mentally keep track of your position in the sequence as you pressed different buttons.

As difficult as that task may seem, it would be far more difficult to deduce your PIN number by *trial and error*. Any error would terminate a trial and result in a new trial in which the digits were displayed in a different config-uration. To determine your PIN, you would have to recall the consequences of any of the 36 types of logical errors you might make while attempting to produce the required sequence (21 types of forward errors and 15 types of backward errors). Further, you would have to determine the first 6 digits without getting any money from the cash machine. This is precisely the type of problem the monkeys had to solve at the start of training on each of the four 7-item lists on which they were trained. Instead of numerals, the mon-keys had to respond to photographs. Instead of cash, they were given banana pellets.

All four monkeys learned all four of the 7-item lists and also demonstrated that they could execute all of those lists when they were selected at random during a single session. As shown in Figure 2, each monkey became progres-sively more efficient at deducing the correct order in which to respond dur-ing the course of learning four 7-item lists. On the final 7-item list, they barely exceeded the minimum number of logical guesses needed to identify the first 2 items.

In a separate experiment, monkeys were tested on their ability to apply their knowledge of four different 7-item lists on a novel task. The monkeys were shown all of the 336 pairs that could be derived from the 28 items used to construct the four 7-item lists on which they were trained. (None of the

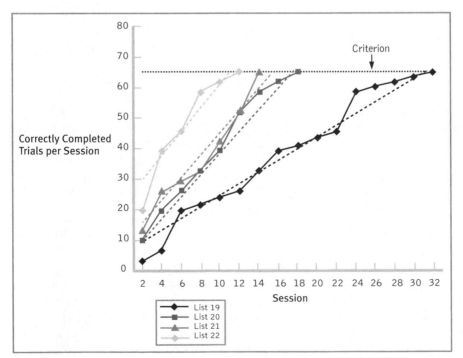

FIGURE 2   Serial expertise in four monkeys. The mean accuracy of responding on each 7-item list during even-numbered sessions. The probability of executing a new 7-item list cor-rectly by chance, assuming no backwards errors, is $1/5040 = 1/7!$ Note that the X axis is session (not list). (Terrace, Son, & Brannon, 2003)

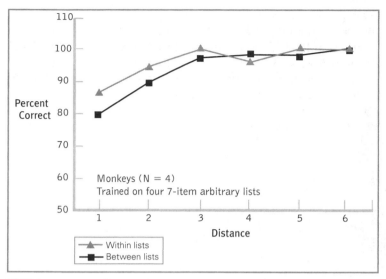

FIGURE 3 Distance effects with arbitrary stimuli. Mean accuracy to between- and within-list subsets as a function of distance between items on original lists in the Terrace, Son, & Brannon (2003) experiment.

subsets had the same ordinal position on each list—for example, B_{list1} and B_{list3}— because there was no correct answer for those subsets.) Monkeys were rewarded for responding to the items in each pair in the order specified by their ordinal positions on the original list. As shown in Figure 3, monkeys responded at the same high level of accuracy (91 percent) on the *first* occasion on which each pair was presented, whether the items were drawn from the same or from *different* lists. For example, they were equally adept at responding in the correct order to the second item of the third 7-item list and the sixth item of the first 7-item list (a between-list pair) as they were to the second and the sixth item of the fourth 7-item list (a within-list pair).

The sequences that the monkeys learned in these experiments are by far the most difficult lists ever mastered by any nonhuman primate, including those trained in experiments on the linguistic and numerical abilities of apes (Premack, 1976; Rumbaugh, 1977). Their performance probably does not reflect the upper limit of a monkey's serial capacity. The ease with which they learned 7-item lists and the steady decrease in the number of sessions they needed to master new lists suggests that they could master longer lists. The monkeys' performance on the pair-wise test is significant because it showed that they could compare representations of the ordinal position of each item from each list and then apply that knowledge to solve a novel problem. Specifically, their performance shows that each monkey represented, in long-term memory, the ordinal position of items from each of the four 7-item lists they had learned and that they were able to compare, in working memory, the ordinal positions of any two items from any of the 7-item lists. The ability to perform such comparisons is beyond the scope of any contemporary theories of animal cognition.

Having observed monkeys perform so well on 2-item subsets that were composed of items from different lists, I felt encouraged to train them on various other tasks. For example, during the last 10 years, we have trained monkeys to learn lists based on numerical quantity (Brannon & Terrace, 1998) and to engage in a metacognitive task that requires them to indicate their confidence in the accuracy of their response (Kornell et al., 2007). These and other experiments suggest that we have just scratched the surface of a monkey's ability to think without language.

Suggested Further Reading

Terrace, H. S. (1979). *Nim.* New York: Knopf.

Wasserman, E. A. , & Zentall, T. R. (Eds.). (2006). *Comparative cognition: Experimental explorations of animal intelligence.* New York: Oxford University Press.

References

Brannon, E. M. & Terrace, H. S. (1998). Ordering of the numerosities 1–9 by monkeys. *Science, 282,* 746–749.

Gardner, B. T. and Gardner, R. A. (1969). Teaching sign language to a chimpanzee. *Science 162,* 664–672.

Kornell, N., Son, L. K., & Terrace, H. S. (2007). Transfer of metacognitive skills and hint seeking in monkeys. *Psychological Science, 18*(1), 4–71.

Lashley, K. S. (1951) The problem of serial order in behavior. In L. A. Jeffress (Ed.), *Hixon symposium on cerebral mechanisms in behavior.* New York: John Wiley & Sons, 112–136.

Nelson, K. (1981). Individual differences in language development: Implications for development and language. *Developmental Psychology, 17,* 170–187.

Premack, D. (1976). *Intelligence in ape and man.* Hillsdale, NJ: Lawrence Erlbaum Associates.

Rumbaugh, D. M. (1977). *Language learning by a chimpanzee: The Lana project.* New York: Academic Press.

Terrace, H. S. (1979). *Nim.* New York: Knopf.

Terrace, H. S. (2002). Serial expertise and the evolution of language. In Wray, J. H. A., & Newmeyer, F. J. (Eds.), *The Transition to Language.* New York: Oxford University Press. 64–90.

Terrace, H. S. (2005). The simultaneous chain: A new approach to serial learning. *Trends in Cognitive Science, 9,* 202–210.

Terrace, H. S., Petitto, L. A., Sanders, R. J., & Bever, T. G. (1979). Can an ape create a sentence? *Science, 206,* 891–902.

Terrace, H. S., Son, L. K., & Brannon, E. M. (2003). Serial expertise of rhesus macaques. *Psychological Science, 14*(1), 66–73.

Thompson, C. R., & Church, R. M. (1980). An explanation of the language of a chimpanzee. *Science, 208,* 313–314.

Consciousness

Bernard J. Baars

Thinking About Consciousness

Daniel M. Wegner

When You Put Things Out of Mind, Where Do They Go?

Thinking About Consciousness
Bernard J. Baars
The Neurosciences Institute

▶ *Please describe your current position and research interests.*
I constantly work to update my college textbook, *Cognition, Brain and Consciousness: An Introduction to Cognitive Neuroscience*. I am also affiliated with the Neurosciences Institute, headed by Nobel Laureate Gerald Edelman, and I do collaborative research with Professor Stan Franklin at the University of Memphis on large-scale artificial intelligence systems that perform human-like functions, including approximations to computational consciousness. The ethical and legal implications of the return to the study of consciousness is another major focus of interest.

▶ *What drew you to studying consciousness as such?*
How could anybody who is interested in the human condition avoid it? I found it difficult as a student to understand why it was so much avoided. One of my hopes is to promote integration of the great philosophical and humanistic traditions of consciousness studies with science.

▶ *What has been the real-world impact of this work?*
The journal and scientific association I cofounded have helped to bring out a large amount of excellent scientific and medical research. For example, we are getting closer to a brain index for conscious processes—a very difficult feat. Medical research has also shown that diagnosed coma patients have intermittent conscious experiences about 40 percent of the time. We know much more about consciousness in other species. The old saying is that "nothing is as practical as a good theory." We are beginning to see how that works in consciousness science.

We are all conscious beings, as we discover every morning when we wake up to a new day. But consciousness is not something that can be observed directly, at least not in the public domain of normal science. People can, of course, tell others about their conscious experiences, or they can signal their experiences through some voluntary action like pressing the accelerator in an automobile when the traffic light turns green. In brain science, we can record the activity of neurons and use the resulting overall record (an electroencephalogram, or EEG) to detect gross differences in brain activity between normal waking and deep (slow-wave) sleep. (Edelman & Tononi, 2000; Crick & Koch, 2003).

In contrast to people's ability to accurately report conscious events, we have no access to the unconscious processes that are constantly ongoing in our brains. For example, over-learned habits, like the details of riding a bicycle, tend to become unconscious. Our own speech movements—of the tongue, lips, and vocal cords—are not under direct voluntary control, unless we get very clear conscious feedback about their movements. The cerebellum, a giant clump of neurons tucked under the back of the cortex, is believed to function unconsciously. People with bilateral damage to the cerebellum are conscious, but they lose the ability to control fine motor movement. And in the last 10 years or so, evidence has grown that the brain has an unconscious pathway through which visual information flows (called the dorsal stream), stretching from the visual cortex to the parietal regions, which is used for spatial framing and even visually guided reaching for objects within arm's reach. So even in the waking brain, many unconscious processes are active every second of the day.

The first obstacle in dealing with consciousness as a scientific topic arises from the tangled thicket of conflicting ideas that surrounds the topic. One philosophical debate alone, the mind-body debate, has a relevant literature extending from the Upanishads to the latest philosophical journals—4,000 years of serious thought. But one time-honored strategy in science is to put aside philosophical issues for a time by focusing on empirically decidable ones.

The Evidence

How are we to discover empirical evidence about consciousness? Nineteenth-century psychologists like Wilhelm Wundt (1832–1920) and William James (1842–1910) believed that the nature of consciousness was the fundamental problem for psychology, but they had remarkably little to say about it as such. In a way, they took the reality of personal consciousness to be so obvious that it could not be doubted or explained. Freud and thinkers in the psychodynamic tradition have much to say about unconscious motivations, but they also took conscious experience largely for granted. Behaviorists working in the first half of the twentieth century tended to discourage a consideration of consciousness, and even cognitive psychologists avoided it until the last decade or two.

In truth, the facts of consciousness are all around us, ready to be studied. Practically all findings in psychology involve conscious experience, as you know if you've been a subject in an experiment. A psychologist can no more avoid consciousness than a physicist can evade gravity. A number of scientists have been focusing on consciousness by comparing conscious versus unconscious events—the ones people can tell us about versus the ones they can't.

This idea goes back to William James' *The Principles of Psychology* (1890). James proposed contrasting comparable conscious and nonconscious events as a way of focusing on the issue of consciousness as such. We call the resulting method contrastive analysis. One can think of contrastive analysis as an experiment in which consciousness is an experimental variable and everything else is held as constant as possible. A wealth of information has now accumulated based on this reasoning. In recent years, thousands of experiments have been published on the topic of human consciousness, many of them using this kind of comparison.

In one famous, well-studied technique, called binocular rivalry, one image is presented to the left eye, and a very different image is presented to the right eye. The two images are so different that the brain cannot fuse them into a single image, the way it does in normal vision when we look at a coffee cup on a table in front of us. Instead, the conscious part of the brain flips back and forth between the two images, often for several seconds each. We see one image (for instance, a smiley face) or another (a sunburst image). But when the smiley face is not conscious during binocular rivalry, it still is projected on the retina, just as before. The switch between the two stimuli takes place inside the brain.

Where and how does the brain decide which image is going to be conscious and which is not? Current evidence from animal and human studies suggests that visual objects "become conscious" when the brain is able to put together multiple maps of the visual input. You can think of the visual brain as a stack of maps of the scene your eyes are looking at, at any given moment in time. Every fraction of a second, the retina takes a detailed snapshot, a "map" of the visual input, which is echoed at the next level of the thalamus and the first visual area of cortex. Next, the detailed map is taken apart into separate visual maps for colors, for edges between light and dark regions, for movement and for shapes. All of those maps preserve the spatial location of the thing you are looking at, so that there is a point-to-point correspondence, a consistent stack of "visuotopic" maps. But we do not see a world of separate visual features—no points of light, no isolated patches of color, and not just one momentary snapshot at a time. Rather, we see a white cat jumping in a single graceful bound from the floor to the kitchen counter. Our conscious experiences are about an integrated world of objects in motion.

The best evidence we have today is that all the separate "feature maps" for visual location, color, shape, movement, and object identity are put together in the posterior half of the brain, terminating in the lower part of the temporal lobe. Studies of binocular rivalry in monkeys and humans show that this is where the information for the conscious stream comes together to make an integrated visual experience (Logothetis, 1998). Because all the visual maps are firing neurons in the same map coordinates, we find regular synchronized oscillations among the input maps, like a surfers' beach wave that just builds and builds on itself. In the brain, those oscillations among visual maps are believed to run around 30 Hz and above. Like the surfers' wave, the activity in these maps becomes higher and higher as long as its locations and features are mutually consistent. A conscious visual object like a coffee cup seems to be made up of a lot of such visual maps synched together to produce high, synchronous waves, to bring the location, shape, and colors of the coffee cup into an integrated wave of brain activity (Varela et al., 2001).

But is that enough for conscious perception?

Global Workspace Theory: A Chat Room on the Brain Web

What about the rest of the brain? Is it enough for the visual cortex to have synchronized input maps of a visual coffee cup to make it conscious? More than 20 years ago, I argued that stimulus integration is not enough for consciousness (Baars, 1988). After all, if you were to try to listen to your favorite music and understand this essay at the same time, you'll find out pretty quickly that you can't do both. Listening and studying interfere with each other. (I'm sorry, but it's true!)

And yet, why couldn't the brain, with its tens of billions of active neurons, just integrate those two streams of information at the same moment in time? If stimulus integration is enough for consciousness, you could be conscious of a textbook, and a conversation with a friend, and the heavy traffic around your car, and all the good things you might eat for lunch. Why can't we be conscious of everything all at once, even with different or contradictory streams of information?

The trouble with the "stimulus integration" explanation for conscious perception is that it doesn't explain the radical limited capacity of moment-to-moment conscious events. Consciousness is often compared to a stream, with one thought or percept coming after the next. And very careful experiments on the moment-to-moment limitations on conscious contents show that the window of consciousness is even smaller than we think. For example, the snapshots of the visual world that our eyes take in at any single moment are keyhole-sized. Our eyes jump from one place to another in the visual scene in front of us and take in narrow snapshots. The brain puts all of these foveal fixations, or snapshots, together, so that we have the sense of seeing the entire scene in front of us. But momentary input is remarkably small. That's why magicians can trick your eyes, by drawing your conscious vision in one place, while right in front of you (but outside of the fovea) the trickster is making tennis balls disappear or slipping new playing cards into a deck.

But notice a huge advantage of consciousness, namely its ability to access large amounts of information. An educated person may have a vocabulary of 100,000 words. Each word that we know can connect to a whole network of related ideas, sounds, and speech gestures. We can recognize literally thousands of different people (which doesn't mean we remember their names, of course). We can recognize a movie scene from many years ago, without trying to memorize it. Our access to information stored in the brain and in the world is huge even though our momentary conscious snapshots are small (Baars, 2002).

Do other systems have these properties? I believe so. Examples are the World Wide Web, radio stations, and gigantic stadiums. These systems involve massively parallel processing: Many complex and sophisticated things are happening at the same moment in time. The Web is constantly buzzing with activity all around the world. A radio station may broadcast a simple song, but it can be heard by thousands of people, all with their own thoughts and feelings associated with the song. Such massively parallel information-processing systems often operate through a narrow, limited capacity channel. The radio station plays only one song at a time, and in fact, only one note of a song in any fraction of a second. A gigantic stadium might have tens of thousands of people all watching the same football player carry the ball across the field. All those systems combine massive capacity with a narrow focal series of events.

The brain looks like such a system. With 30 or 40 billion neurons, working away at the same time, with a massive highway system of connections between all the different regions of the cortex, and with literally trillions of axons firing, and even more synapses, the brain is of a level of complexity comparable to the World Wide Web.

But now imagine having a chat room with half a dozen people participating. Only one person can speak at any moment of time. Over time, as different people jump into the conversation and then start doing their own thinking because somebody else is talking, the chat room looks like a serial, one-at-a-time stream of events. But in fact, we know there are many parallel events happening. And if we imagine that the chat room discussion is being Webcast to dozens or hundreds of other people, we have a huge "unconscious" system, with a very small "conscious" focal stream.

A Prediction That Seems to Be Working Out

In 1983, and in later publications, I predicted that conscious events should be "broadcast" in the brain, far beyond the stimulus-processing regions. I based my argument on what cognitive scientists already knew: Artificial intelligence architectures are built in precisely that way (Baars, 1983, 1988, 1997, 2002; Newell, 1992). And we knew that those systems—parallel-interactive ones, sometimes called society models—are very good at solving difficult problems, like computerized speech perception. Our knowledge of the brain is still very fragmentary. There are vast gaps in our knowledge about consciousness, but one testable prediction is that conscious events would trigger very widespread activation in the brain (Dehaene & Naccache, 2001).

That prediction has now been supported by brain imaging methods. Apparently, our consciousness of a coffee cup on a table in front of us requires more than just the visual brain. In addition to stimulus integration, consciousness seems to involve forward spread of brain activity from the sensory regions at the back of the brain to the parietal and frontal lobes. That is at least what studies with functional magnetic resonance imaging (fMRI), magnetoencephalography (MEG), and EEG are showing. We always have to be aware of our limitations, and no doubt we will get more evidence that will force us to refine that hypothesis. But it's encouraging that we can make a rather surprising prediction about the role and effects of conscious events in the brain and obtain evidence suggesting that we are on the right path.

The Need to Understand Conscious Experience

Imagine the enterprise of scientific psychology as a great effort to solve a jigsaw puzzle as big as a football field. Several communities of researchers have been working for decades on the job of finding the missing pieces in the puzzle, and in recent years many gaps have been filled. However, one central missing piece—the issue of conscious experience—has been thought to be so difficult that many researchers have sensibly avoided that part of the puzzle. Yet the gap left by this great central piece has not gone away, and surrounding it are numerous issues that cannot be solved until it is addressed. If that is a reasonable analogy, it follows that the more pieces of the jigsaw puzzle we discover, the more the remaining uncertainties will tend to cluster about the great central gap where the missing piece must fit.

Suggested Further Reading

Baars, B. J., & Gage, N. M. (2007). *Cognition, brain and consciousness: An introduction to cognitive neuroscience.* London: Elsevier/Academic Press.

Edelman, G. M., & Tononi, G. (2000). *A universe of consciousness.* New York: Basic Books.

References

Baars, B. J. (1983). Conscious contents provide the nervous system with coherent, global information. In R.J. Davidson, G. E. Schwartz, & D. Shapiro (Eds.), *Consciousness and self-regulation: Vol. 3. Advances in Research and Theory.* New York: Plenum Press.

Baars, B. J. (1988). *A cognitive theory of consciousness.* New York: Cambridge University Press.

Baars, B. J. (1997). *In the theater of consciousness: The workspace of the mind.* New York: Oxford University Press.

Baars, B. J. (2002). The conscious access hypothesis: Origins and recent evidence. *Trends in Cognitive Sciences, 6*(1), 47–52.

Crick, F., & Koch, C. A. (2003). A framework for consciousness. *Nature Neuroscience, 6,* 119–126.

Dehaene, S., & Naccache, L. (2001). Towards a cognitive neuroscience of consciousness: Basic evidence and a workspace framework. *Cognition, 79,* 1–37.

Edelman, G. M., & Tononi, G. (2000). *A universe of consciousness.* New York: Basic Books.

James, W. (1890). *The principles of psychology.* NewYork: Holt.

Logothetis, N. K. (1998). Single units and conscious vision. *Philosophical Transactions of the Royal Society B: Biological Studies, 353,* 1801–1818.

Newell, A. (1992). SOAR as a unified theory of cognition: Issues and explanations. *Behavioral and Brain Sciences, 15*(3), 464–492.

Varela, F., Lachaux, J.-P., Rodriguez, E., & Martinerie, J. (2001). The brainweb: Phase synchronization and large-scale integration. *Nature Neuroscience, 2,* 229–239.

When You Put Things Out of Mind, Where Do They Go?

Daniel M. Wegner
Harvard University

▶ *Please tell us about your current position and research interests*

I am Professor of Psychology at Harvard University. My research examines the role of thought in self-control and social life. This includes the study of thought suppression (why we have trouble keeping unwanted thoughts out of mind), transactive memory (how we remember things cooperatively with others), and apparent mental causation (what gives us the sense that we are consciously causing our actions). The past few years I've also become fascinated by mind perception—how people try to make sense of minds that are very different from their own, from the minds of animals to those of robots, infants, people in persistent vegetative states, fetuses, groups such as corporations, and even the nonliving or supernatural.

▶ *What got you interested in studying how we perceive and control the mind?*

I'd have to say that the early seed of this interest was a sleazy politician. I noticed that when a headline aired someone's denial of an accusation (for example, "Mayor claims she took no bribes"), I often ended up thinking the accusation was true anyway. This got me to wondering if denials ever really work—if you can erase ideas or possibilities with denials once they are known and the "cat is out of the bag." Eventually, this led to experiments on what happens when people are specifically asked not to think about something.

▶ *What has been the real-world impact of this work?*

I'm not a clinical psychologist, but this work has real-world clinical implications. People who have unwanted thoughts—thoughts that make them anxious or depressed or disgusted or afraid—often come to clinical psychologists hoping that there will be treatments that can ease their struggle. Our studies of people who are simply asked in the lab to try to stop thinking about some neutral item provide a window into what people who are truly troubled by real-world unwanted thoughts can do to cope with them. And it turns out that people can sometimes overcome these thoughts by reversing the impulse to avoid them. Therapies that encourage people to talk about their unwanted thoughts, think about them, or otherwise confront them, often provide surprisingly useful pathways *away* from the thoughts. Research on the disclosure and acceptance of unwanted thoughts is helping to create useful new therapeutic strategies.

Have you ever tried to stop thinking about something? Try right now to stop thinking about your nose. Yes, the nose right there on your face. Put it out of mind. Really. Just stop everything for a minute and don't think about your nose.

Bet you couldn't. In fact, if you're like me, you may go a bit cross-eyed trying to sneak peeks at the darn thing. Fortunately, as soon as you give up the project of not thinking about it, the thought of your nose will settle back into the netherworld of things you've successfully *not* been thinking about all day. But the lesson is clear: Putting things out of mind brings them to mind. As Fyodor Dostoyevsky observed in *Winter Notes on Summer Impressions*, "Try to pose for yourself this task: not to think of a polar bear, and you will see that the cursed thing will come to mind every minute."

Dostoyevsky's Challenge

As it turns out, the Russian novelist was exactly right. My research team learned this a number of years ago in experiments that called for participants to accept the challenge of thought suppression (Wegner et al., 1987). We escorted individuals into a recording room and asked them to think aloud—saying anything that came to mind. After a while, we broke in and added a further instruction: Please try not to think about a white bear.

On average, people mentioned the bear about once per minute—just as Dostoyevsky had said. And, when we continued the experiment, we learned something new. After 5 minutes, we released participants from the suppression instruction and asked instead that they go ahead and *think* about the white bear. During this release, we found a further effect of suppression—a kind of rebound effect in which participants talked almost continuously about the bear. In fact, they had much more to say about it than did others who had been asked to discuss it from the outset. If your nose suddenly has come to mind, you are experiencing the rebound.

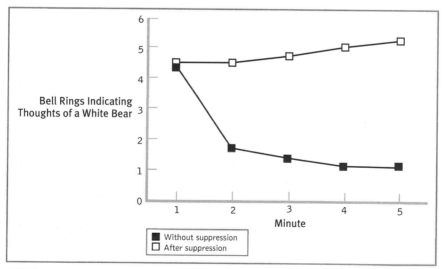

FIGURE 1 Rebound effect. Participants were asked to try not to think about a white bear, and then were asked to think about it and to ring a bell whenever it came to mind. Compared to those who were simply asked to think about the bear without prior suppression, those who first suppressed the thought showed a rebound of increased thinking. (Wegner et al., 1987)

Why then would anyone ever try to suppress a thought? It's useless, right? Dostoyevsky had a wise observation about this as well. In *Notes from the Underground,* he wrote, "Every man has reminiscences which he would not tell to everyone but only to his friends. He has other matters in his mind which he would not reveal even to his friends, but only to himself, and that in secret. But there are other things which a man is afraid to tell even to himself, and every decent man has a number of such things stored away in his mind." In other words, we all have thoughts that we may desperately want to suppress. We try not to think about that stupid boast to a friend, the little mole that could be cancer, the tempting ice cream in the freezer, the ridiculous fear that no one seems to share, or perhaps the pesky secret we promised never to reveal (Wegner, 1989).

One of Sigmund Freud's major discoveries was that people are driven by their emotions to try to put things out of mind (for example, Freud, 1915/1957). When thoughts make us anxious, sad, disgusted, afraid, or worse, we try to keep them at bay. Freud suspected that suppression might involve both conscious efforts and unconscious forgetting, which he called repression.

Avoidance processes happen spontaneously when thoughts are too emotional, and that has made such processes notoriously opaque to scientific investigation. Freud and other psychoanalysts found it impossible to observe the way people put things out of mind because the observations could only start after the fact, when emotions had already led people to try to control their thoughts. Figuring out what had happened was a bit like trying to see whether the light is on after the refrigerator door is closed. Freud had to invent methods such as dream interpretation and free association to "uncover" thoughts he believed people might have actively avoided. My colleagues and I found a scientific solution to this problem: Our white bear technique—manipulating suppression by asking people to try not to think about an unemotional thought—offers a new experimental window on the mind.

Sticky Thoughts

What has the experimental study of thought suppression taught us? We now know that suppression can be superficially effective, in that people can keep things out of mind briefly or intermittently. Some people even tell us that they're pretty good at not thinking about things. Unfortunately, they happen to be the same sort of folks who claim that they floss daily, always wait for the green light to cross the street, and never get sad. Actually, almost anyone can succeed at suppression—if the target is a long list of unrelated items. But research following up on the white bear studies (Najmi & Wegner, 2008; Rassin, 2005; Wenzlaff & Wegner, 2000) reveals that when you try to keep a single neutral thought out of mind:

- You are likely to notice it returning to mind for days.
- Distractions will make you think of it *more* rather than less often.
- Related ideas may remind you of it, but the thought itself is unlikely to remind you of those related ideas.

- You may think about it without even realizing it is on your mind but become conscious that you were thinking of it when someone asks.

- You may find it surfacing in your dreams, more so than if you had tried to think about it on purpose.

- The brain structure linked with remembering what you are doing (the dorsolateral prefrontal cortex) will be persistently activated even if you've pushed the thought out of mind.

One way to account for these findings is to suggest that part of the mind is *looking* for the very thought you are trying to suppress. This insight underlies the theory of ironic processes of mental control (Wegner, 1994). According to the theory, the attempt to stop a thought initiates two mental processes—a conscious operating process that searches for anything to think about other than the unwanted thought, and an automatic monitoring process that searches for the unwanted thought. The two processes normally work together to produce mental control.

When you try not to think of a white bear, for instance, the conscious operating process leads you to think of possible distracters: What's interesting in this room to think about? What will I be doing later today that I can review now? What's over there on the shelf that I can look at for a while? The automatic monitoring process must remain active too, so you can renew your efforts to find distracters if you happen to think of the white bear. This unconscious monitoring process alerts you when the unwanted thought enters consciousness. The two processes usually cooperate to keep the white bear out of mind, but, ironically, the monitoring process increases the mind's sensitivity to the unwanted thought and so increases the likelihood it will return.

Train Wreck

Does thought suppression begin to sound like a psychological train wreck? When profound motivation to suppress certain thoughts collides with an unconscious process that renders the effort useless, the result can be mental turmoil—cyclic attempts to suppress, punctuated by the thought's return. Unfortunately, this isn't even the worst part.

Suppression produces a cascade of additional unintended effects (Wenzlaff & Wegner, 2000). Many emotions associated with the unwanted thought re-emerge larger than life when the thought surges back to mind. When people try not to think about sex, for example, measures of skin conductance level indicate that their hands perspire and they get every bit as excited as if they were thinking about sex. When people who have no particular fear of visiting the dentist are asked not to think about it before a visit, they report increased anxiety and increased levels of intrusive distressing thoughts about what will happen. And when people are asked not to think about a past relationship with an old flame for whom they still are burning, their skin conductance levels rise to show increased emotionality as soon as they complete the suppression session.

Suppressing emotional thoughts seems to supercharge the thoughts, making them trigger the very emotion the person is trying to avoid through thought suppression. The eventual effect of suppressing thoughts, then, can be to leave the person overwrought, a bundle of emotions. This is not good. In fact, researchers examining the effects of thought suppression on the body have found that just a few hours spent suppressing emotional thoughts (for example, the feelings of depression and loneliness that come from moving away from home) can undermine bodily immune responses (Petrie, Booth, & Pennebaker, 1998). Perhaps thought suppression breaks down normal defenses and increases people's susceptibility to illness.

And we've not even begun to talk about *mental* disorders. Some psychologists believe that thought suppression may be involved in psychological disorders such as depression, anxiety, and obsessive-compulsive disorder (OCD). People may develop these disorders because they are particularly poor at suppressing and so find that unwanted thoughts plague their minds. People with OCD who experience repetitive unwanted thoughts or find themselves performing compulsive behavioral rituals might have a deficit in mental control abilities. In fact, OCD sufferers have been found to be particularly poor at suppressing even a neutral thought. Perhaps this deficit precipitates their serious hassles with unwanted thoughts in everyday life.

For a wider range of psychological problems, however, thought suppression difficulties are more likely to be a *complication* rather than a cause. Doesn't it stand to reason that people who have unpleasant thoughts, emotions, or mental symptoms would try not to think about their problems? If you are hearing voices, for example, or are not able to stop crying, or are fearful of being outside, trying not to think about the disturbing symptom might at first seem like a sensible thing to do. Suppression may offer a flash of relief, a respite in the face of an alarming realization about oneself. So one possibility is that thought suppression is a common personal response to psychological disorders.

The Amplifier Hypothesis

The suppression response is not just a minor side effect of psychological disorders. Given what we know about the way suppression can echo in the mind, we might expect that suppression might help briefly but would eventually amplify the person's problem. The process could work like this: Thinking more about the problem would result in more frequent awareness of emotions associated with the problem. Alarmed by these snowballing difficulties and suppressing that response as well, the problem could grow even larger. Thus, a person who started with a minor fear of speaking in public could find that this fear has escalated into a full-blown social phobia.

There is evidence consistent with this amplifier hypothesis (Najmi & Wegner, 2008; Wegner & Zanakos, 1994). People who chronically use conscious thought suppression as a strategy for coping with distressing thoughts are more likely than others to be anxious and depressed and to report symptoms of OCD. This link between suppression and the severity of psychological symptoms is common in other disorders as well. For example, people who report engaging in self-mutilation or self-harm are more likely than others to engage in thought suppression, and people who use thought suppression as a strategy for quitting smoking are more likely to experience return of thoughts about smoking when they are trying to quit. Children and adolescent victims of traumatic accidents who report using thought suppression are more likely than other accident victims to suffer from post-traumatic stress disorder.

Findings like these are evidence of an association between suppression and increases in the intensity of psychological disorders, but they cannot be interpreted to mean that suppression *causes* the amplification of disorders. In fact, experimental studies to test this idea could be unethical—the predicted effect of instructing people to suppress could possibly make a disorder worse! But an opposite strategy is ethically quite acceptable: In studies of what happens when people are encouraged to *relax* their attempts to suppress thoughts, researchers have reported the expected causal relationship: When people in psychotherapy are led to accept their symptoms and face the thoughts they've been striving to avoid, they can experience noteworthy alleviations of the symptoms of a disorder (for example, Marcks & Woods, 2005).

Facing unwanted thoughts isn't easy. The emotional motivation behind suppression can sometimes push so hard that there is no way to push back. If you fear spiders, for example, sitting and thinking about a spider even for a few minutes might be an emotional nightmare. People think of all kinds of ways to try to escape their unwanted thoughts because thinking such thoughts is exquisitely painful. Psychotherapists who help people stop knee-jerk suppression must often be masterfully persuasive and encourage clients to undertake change one step at a time.

Apparently, hypnosis can help people to suppress thoughts, but it's not an approach that we recommend. Overcoming the emotional urge to suppress is the key, and this can only be done by thinking the unthinkable. As Bertrand Russell (1930, p. 64) observed in *The Conquest of Happiness*:

> Now every kind of fear grows worse by not being looked at. The proper course is to think about it with great concentration until it has become completely familiar. In the end familiarity will blunt its terrors; the whole subject will become boring, and our thoughts will turn away from it, not, as formerly, by an effort of will, but through mere lack of interest in the topic. When you find yourself inclined to brood on anything, the best plan is always to think about it even more than you naturally would until at last its morbid fascination is worn off.

Suggested Further Reading

Wegner, D. M. (1989). *White bears and other unwanted thoughts: Suppression, obsession, and the psychology of mental control.* New York: Viking/Penguin.

Wenzlaff, R. M., & Wegner, D. M. (2000). Thought suppression. In S. T. Fiske (Ed.), *Annual Review of Psychology* (Vol. 51, pp. 51–91). Palo Alto, CA: Annual Reviews.

References

Dostoyevsky, F. (1955). *Winter notes on summer impressions* (R. L. Renfield, Trans.). New York: Criterion Books.

Dostoyevsky, F. (2004). *Notes from the underground* (R. Pevear & L. Volkhonsky, Trans.). New York: Knopf.

Freud, S. (1915/1957). Repression. In J. Strachey (Ed.), *The standard edition of the complete psychological works of Sigmund Freud* (Vol. 14, pp. 146–158). London: Hogarth.

Marcks, B. A., & Woods, D. W. (2005). A comparison of thought suppression to an acceptance-based technique in the management of personal intrusive thoughts: A controlled evaluation. *Behaviour Research and Therapy, 43,* 433–445.

Najmi, S., & Wegner, D. M. (2008). Thought suppression and psychopathology. In A. J. Elliott (Ed.), *Handbook of approach and avoidance motivation* (pp. 447–460). Mahwah, NJ: Erlbaum.

Petrie, K. P., Booth, R. J., & Pennebaker, J. W. (1998). The immunological effects of thought suppression. *Journal of Personality and Social Psychology, 75,* 1264–1272.

Rassin, E. (2005). *Thought suppression.* New York: Elsevier.

Russell, B. (1930). *The conquest of happiness.* New York: Horace Liveright.

Wegner, D. M. (1989). *White bears and other unwanted thoughts: Suppression, obsession, and the psychology of mental control.* New York: Viking/Penguin.

Wegner, D. M. (1994). Ironic processes of mental control. *Psychological Review, 101,* 34–52.

Wegner, D. M., Schneider, D. J., Carter, S., & White, T. (1987). Paradoxical effects of thought suppression. *Journal of Personality and Social Psychology, 53,* 5–13.

Wegner, D. M., & Zanakos, S. (1994). Chronic thought suppression. *Journal of Personality, 62,* 615–640.

Wenzlaff, R. M., & Wegner, D. M. (2000). Thought suppression. In S. T. Fiske (Ed.), *Annual Review of Psychology* (Vol. 51, pp. 51–91). Palo Alto, CA: Annual Reviews.

9

Intelligence

Howard Gardner
The Theory of Multiple Intelligences

Robert J. Sternberg
The Rainbow Project: Using a Psychological Theory of Intelligence to Improve the College Admissions Process

The Theory of Multiple Intelligences
Howard Gardner
Harvard Graduate School of Education

▶ *Please describe your current position and research interests.*
I am the Hobbs Professor of Cognition and Education at the Harvard Graduate School of Education and Senior Director of Harvard Project Zero. Since the middle 1990s, colleagues and I have been studying the nature of good work: Work that is excellent technically, personally meaningful, and carried out in an ethical manner. Since 2005, we have also been studying good play: How young people are being changed by the new digital media.

▶ *What made you question the idea that intelligence is a single entity?*
In the 1970s, I was conducting research with two groups: adults who had suffered brain damage and children who were artistically talented. Every day I was seeing dramatic examples of jagged intellectual profiles: Individuals excellent in some areas were average in others and had marked difficulties with some materials. These daily experiences convinced me that the notion of a single, undecomposable intellect could not possibly be correct.

▶ *What has been the real-world impact of this work?*
The real-world impact of this work is much greater than I could ever have anticipated. All over the world, educators found the ideas of interest and began to institute changes that could better serve the "multiple intelligences" of their students. My colleagues and I chronicle some of these educational experiments in *Multiple Intelligences Around the World* (see suggested reading). The work has also had influence in other institutions, such as museums, and at the workplace, particularly in the areas of human resources and the identification and cultivation of talent.

In 1969, while a graduate student in developmental psychology at Harvard University, I had one of those experiences that, in retrospect, changes one's life. I was part of a research team at a fledgling research group called "Project Zero"—a group concerned primarily with the nature of human artistic activity—headed by the renowned philosopher Nelson Goodman. Researchers at Project Zero were interested in artistic cognition—how artists make and create worlds through the use of various symbol systems, and how the rest of us relate to, make sense of, fall in and out of love with symbolic creations in the several art forms.

Our team had heard about the research of Boston-area neurologist Norman Geschwind, and so we invited him to give an informal seminar. This was the era when nonspecialists first heard about the division of labor between the two cerebral hemispheres. In most individuals, particularly right-handers, the left hemisphere is "dominant" for language; an injury to areas in that part of the brain cause aphasia (acquired loss of language). Language is seldom represented in the complementary right hemisphere; instead, injuries there typical impair spatial and musical capacities and produce an unusual emotional profile as well. Perhaps, we reasoned, this line of work might provide clues about human symbol-using capacities in the arts and other realms.

I was mesmerized by Geschwind's presentation—his impressive command of the field and (I must admit) his charismatic personality. At this time behaviorist ways of thinking were predominant, and I had never thought much about the organization of capacities in the human brain. As part of my work at Project Zero, I had been trying to understand the nature of artistic activities in artists and in ordinary persons, and particularly the relationships among different kinds of artistic skills. For example, I wondered about the connections between language and music: Did musical capacity piggyback on linguistic capacities, or vice versa, or were they largely independent from one another? I also was puzzling about the nature of artistic talent: From where did it come, how did it develop, and was it independent of other human capacities, other facets of intellect?

As I recall, the session with Geschwind lasted from early afternoon until well into the evening (we broke for dinner). I was particularly fascinated when, prompted by our questions, Geschwind told us about what had happened to famous artists—like the composer Maurice Ravel—after damage to the brain had been sustained. By the end of the session, I had become convinced that the representation of cognitive capacities in the brain might provide a clue to some of the issues about artistry that had puzzled me—and for which I had lacked a means for investigation.

And so, throwing caution to the winds, I decided to apply for a postdoctoral fellowship with Geschwind at the Harvard Medical School and the Aphasia Research Center of the Boston Veterans Administration Medical Center. I say "throwing caution to the winds" because most of my peers were applying for academic positions, and none of my professors thought that I could learn much from studying the cortical representations of human capacities. They still subscribed to the mid-twentieth-century dogma that the brain was off limits for psychology. The postdoctoral fellowship grew to 2 and then to 3 years; and it turned out that I ultimately spent 20 years carrying out neuropsychological research, in the process learning a great deal about the nature of artistic capacities and how they relate (and when they do not relate) to other human cognitive faculties.

But I did not abandon my work as a developmental psychologist, carried out under the auspices of Project Zero. While I was studying the breakdown of artistic (and other) capacities under conditions of damage to the brain, I was at the same time examining how various cognitive capacities developed in typical children, as well as children who showed unusual cognitive profiles (gifted children, prodigies, savants and, on occasion, young persons with severe learning deficits). And so, in the aggregate, I was examining the human mind from three distinct vantage points: how abilities are organized in artists in their prime; how such symbol-using capacities develop under ordinary conditions; and how they can be disrupted by damage to the human brain—the "experiment of nature" caused by stroke and other kinds of trauma.

Among my colleagues in psychology, I am unusual. Nearly all empirically oriented psychologists spend the bulk of their time carrying out experiments and writing articles thereafter. Rarely do psychologists write books, and especially rarely before they earn tenure! And when they write books, they are often textbooks or popular accounts of their own work. From the first, however, I was a book writer. By the time I began my postdoctoral studies, I had finished three books, and I had begun a series of books about my favorite subject—the human mind. (By now, at least ten of my books feature the word *mind* in the title.) In 1975, having spent a few years carrying out neuropsychological research, I published yet another mind-focused work: *The Shattered Mind: The Person After Brain Damage.*

By that time, thanks to my work with Norman Geschwind and other outstanding researchers in neurology and neuropsychology, I had already become convinced that the notion of the mind as a single, all-purpose computer could not be correct. Every day I was seeing young people who might be excellent in one area of study, art, or craft, while completely undistinguished in other spheres. Even more dramatically, I was daily seeing patients who exhibited unusual combinations of abilities and disabilities. One person might lose his ability to sing but be able to carry on ordinary conversation; a second might exhibit the reverse profile of symptoms. Similarly, the relation between proficiency in the visual arts and other competences was vexed; it even seemed, on occasion, that a stroke might free up artistic potential that had hitherto been latent.

And so I began to outline a book, provisionally entitled *Kinds of Minds,* in which I proposed to define the different spheres of human competence—as I might put it today, the several computers of the mind. Yet something told me that I was not quite ready to write this book, and so I put my notes aside and actually forgot this stalled project until 25 years later. Instead, I continued my parallel lines of research, contributing a few bricks to the edifices of developmental psychology and neuropsychology.

A New View of Intelligence

Enter another unexpected event. In 1979, the Harvard Graduate School of Education received a large grant from a Dutch foundation, the Bernard van Leer Foundation. I was chosen to be a Principal on The Human Potential Project. And I was given an intriguing assignment: Summarize what has been established about human cognition from the biological and cognitive sciences. The project lasted 5 years, covered much of my salary, provided research assistants, and, invaluably, gave me an opportunity to travel around the world, thereby broadening my notions of human cognitive potential.

In effect, I was picking up the pieces of *Kinds of Minds.* With a wonderful team of researchers, I embarked on a massive survey and synthesis of the various bodies of knowledge pertinent to human intellectual capacities: what was known from the realms of biology, psychology, anthropology, and other relevant disciplines. From my work with children and brain-damaged adults, I had a premonition of possible categories, the identity of the several "computers" that together constitute the human mind. But I was determined not to be aprioristic: I wanted to cut nature at its proper joints, come up with the optimal taxonomy, and so I was guided by what the data revealed.

I made a number of crucial decisions. First of all, I decided that I would not begin with the several sensory organs. My work in neuropsychology had convinced me that the human intellect operates on information, irrespective of the particular sensory organs that happen to be involved in taking in that information. Thus, the language faculty can be activated by hearing (spoken language), by sight (written language), and even tactilely (as in Braille). So, too, spatial capacities operate even in those who are blind.

Second, and fatefully, I decided to call these capacities human intelligences. I wanted to underscore the importance of the distinctions that I was making. I had a premonition that if I used a neutral word like *talent* or *capacity* or *faculty*, it would be easy to ignore what I was saying. ("Oh, for sure, there are many human talents.") But if I used the charged word *intelligence* I would be able to capture the attention of both psychologists and the general public—nearly all of whom have strong views of what human intellect is. As a tentative definition, I suggested that *an intelligence* is a competence to solve problems or fashion products that are valued in at least one culture. (Since then, I have refined the definition, but I am trying to be historically accurate.)

Third, I made an important methodological decision. I developed a set of eight criteria for what counts as intelligence; only those candidate abilities that scored reasonably well on these criteria would make the ultimate list. Here are the eight criteria:

- An intelligence should be discerned in relative isolation in prodigies, autistic savants, stroke victims, or other exceptional populations.
- It should have distinct representation in the nervous system.
- It should have a distinct developmental trajectory. Different intelligences should develop at different rates and with different patterns.
- It should have some basis in evolutionary biology. In other words, an intelligence should have putative survival value, and simpler manifestations of an intelligence should be discernible in other species.
- It should be susceptible to capture in symbol systems—some form of notation.
- It should be supported by evidence from psychometric measures.
- It should be distinguishable from other intelligences through experimental psychological tasks.
- It should contain core, information-processing capacities. For example, language includes core phonological and syntactic analyzing mechanisms.

Armed with a word, a definition, and a set of criteria, I proposed seven human intelligences. I have since added an eighth (Naturalist) and am considering a provisional ninth (Existential). In the accompanying Table 1, I have listed the intelligences, given a capsule definition, and proposed specimen individuals who excel in that particular intelligence.

TABLE 1. Eight Intelligences

Linguistic intelligence
Enables individuals to process information and create products involving language. Poets, novelists, and journalists exhibit this intelligence in abundance.
Examples: William Shakespeare, Toni Morrison

Logical-mathematical intelligence
Allows individuals to make calculations, consider hypotheses and solve abstract problems. Engineers, scientists, and analytic philosophers are likely to possess a profile of intelligence high in logical-mathematical intelligence.
Examples: Isaac Newton, Marie Curie

Spatial intelligence
Enables individuals to navigate around complex terrains and to manipulate spatial images in their head. Sailors, pilots, architects, and painters stand out in their spatial abilities.
Examples: Frank Gehry, Georgia O'Keeffe

Musical intelligence
Allows individuals to produce and make meaning of different patterns of sound. Composers, conductors, and musical performers exhibit this intelligence.
Examples: Wolfgang Amadeus Mozart, John Lennon

Bodily-kinesthetic intelligence
Involves using one's body to create products or solve problems. Athletes, dancers, crafts-workers, and surgeons all draw upon bodily-kinesthetic intelligence.
Examples: Martha Graham, Tiger Woods

Interpersonal intelligence
Reflects an individual's ability to recognize and interpret other people's moods, desires, skills, motivations, and intentions. Teachers, clinicians, and salespeople are likely to possess considerable interpersonal intelligence.
Examples: Martin Luther King, Jr., Oprah Winfrey

Intrapersonal intelligence
Allows individuals to recognize and assess these characteristics within themselves. Those who excel in introspection exploit this intelligence.
Examples: Sigmund Freud, Virginia Woolf

Naturalistic intelligence
Enables individuals to identify and distinguish among various types of plants, animals, weather formations, and so forth, that are found in the natural world. This form of intelligence is obviously important for those whose survival depends on direct interaction with the natural environment: hunters, farmers, and those who study the natural world. It is possible that this human faculty is now used by most of us chiefly to make distinctions among different consumer goods.
Examples: Charles Darwin, Rachel Carson

There may be a ninth intelligence, which I call existential intelligence—I think of it as the intelligence of "big questions." Young people, religious leaders, artists, and philosophers ponder the nature of life, death, love, and war. We respond to leaders who embody existential intelligence. Before pronouncing this an "official" intelligence, however, I would like firm evidence that distinct brain systems have evolved to allow us to ponder those things that are too big, or too little, to be perceived directly.

These, then, are the set of intelligences that I proposed—initially in 1983 in *Frames of Mind* and about which I've written and lectured in subsequent years. The theory makes two principal claims.

1. All of us have the full range of intelligences. The intelligences are what make us human beings in the cognitive sphere.

2. No two human beings, not even identical twins, exhibit exactly the same profile of intelligences—the same strengths, weaknesses, and patterns of interaction among the intelligences. And that is because even if two people are genetically identical, they have varied experiences and may well be motivated to distinguish themselves from one another. And so, in the end, they may turn out to be quite different from one another.

"Fifteen Minutes" of Fame for *Frames of Mind*

When *Frames of Mind* first appeared, I had certain expectations—none of which was met. First of all, I had thought of the book as addressed to my primary audience of psychologists—especially those in cognitive and developmental psychology. Second, having already published half a dozen books to a modest reaction and equally modest sales, I had expected little hubbub and a gradual silence.

What happened instead? First of all, this was—and remains—my only publication to receive a lot of immediate attention. Second, the primary response to my work came from educators (with whom I had had only a modest amount of contact). Initially in the United States, and then throughout the world, educators glommed onto the idea of multiple intelligences. And perhaps because I had said little about the educational implications of the theory, these educators came up with their own applications—in teaching, in curriculum, in tracking (or nontracking) of students. For the most part, I was impressed by the educational implementations of the theory, which included several schools built around the idea of multiple intelligences. Sometimes I was bemused by the applications. And a few times I was horrified—as when an educational program in Australia classified the major racial and ethnic groups in Australia in terms of the intelligences that they possessed and the ones that they lacked. Fortunately, that program was soon cancelled.

The harshest criticism by far came from the psychometric establishment—the individuals who developed the standard intelligence test, the IQ test, and who believed (and continue to believe) that they have the right to define intelligence, to determine how it is measured, and to resist efforts to pluralize the concept, or to assess it in ways that deviate noticeably from short oral or paper and pencil instruments.

Without having anticipated it, I had walked into a buzz saw. The problem, I think, was my lack of training in the area of psychometrics: I had rarely thought about IQ tests altogether—in either a positive or negative vein. The choice of the term *intelligence* had been primarily strategic—based on calling attention to the idea, not on studied immersion in earlier work on intelligence. Although I did not like being attacked, I got used to it, and, hard as it is to admit it, I did learn from it . . . at least sometimes.

Looking back at this work from the vantage point of 25 years, what would I say? First of all, I have learned to make important distinctions. Despite what many educators say, intelligences are not the same as learning styles. An intelligence is a capacity to compute information, not a way of approaching a range of tasks. Nor is an intelligence the same as a domain or a discipline. Any domain can involve several intelligences, and any intelligence can be drawn on for a variety of pursuits. More concretely, several intelligences are involved in doing mathematics; and someone with logical mathematical intelligence can apply it to a range of areas, from computing to gambling.

Second, if I don't create ways of assessing the intelligences, other people will—and indeed they have. Our own efforts to assess intelligences took the form of Project Spectrum: the development of a rich curriculum for preschool children. The Spectrum curriculum contains all kinds of materials that are attractive to young children; and by observing the young children as they interact with these materials (in the manner of a child making her way through a children's museum), one can infer their profile of intellectual strengths.

The best example of assessing intelligences that I've ever seen was developed with no input from me. Located in southwestern Denmark, Danfoss Universe is a 10-acre "science experience park" with more than 150 activities that strive to combine learning and fun (www.danfossuniverse.com, 2006). Its Explorama is a museum-sized building that houses more than 50 different activities. Each activity is designed to help participants learn about and focus upon one of their specific intelligences. Importantly, the intelligences are probed directly, not through the screen of a multiple-choice, linguistic device. Here is a sample of a few exhibits found in the Explorama:

- A linguistic exhibit offers a recording of words spoken in Japanese. When participants mimic the Japanese words, the exhibit offers a visual representation of their vocalization superimposed over that of a native Japanese speaker. Through this comparison, participants can strive to improve the accuracy of their tone and pronunciation.

- A musical exhibit allows participants to create melodies on a theremin—an electronic instrument played without actually touching the instrument itself. Participants learn about melody by moving their hands within the vicinity of two antennae.

- An interpersonal exhibit called Teambot requires participants to work cooperatively to design a robot arm that can move an object from one location to another.

■ An intrapersonal exhibit called Mindball asks that participants don electrode-equipped headbands attached to a computer that is, in turn, connected to a Ping-Pong table. If the participant can lower his or her stress level as measured by the electrodes, this reduction in stress can be converted by the computer into a force that propels a Ping-Pong ball to the other side of the table.

Before embarking on these and other MI-based activities, visitors to the museum are asked to complete a survey describing their beliefs about their own intellectual profile. After completing their visit to the Explorama, participants are invited to reflect upon whether their performance on the various exhibits bore out their initial beliefs about their profile of intelligences (Gardner, 2006a). In this way, many visitors conclude their visit to Danfoss Universe with a deepened understanding of their own intellectual strengths and weaknesses—and, in the process, have the opportunity to assess and perhaps enhance their own intrapersonal intelligence.

Looking Ahead

Seeing these various applications around the world has moved me deeply. Although I started out as a psychologist trying to map the mind as it is, I am now equally interested in the ways in which ideas are employed and the differences those applications might make in the world. At this point, determining the precise number and boundary of the intelligences has become less important than MI theory's overarching premise that intelligence is better understood as multiple rather than singular (Chen and Gardner, 2005; Gardner, 2006b). As research in the fields of neuroscience and genetics proceeds, our understanding of the ways in which different genes and areas of the brain impact specific intellectual capacities will increase dramatically. Currently identified constructs such as logical-mathematical intelligence will undoubtedly be found to be composed of specific subsets: perhaps subintelligences for processing small numbers, estimation, and deductive reasoning (Gardner, 2006a). Overall, however, I am confident that the concept of multiple intelligences will be substantiated. And I dare to think that its application in various domains—education, museums, the workplace—will be benevolent.

Nowadays, in our competitive global society, young persons feel pressured at increasingly young ages to make career decisions, even irrevocable ones. By the same token, young scholars often feel that they need to get the first job, define a focused area of research, and move straight to tenure and beyond. Reflecting on my own life, at a time when I am definitely a "senior" (as I write these words, I am 65), I am impressed by the extent to which my life trajectory could not have been predicted, and I am better for those chance events that make crucial differences. Had I not heard Geschwind speak; had we not received the grant from the Van Leer Foundation; had I not used the word *intelligence*. . . . And even after *Frames of Mind* was published, I had no idea of the course that its ideas—its memes—would take. I love science and scientific explanations—but my own life's work is a testimony to the importance of history, culture, and, yes, chance.

Acknowledgement

Thanks to Scott Seider for his help in preparing this essay.

Suggested Further Reading

Chen, J., Moran, S., & Gardner, H. (2009). *Multiple intelligences around the world*. San Francisco: Jossey Bass.

Gardner, H. (2006). *Multiple intelligences: New horizons*. New York: Basic Books.

References

About Danfoss Universe. (n. d.) Retrieved November 2006 from http://www.uk. danfossuniverse.com

Chen, J., & Gardner, H. (2005). Multiple intelligences: Assessment based on multiple-intelligence theory. In D. Flanagan and P. Harrison (Eds.). *Contemporary intellectual assessment: Theories, tests and issues*. New York: Guilford Press.

Gardner, H. (1983). *Frames of mind: The theory of multiple intelligences*. New York: Basic Books.

Gardner, H. (1999). *Intelligence reframed: Multiple intelligences for the 21st century*. New York: Basic Books.

Gardner, H. (2006a). *Multiple intelligences: New horizons*. New York: Basic Books.

Gardner, H. (2006b). Response to my critics. In J. Schaler (Ed.), *Gardner Under Fire*. Chicago: Open Court Publishers.

Gardner, H., Kornhaber, M., & Wake, W. (1996). *Intelligence: Multiple perspectives*. Fort Worth: Harcourt Brace.

Kornhaber, M. (1994) *Multiple intelligences: Why and how schools use it*. Unpublished qualifying paper, Harvard Graduate School of Education.

Kornhaber, M., Fierros, E., & Veenema, S. (2004). *Multiple intelligences: Best ideas from research and practice*. Boston: Pearson.

Olson, L. (1988). Children flourish here: Eight teachers and a theory changed a school world. *Education Week, 7*(8), 83–104.

The Rainbow Project: Using a Psychological Theory of Intelligence to Improve the College Admissions Process

Robert J. Sternberg
Tufts University

▶ *Please tell us about your current position and research interests.*
I am Dean of the School of Arts and Sciences and Professor of Psychology at Tufts University. I am also Honorary Professor of Psychology at the University of Heidelberg. My main research interests are in intelligence, creativity, wisdom, and leadership.

▶ *What got you interested in measuring practical and creative intellectual skills?*
I first devised my theory of successful intelligence as a result of my interactions with university students. These interactions made me realize that someone could be high in academic intelligence but not so high in the creative or practical aspects of intelligence, and vice versa. My colleagues and I have also done research on how to teach as well as assess for successful intelligence.

▶ *What has been the real-world impact of this work, or what do you envision that it will be?*
I hope that the world of education sees the light and adopts all or at least most of my ideas with great enthusiasm and energy, preferably before I either become senile or die.

Every scientific study has a story. The story of the Rainbow Project begins in the late nineteenth century, when British scientist Sir Francis Galton (1822–1911) proposed a theory of intelligence based upon the notion that more intelligent people have keener sensory-motor capacities than less intelligent ones. He expected the more intelligent, for example, to have keener eyesight, a firmer grip, greater ability to distinguish between different tones, and so forth. Based on this notion, Galton developed a test of intelligence based upon sensory-motor skills.

As is always true in science, investigators have different ideas about how a story should develop and how it should end. French scientists Alfred Binet (1857–1911) and Theodore Simon (1873–1961) disputed Galton's claims about the nature of intelligence and how to measure it. Intelligence, they argued, is a matter of higher-level thinking and good judgment rather than sensory abilities (Binet & Simon, 1916). The tests they developed required people to demonstrate judgment, interpret proverbs, provide the meanings of words, and solve arithmetic problems, among other school-related skills. Their tests predicted school performance better than did Galton's and came, therefore, to serve as the basis for future intelligence-test development. In fact, Binet and Simon's assessment device became the first IQ test. The term IQ, a translation of the German word *Intelligenz-Quotient*, was coined by William Stern (1871–1938), who suggested that intelligence tests could be scored by using a ratio of mental age divided by chronological age × 100.

An American psychologist, Lewis Terman (1877–1956) of Stanford University, imported Binet and Simon's tests into the United States. He used them in his research and published a version and revisions (for example, Terman & Merrill, 1937). The fifth edition of this test—called the Stanford-Binet Intelligence Scale—is in use today. Binet and Terman had created tests to measure the intelligence of individuals, one at a time. However, others were soon taking mental measurement in another direction. Researchers such as Arthur Otis (1886–1964) and Carl Brigham (1890–1943) were interested in group testing of individuals. Brigham was the inventor, in the early twentieth century, of what is today called the SAT.

The SAT has a long history. Originally, the initials were an acronym for "Scholastic Aptitude Test." This name implied to many people that the test measured innate intellectual qualities, so the name was changed to "Scholastic Assessment Test." Perhaps because this name was too vague, the acronym was later made to be the test name. At present, "SAT" stands for nothing but itself!

Although its owner, the College Board, insists that the SAT is not an ability test, research suggests that scores on the test are very highly correlated with scores on tests of intelligence (Frey & Detterman, 2004). Indeed, the test is about as related to any one intelligence test as intelligence tests are related to each other. British psychologist and logician Charles Spearman (1863–1945) had argued as long ago as 1927 that all tests of mental abilities are positively related to each other, and the SAT is no exception.

The SAT has been a good predictor of college performance (Bridgeman, McCamley-Jenkins, & Ervin, 2000; Hezlett et al., 2001), but no test, including this one, provides perfect prediction. Moreover, there is another problem. Tests such as the SAT originally were introduced to counter decisions being made largely on the basis of social class. The world was changing. Whereas a person's last name, social standing, or private school had once mattered more to future outcomes than his or her ability, college was proving to be a gateway to a successful life. Thus, the goal underlying group testing was the introduction of a merit- rather than class-based basis for admission to college. But as the diversity of the college applicant pool increased, an unfortunate fact emerged: Test scores are highly correlated with social class.

The SAT, ACT (the American College Testing Program, a national college admissions and placement exam), and similar tests are not based on any particular theory of abilities, and some psychologists argued that a test based more closely on a psychological theory, especially a broad theory of abilities, might improve prediction of performance beyond what the SAT current yields (for example, Gardner, 1983; Sternberg, 1985). A related hope was that such tests might better recognize the wide diversity of abilities students can bring to college life. So, in 2000, my collaborators and I initiated an effort to devise a test that might turn these hopes into reality.

The Rainbow Assessment: Underlying Theory

The Rainbow Project was carried out when I was a professor at Yale University. My collaborators and I called the project "Rainbow" to underscore the notion that abilities, like light, can be decomposed into different aspects like the spectrum of light. Intelligence, like light, may appear to be of just one "color." But it represents a rainbow array of different kinds of abilities. Underlying the new assessment are ideas that I first proposed more than two decades ago. In a book called *The Theory of Successful Intelligence* (Sternberg, 1997), I argued that intelligence is one's ability to achieve one's goals in life, within one's sociocultural context. Such success depends on capitalizing on one's strengths and compensating for or correcting one's weaknesses so as to adapt to, shape, and select environments through a combination of creative, analytical, and practical abilities. My theory distinguishes three aspects of intelligence: creative abilities to generate novel ideas, analytical abilities to evaluate whether the ideas are good ones, and practical abilities to execute one's ideas and to persuade others of their value.

I have argued that conventional tests of intelligence and the SAT measure primarily analytical abilities, as well as memory. Thus, a new, theoretically based test would contribute the most in its assessments of creative and practical abilities, the two kinds of abilities not directly measured by conventional tests.

The Rainbow Project Team

The team working on the Rainbow assessment was unusual in two ways. First, among its more than a dozen members from all around the United States were researchers with a range of viewpoints on what intelligence is and how to measure it. On most projects, collaborators share a single point of view, or at least, their points of view differ relatively little. In contrast, the team's views varied all over the map! Second, the team was highly interdisciplinary, involving cognitive psychologists, measurement psychologists, educational psychologists, developmental psychologists, cultural psychologists, and others from outside psychology altogether. I was the team leader (Sternberg & The Rainbow Project Collaborators, 2006).

The College Board, publishers of the SAT, provided funding. Some collaborators were from the Board, but it made no attempt, ever, to influence the outcome.

Who Did We Test and How?

Roughly 1,000 participants—mostly college freshman—were attending a diverse group of schools, ranging from those that are not at all selective in their admissions procedures to some that are highly selective. Thirteen colleges and universities and two high schools were represented in the sample. Tests were administered at the universities by proctors under controlled conditions, either in paper-and-pencil format or over the Internet.

We used a variety of tests that measured analytical, creative, and practical skills. All of the analytical tests were multiple choice, but only some of the creative and practical tests were of this kind. Other performance-based tests required participants to solve problems using relatively divergent thinking.

There were three creative-performance tests. In one, cartoons like those in the *New Yorker* magazine were presented without captions, and participants were asked to think up good captions. In a second test, participants were given unusual titles, such as *Beyond the Edge* or *The Octopus's Sneakers*, and were asked to write creative stories. In a third test, participants were shown visual collages, such as different pictures of musicians, and asked to dictate a story. The creative performance tests were scored for three attributes—the originality or novelty of a response, the quality of that response, and the extent to which the response was appropriate to what was asked on the assessment.

Three practical tests measured problem-solving skills. One presented participants with situations similar to those they might encounter in college—for example, resolving a dispute with a roommate. A second test was similar, but the scenarios were work related. A third test consisted of scenarios presented visually—for example, a video of a student entering a room filled with party-goers, with the expression on his face suggesting that he did not know anyone at the party. Test takers had to figure out what to do. Various options were presented, and students had to rate their quality. They included options such as leaving the party, staying at the party but primarily observing what is going on, actively making efforts to meet people, and so on (see Table 1).

TABLE 1. Movies Used in the Rainbow Project to Assess Practical Intelligence	
Title	**Theme**
The Party	Entering a party where one does not know anyone
A Fair Portion	Discussing shares of rental payments for a flat
Professor's Dilemma	Asking for a letter of recommendation from a professor who does not know you very well
No Free Lunch	Having eaten a lunch and discovering that you do not have the money to pay for it
The Unwanted Guest	Dealing with a friend in need of help at a time when you are just seeing your significant other for the first time in a long time
Pressing Corporate Matter	Making a decision regarding proactive actions that can be taken before a wave of firings commences in your company
Jerry's "Beautyrest Sleeper"	Organizing your friends to move your furniture to a new flat

Prediction of Freshman-Year Academic Success

In considering our findings, keep in mind that our goal was not excellent prediction of freshman-year performance but rather something even better:

prediction of first-year grade point average (GPA) *above and beyond* what we could get from SAT scores and high school GPA. In other words, we would measure the success of our venture in terms of what it added to existing predictors.

However, our decision to test students at community colleges and universities around the country introduced a kind of handicap: Because the dependent (predicted) variable was freshman GPA and colleges differ widely in their grading systems, we expected that our level of prediction would be lower than if only one college were studied.

We did not expect our analytical measures to add much prediction beyond what is obtained from the SAT because the SAT already is an analytical test. And, in fact, they added only 0.1% prediction over and above that of the SAT, raising the percentage of the variation in scores explained from 9.8% to 9.9%. (If you imagine a pie, where the whole pie represents perfect prediction and none of the pie represents no prediction, then our analytical measure added only 0.1% of the pie to our equation!)

We hoped, however, that our creative and practical measures would add significant predictive power, and they did. The creative measures increased prediction from 9.8% to 12.8%, and the practical measures increased prediction from 9.8% to 10.7%. If we allowed the measures we used to enter freely into the prediction equation, the combination of all our new measures increased prediction from 9.8% to 19.9%, roughly doubling our ability to predict freshman success. If we included high school GPA in the equation, our new measures increased prediction of freshman GPA 1½ times (rather than double, as in the case of adding the new assessment to the SAT alone).

So, we now know our measures do seem to make a significant difference in predicting freshman academic success in college, at least in our sample. Among the roughly 1,000 students who took our tests, creative and practical abilities made a difference to academic success beyond the difference made by the analytical abilities as measured by the SAT and beyond what high school GPA measures.

Effect on Ethnic-Group Differences

An issue of concern for colleges and universities in general has been the persistence of gaps in SAT scores between racial and ethnic groups. A key question, therefore, was what would happen to differences among ethnic groups in their potential for admission if new tests were used. Would the new tests increase, decrease, or leave unchanged the level of diversity on college campuses? A test that decreased diversity would certainly be viewed as suspect for practical use.

In fact, use of the Rainbow assessment showed promise of *increasing* diversity. We assessed the impact of our tests on five ethnic groups: European Americans, Latino Americans, African Americans, Asian Americans, and Native Americans. Two different types of data analysis revealed the same results: Ethnic group differences, overall, *decreased* when assessments of creative and practical abilities were added to assessments of analytical ones.

Why? Because, on average, backgrounds and methods of socialization differ among racial and ethnic groups, and so broader tests are more likely to capture the full range of their abilities than are narrower ones. For example, Native Americans (although limited in numbers in our sample), on average, did worse on the analytical tests than most other groups, but better on oral story telling than did any other groups.

Follow-Up

We had hoped for a second phase of the Rainbow Project, but the College Board did not provide funding, arguing that the tests were not practical on a large scale. I was disappointed because the data had been so good and because our empirical article had been published as the lead article in the leading journal in the field of intellectual abilities. Their argument led me to reflect on how one can turn data into action.

My arrival at Tufts University in the fall of 2005 gave me an opportunity to find out. As Dean of the School of Arts and Sciences at Tufts, I have been interested in applying the latest findings in psychology to the education of students at Tufts. After all, we study psychology, at least in part, so that our findings can make a difference to the world. Beginning in the fall of 2006, Tufts added to its college-specific application a section that encourages students, on an optional basis, to select an activity that gives them an opportunity to demonstrate their creative, analytical, and practical skills in ways that conventional tests and college applications perhaps have not fully allowed.

The project has been called "Kaleidoscope" in order to emphasize the array of skills the assessments would measure. Our goal is to select future leaders who will make a positive and meaningful difference to the world. We did not necessarily expect to enhance prediction of grades in this project, but rather, to enhance prediction of leadership skills, in general. One item asks applicants what book they would most like on their bookshelf and why (analytical). Another asks applicants to write a story with a title such as "The End of MTV" (creative). A nonverbal item allows students to draw an advertisement for a new product (creative). Another item asks applicants how they would convince other students of an idea to which the other students did not initially respond favorably (practical). In carrying out these tasks, students have a fairly free opportunity to demonstrate a broad range of skills needed for college success—skills often hidden from college admissions officers. The essays we use are not the only ways to assess creative and practical skills, but they supplement other ways in providing a concrete opportunity for applicants to display these skills.

Putting the items on the college application rather than having them in a separate test (as in the Rainbow Project) has both advantages and disadvantages. An advantage is that students can ponder their responses rather than being forced to produce them rapidly—a situation particularly advantageous for creative thinking. A disadvantage, however, is that parents, counselors, or others can help the students write their answers. There is no way to know for sure. In measuring skills, no one perfect way exists that can produce a true reading of what anyone can do.

We already have some interesting data, although the data are correlational, and so it is not possible definitively to determine causality. In the first year that we used Kaleidoscope, the number of applications, SATs, and GPAs of our applicants rose. In particular, we had substantially fewer weaker applicants than we had had before. In that year, the number of applications by and acceptances of under-represented minorities increased substantially.

After the students' freshman year, we followed them to ascertain how they were performing at the university. We found no statistically significant difference in grades between people who excelled in Kaleidsocope and others who were admitted with comparable academic credentials but whose admission depended more on reasons other than Kaleidoscope. So we were able to enhance leadership credentials of our students without adverse effects on academic performance. Students who were top performers on Kaleidoscope showed signs of greater participation in leadership activities after their first year.

Conclusion

Our goal was to devise assessments that were based on validated psychological principles and would build on already existing assessments. The kinds of abilities measured by the SAT and the ACT—primarily memory and analytical abilities—are important for success in school and in life. But they are not the only abilities that matter. Future citizens also need to be able to adapt to rapidly changing environments (the creative aspect) and to apply what they learn in school to their everyday lives (the practical aspect). For example, 2008 was a year of massive financial challenges not experienced before by most people in their lifetimes. The "old rules" just no longer seemed to apply. People needed not only analytical, but also creative and practical abilities to negotiate the new world that these challenges presented.

Every scientific study has a story. The story of the Rainbow Project began, in a sense with Galton and Binet, but it is hard to know where it will end!

Suggested Further Reading

Sternberg, R. J. (2003). *Wisdom, intelligence, and creativity synthesized.* New York: Cambridge University Press.

Sternberg, R. J., & Grigorenko, E. L. (2007). *Teaching for successful intelligence* (2nd ed.). Thousand Oaks, CA: Corwin.

Sternberg, R. J., Kaufman, J. C., & Grigorenko, E. L. (2008). *Applied intelligence.* New York: Cambridge University Press.

References

Binet, A., & Simon, T. (1916). *The development of intelligence in children* (E. S. Kite, Trans.). Baltimore, MD: Williams & Wilkins.

Bridgeman, B., McCamley-Jenkins, L., & Ervin, N. (2000). *Predictions of freshman grade-point average from the revised and recentered SAT I: Reasoning test.* (College Board Report No. 2000-1). New York: College Entrance Examination Board.

Frey, M. C., & Detterman, D. K. (2004). Scholastic assessment or g? The relationship between the scholastic assessment test and general cognitive ability. *Psychological Science, 15,* 373–378.

Gardner, H. (1983). *Frames of mind: The theory of multiple intelligences.* New York: Basic Books.

Hezlett, S., Kuncel, N., Vey, A., Ones, D., Campbell, J., & Camara, W. J. (2001). *The effectiveness of the SAT in predicting success early and late in college: A comprehensive meta-analysis.* Paper presented at the annual meeting of the National Council of Measurement in Education, Seattle, WA.

Spearman, C. (1927). *The abilities of man.* New York: Macmillan.

Sternberg, R. J. (1985). *Beyond IQ: A triarchic theory of human abilities.* New York: Cambridge University Press.

Sternberg, R. J. (1997). *Successful intelligence.* New York: Plume.

Sternberg, R. J., & The Rainbow Project Collaborators. (2006). The Rainbow Project: Enhancing the SAT through assessments of analytical, practical, and creative skills. *Intelligence, 34*(4), 321–350.

Terman, L. M., & Merrill, M. A. (1937). *Measuring intelligence.* Boston: Houghton Mifflin.

Emotion and Motivation

Paul Ekman and David Matsumoto
**Reading Faces: The Universality of
Emotional Expression**

E. Tory Higgins
Human Self-Regulation and Emotion

Reading Faces: The Universality of Emotional Expression

Paul Ekman
University of California, San Francisco
The Paul Ekman Group, LLC

David Matsumoto
San Francisco State University

▶ *Please tell us about your current position and research interests.*
Paul Ekman: Until I retired in 2004, I was a professor of psychology in the Department of Psychiatry at the University of California at San Francisco. I am currently Manager, Paul Ekman Group, LLC. My research interests include emotion, nonverbal behavior, and deception.

David Matsumoto: I am Professor of Psychology, San Francisco State University. My research interests include cross-cultural communication, intercultural communication, and emotion.

▶ *What got you interested in the face and reading its expressions of emotion?*
Paul Ekman: The ability to detect signs of deception in psychiatric patients.

David Matsumoto: Questions concerning why infants and young children could understand the emotional states of their parents and adults around them when they didn't understand language.

▶ *What has been the real-world impact of this work or what do you envision that it will be?*
As explained in the essay, we hope that our work will help to create a more humane, compassionate, and safe society for all people of the world.

The universality of facial expressions of emotion is perhaps the most important contribution that basic science has made to our understanding of emotional states in human beings. The idea that specific expressions accompany specific emotions and that these expressions occur in humans everywhere was first proposed by Charles Darwin (1872/1998) more than 100 years ago. Indeed, his ideas about emotions were central to his theory of evolution, suggesting that emotions and their expressions were biologically innate and evolutionarily adaptive, and that similarities could be seen as part of our primate heritage.

But, until the 1960s, the findings on this issue were admittedly inconclusive, and the dominant perspective in psychology at the time was exactly the opposite—that facial expressions were culture-specific, much like language. Darwin's claims were resurrected by Sylvan S. Tomkins (1962), who suggested that emotion was the basis of human motivation and that the seat of emotion was in the face. Tomkins and I (Paul Ekman) joined forces to conduct what are known in the field today as the original universality studies.

Four sources of evidence comprise these studies. In the first, we showed pictures of many different facial expressions to observers in different cultures and asked them to judge which emotion was portrayed in the face. If emotional expressions were universal, we expected to find high agreement within and across cultures in judgments. If emotional expressions were culture-specific, we thought we would find agreement within a culture, but disagreement across cultures. The results revealed high agreement both within and across cultures for six emotional expressions–anger, disgust, fear, happiness, sadness, and surprise. These data were the first systematic evidence for the universality of emotions and their expressions (Ekman, Sorenson, & Friesen, 1969).

Our next two studies assessed the possibility that the cross-cultural similarity in interpretation might be due to shared visual input. (All previous participants were from relatively industrialized countries and might have learned to recognize emotion through mass media—television, movies, magazines, and so forth.) To address this issue, Wallace Friesen and I went to the highlands of southeast New Guinea to study an isolated, preliterate, Stone Age culture devoid of mass media.

In one study, the tribespersons accurately matched the facial expressions of Western adults with stories depicting the relevant emotions (Ekman & Friesen, 1971). This finding was the second source of evidence for universality and addressed the concern about shared visual input; with no access to mass media, the tribespersons had never seen Westerners before. For the next study, we filmed the faces of individual tribespersons as they portrayed what they would look like if they were the person in the stories. We showed those film clips to Americans. Although they had never before seen anyone from the tribe, they accurately identified the emotions the New Guineans intended to portray. We now had two different, additional sources of evidence for universality of facial expression of emotion.

Still critical of our findings, opponents argued that our studies measured judgments—that they did not show that people in different cultures actually produced those expressions when emotions were spontaneously aroused. We therefore conducted another study in which we individually videotaped American and Japanese participants alone in a room as each watched a highly emotion-provoking film. We analyzed the specific facial muscles that moved in the participants and showed that Americans and Japanese produced the same expressions of emotion—the same six universally recognized emotions (Ekman, 1972). These data provided the fourth source of evidence for universality of facial expression of emotion.

Since then, in judgment studies undertaken around the world, David Matsumoto and others have demonstrated convincingly that a small set of facial expressions are universally recognized, and when emotions are aroused, the same facial expressions of emotion are reliably produced by people from all walks of life everywhere (Matsumoto et al., 2008). In other research, we demonstrated the existence of a seventh universal expression: contempt (Ekman & Friesen, 1986; Matsumoto, 1992). We now know that facial expressions are part of a coordinated response system that involves unique physiological responses, specific cognitive activities, preparation for motor behaviors, and specific feelings. Facial expressions are signals of a rich, complex response system we *all* have.

Microexpressions

A second important discovery was the existence of microexpressions, which are expressions of intense emotions that go on and off the face in a fraction of a second, sometimes as fast as 1/30 of a second. They occur so rapidly that if you blink, you miss them. Wallace Friesen and I (PE) discovered microexpressions almost 40 years ago while investigating a problem that had long plagued psychiatric hospitals: determining the risk for suicide in depressed inpatients who had asked for weekend passes. We carefully reviewed films of inpatients who, although apparently improved, nonetheless attempted suicide during their leave. One patient admitted both to wanting to take her life and lying about it during the interview, but we could find nothing in the interview film that betrayed the lie. The patient smiled frequently, spoke optimistically, and was convincingly cheerful.

We then viewed the film in painstaking detail—frame by frame. With 24 frames per second and a 12-minute interview, it literally took over 100 hours to review the film. What we found was amazing: When the doctor asked the patient about her future plans, we noticed a brief but intense expression of anguish that lasted only 2 frames (1/12 of a second), followed by a smile. In freeze frame, her true emotion was obvious but then deliberately concealed. Finally knowing what to look for, we then found other examples of these extremely fast expressions in the same film. We did further research on microexpressions and found that microexpressions are signs of both deliberately concealed emotions (the person does not want to show his or her true feelings) and repressed emotions (the person does not know what he or she feels) (Ekman & Friesen, 1974).

Real-World Applications

Our rigorous demonstration that specific facial expressions reflect specific basic emotions in humans everywhere confirmed Darwin's insight that there are reliable, observable signs to any person's feelings, regardless of culture, race, ethnicity, gender, class, religion, or age. Our discovery of microexpressions meant that discerning people's true feelings—whether deliberately concealed or repressed from memory—is now possible. Two widely used training programs emerged from our discoveries: In one, people can learn to improve their emotional skills. The second involves improving the ability to evaluate truthfulness.

Improving Emotional Skills

The ability to understand basic emotions is important in many professions and improving those skills often increases the effectiveness of job performance. For example, health professionals skilled in reading others' emotions can develop better rapport with their patients—understanding and reflecting upon the patients' strong feelings about their illnesses, health care providers, caretakers, and themselves.

Physicians often need "ground truth" to make an accurate diagnosis. Yet, if their questions about sexual activity, alcohol consumption, and other behaviors arouse strong emotions, their patients may be unwilling or unable to disclose information essential to diagnosing their condition. Practitioners who can correctly assess a patient's emotional state and who can respond with empathy and compassion provide a comfortable and safe environment where ground truth is likely to emerge.

Learning to understand and regulate one's *own* emotions is key to becoming an effective health care practitioner. Blood, vomit, saliva, and excrement often elicit strong emotions. Burns and lacerations are common, and patients themselves may elicit strong emotions if they are dirty or out of control. Thus, professional and competent healers need considerable emotional control—as medical schools, other health care training institutions, and hospitals have recently come to realize. Our training programs have been delivered to many health care organizations, including the Mayo Clinic.

Emotional skills are also important in school settings. Teachers who accurately read the emotions of their students can more effectively adjust their lesson plans to students' needs. Burnout, a major issue, is less likely among teachers who understand their own emotions. And in schools where administrators have learned to accurately read the emotions of the staff, burnout is reduced and teacher effectiveness improved. We have also found that administrators who undergo our training programs are better able to intervene effectively in cases of possible child abuse and other problematic situations. For these reasons, our programs are a centerpiece of teacher training programs at institutions such as San Francisco's Center for Emotional Balance.

In the business world, success—whether you are a senior manager or the most junior assistant—depends on successfully nurturing mutually prosperous interpersonal relations and understanding one's own and others' emotions. Reading emotions in others incorrectly can lead to broken deals, destructive office politics, lost sales, and more. Our emotional skills training programs have been offered to businesses in several countries, as well as to organizational consultants. These programs deliver science-based knowledge to a growing corporate market interested in the assessment and training of emotional intelligence.

Improving emotional skills is also important for moms and dads, husbands and wives, friends and neighbors, and anyone with a vested interest in building strong and constructive relationships. We receive inquiries about training almost daily, and interest is growing.

Evaluating Truthfulness

People are often very emotional when they lie, especially when the stakes are high, and facial expressions, especially microexpressions, can be signs of these emotions. Individuals and organizations with an interest in detecting lies have used programs that we have developed (together with Mark Frank).

The programs are based on substantiated scientific research as well as the real-work experience of officers and agents who have worked with us. We have offered training to police interrogators in the United States, Great Britain, and Canada, and because police are often skeptical about academics, an experienced law enforcement officer and a scientist jointly teach the classes. Participants often discover after training that they see and better understand behavior that previously they misunderstood or misinterpreted. These additional skills invariably help them find ground truth in testimony, depositions, and interrogations.

We have also provided training to military intelligence officers who conduct interrogations of people encountered during military action, people who are suspected of intending harm against the United States. One group of military intelligence officers trained in our noncoercive methods for evaluating truthfulness were assigned to Abu Ghraib prison in Iraq after the exposure of the controversial interrogations that had taken place there. They have reported that our training was very useful in that highly charged setting. We have also taught counterintelligence officers these same skills.

The U.S. State Department Foreign Service Institute has also used our programs to train personnel whose assignments are to conduct visa interviews with citizens of other countries seeking to visit the United States. Our training helps identify people who might be lying during an interview—trying to conceal the intention to work illegally, smuggle drugs, launder money, or engage in terrorist operations. The same skills are needed when interviewing Americans who come to an embassy or consulate to obtain advice, get a passport renewed, or arrange to take home an adopted child.

One trained Foreign Service Officer reported that when interviewing an American abroad, the "passport applicant's face drew up for a split second in a classic disgust microexpression when asked about his supposed hometown. It was enough to raise the suspicion of the Vice Consul, who investigated further and discovered that the true holder of the identity used by the applicant was locked up in a Florida prison. The applicant himself [was] a U.S. citizen wanted for robbery and rape in another state. He had been on the run for several years and had been previously issued a passport in the false identity. Dutch police arrested him."

The Transportation Security Agency (TSA) also includes our training on evaluating truthfulness. The program, called SPOT for "Screening Passengers by Observational Techniques," is currently used in several airports, including some in Great Britain. Thus, in addition to checking tickets, scanning baggage, comparing names to a watch list, and many new technologies, security procedures now include behavioral observation.

To be sure, despite all of the research we and our colleagues have done over the years, we cannot point to one single behavioral sign that on its own signifies deceit. In fact, the only person in history with a reliable and observable sign of lying is Pinocchio! Instead, facial expressions can be evidence of emotions that don't match context; we call these hot spots. Our programs train individuals to identify hot spots, and provide interviewers with advanced analytic interviewing skills to further probe the nature of the person's state and intent. In the SPOT program run by the TSA, for example, when an individual shows a behavior of concern, a SPOT officer approaches the person and asks a few questions while the person remains in line. In an overwhelming number of instances, they discover an innocent reason for the unusual behavior. For example, a person showing many signs of worry is trying to remember if he or she turned off the stove before leaving home or is concerned that he or she might miss the flight. In some instances, the person is detained for further interviews, and of those, a few turn out to be people who are wanted by local, state, or federal agencies.

Although very important, facial expressions are just one of several demeanor cues that reveal emotions associated with lying. Other cues include gestures and physiological responses (for example, sweating). When all of these cues are considered simultaneously, the hit rate for detecting lies is very high. We are currently conducting studies to determine the ceiling for this hit rate and how to reduce errors in detecting lies. We are also conducting studies that examine whether people can be trained to conceal the cues, and thus avoid detection.

Conclusion

The discovery of universal facial expressions of emotion and microexpressions has opened the door to many applications in real-world contexts, and we have been touched by the ways our lifework in basic science has been translated to real-world applications that can create a more fruitful partnership at work and home, more effective team performance, and help get the bad guys off the streets, hopefully helping to create a more humane, compassionate, and safe society. And these real-world applications inform basic research of the future, in a healthy and productive cyclical relationship between science and practice. For example, we know everyone lies sometimes, and some people are better than others at detecting lies. But what makes one person better than another at lying or detecting lies? What do natural lie detectors see that we miss? And how exactly does culture influence universal emotions and their expressions? Although we have some ideas, research has yet to address these fundamental and important questions thoroughly. Although the basic findings we helped to create have been important in their own right, we strongly look forward to the future, where new findings will build on the old and create even further insights into the nature of emotions and expressions.

Suggested Further Reading

Ekman, P. (2003). *Emotions revealed* (2nd ed.). New York: Times Books.

Matsumoto, D., & Willingham, B. (2009). Spontaneous facial expressions of emotion of congenitally and non-congenitally blind individuals. *Journal of Personality and Social Psychology, 96*(1), 1–10.

References

Darwin, C. (1872/1998). *The expression of emotion in man and animals*. New York: Oxford University Press.

Ekman, P. (1972). Universal and cultural differences in facial expression of emotion. In J. R. Cole (Ed.), *Nebraska Symposium on Motivation, 1971* (Vol. 19, pp. 207–283). Lincoln, NE: Nebraska University Press.

Ekman, P., & Friesen, W. V. (1971). Constants across culture in the face and emotion. *Journal of Personality and Social Psychology, 17,* 124–129.

Ekman, P., & Friesen, W. V. (1974). Nonverbal behavior and psychopathology. In R. J. Friedman & M. Katz (Eds.), *The psychology of depression: Contemporary theory and research* (pp. 3–31). Washington, DC: Winston and Sons.

Ekman, P., & Friesen, W. V. (1986). A new pan-cultural facial expression of emotion. *Motivation and Emotion, 10*(2), 159–168.

Ekman, P., Sorenson, E. R., & Friesen, W. V. (1969). Pancultural elements in facial displays of emotion. *Science, 164,* 86–88.

Matsumoto, D. (1992). More evidence for the universality of a contempt expression. *Motivation & Emotion, 16*(4), 363–368.

Matsumoto, D., Keltner, D., Shiota, M. N., Frank, M. G., & O'Sullivan, M. (2008). What's in a face? Facial expressions as signals of discrete emotions. In J. M. Haviland, M. Lewis, & L. Feldman Barrett (Eds.), *Handbook of emotion* (pp. 211–234). New York: Guilford Press.

Tomkins, S. S. (1962). *Affect, imagery, and consciousness: Vol. 1, The positive affects.* New York: Springer.

Human Self-Regulation and Emotion
E. Tory Higgins
Columbia University

▶ *Please describe your current position and research interests.*
I am Stanley Schachter Professor of Psychology, Professor of Business, and Director of the Motivation Science Center at Columbia University. My current research addresses the general question, "Where does value come from?" Beyond the contribution of pleasure and pain to value, my lab is examining another source of value experience—how strongly we are engaged in what we do. Importantly, factors that strengthen engagement, such as obstacles and difficulties, can themselves be unpleasant, but by strengthening engagement, they can increase the value of the goal we are pursuing.

▶ *How did you get interested in self-regulatory processes in human motivation and emotion?*
My personal interest began when I suffered from depression and could not understand, as a psychologist, what was happening to me. After my recovery, I wanted to study what makes people depressed and how it differs from what makes people anxious.

▶ *What has been the real-world impact of this work?*
Over the last decade, new clinical treatments for depression have been developed and used that are directly based on self-discrepancy theory. Currently, my colleagues and I are developing new theory-based distinctions between the psychologies of depression and anxiety that we plan to translate into new and distinct treatments that will be tailored specifically for patients suffering from clinical depression or from generalized anxiety disorder.

Humans share with other animals the general motives of wanting to approach pleasure and avoid pain—the classic hedonic principle of motivation: We experience pleasant emotions when we are successful in our pursuit of goals, and painful emotions when we are unsuccessful. But our motivations and emotions also differ from those of other animals in important ways. In this essay, I will consider two questions about these differences—questions that have shaped the course of my investigations into the sources of human vulnerability: What is special about the motivations of the human animal, and what are the emotional implications of these special motivations?

Most psychologists would argue that humans' capacity for reflective self-consciousness—our ability to think consciously about our self—distinguishes us from nonhuman animals. Although the cognitive consequences of this evolutionary development have received the most attention from researchers, significant motivational consequences have been demonstrated as well (see Higgins & Pittman, 2008).

The ability of humans to engage in reflective self-consciousness is not the only motivationally significant aspect of our inner world, however. As

Charles Horton Cooley (1864–1929) noted many years ago, ". . . most of our reflective consciousness, of our wide-awake state of mind, is social consciousness, because a sense of our relation to other persons, or of other persons to one another, can hardly fail to be part of it" (1964/1902, p. 5). Such social consciousness involves awareness that the outcomes of our actions are determined by others' responses to those actions. People are motivated to behave in ways that result in the power and influence of others being used for them and not against them.

Importantly, human children by 3 to 6 years of age also recognize that the inner states of another person, such as a parent's beliefs, feelings, expectancies, and desires, mediate that person's positive or negative response to their behavior. Equally significant, humans are aware that their own inner states—their own beliefs, competencies, and motives—can be the source of others' feelings, expectancies, and desires: Children have no difficulty, for example, in recognizing a parent's desire that they acquire a particular competency (for example, the ability to work hard). This crucial human discovery has profound effects on motivation (Higgins & Pittman, 2008).

Perhaps because of this discovery, humans are unique in their capacity to imagine future-self competencies—whom they might become, hope to become, dream of becoming, fear becoming—and then using these future-self competencies as reference values for self-regulation in the present (Higgins, 1987; Markus & Nurius, 1986; Oettingen, Pak, & Schnetter, 2001; Oyserman et al., 2004). Scholars have recognized for a long time that people imagine their future selves—their "potential" self (James, 1890/1948) or their "ideal" self (Rogers, 1961). Not until the late 1980s, however, did psychologists begin to investigate extensively two important functions of imagined future selves: (1) as goals or incentives that influence current planning and decisions and (2) as standards or reference points for evaluating and interpreting the current self (Higgins, 1987; Markus & Nurius, 1986).

Imagined Future Selves as Goals or Incentives

In a landmark study of college students, Hazel Markus and Paula Nurius (1986) demonstrated the importance of future selves as an element in a person's self-knowledge. Two-thirds of their student-participants reported that they thought about their possible selves in the future a great deal of the time or all the time. The ratio of positive, "hoped-for" selves to negative, "feared" selves was almost 4 to 1. The positive and negative possible selves, these researchers argued, provide direction and impetus for action and change. Imagining that a desired future self—say, a successful self, a creative self, a loved and admired self—is possible is a form of optimism, and imagining that such selves are not possible is a form of pessimism, and, generally speaking, optimistic thinking about the future yields higher motivation and better performance than does pessimistic thinking. But imagining desired future selves alone or possible selves alone is not sufficient for effective self-regulation. What is effective is imagining future selves that are both desirable *and* possible.

Also effective is imagining not only desired future selves but also future difficulties and obstacles to attaining these desired selves. For example, commitment to and energizing of goal-directed actions increases when people both fantasize a desired (and possible) future self and imagine how to overcome realistic obstacles that could hinder their success (Oettingen et al., 2001). People are also more likely to experience an imagined desired self as being a truly possible self in the future if they can image themselves carrying out a strategy to reach that desired self. In one study, eighth graders from low-income families who possessed possible selves with a strategic self-regulator quality (that is, who believed that they could make it to high school by paying attention in class) had academic outcomes that were superior to classmates with purely self-enhancing possible selves (Oyserman et al., 2004).

Imagined Future Selves as Evaluative Standards or Reference Points

Imagined future selves function not only as directive goals but also as standards to evaluate current actual selves. This self-evaluation process also has major motivational and emotional effects as the self-evaluative process produces pleasant and painful emotions. Some of these self-evaluative emotions, such as pride or shame, are unique to humans because the self-evaluative process involves an awareness that one's actual self is, respectively, congruent with or discrepant from others' expectations (Higgins, 1987). Such socially conscious emotions can be highly motivating.

Emotional Consequences of Imagined Future Selves as Evaluative Standards

Fascinating questions arise when considering the emotional implications of human self-evaluation processes. In particular, why does success in achieving the same objective make some people feel happy or joyful while others feel relaxed or peaceful? Why does failure to achieve the same objective make some people feel sad or discouraged while others feel nervous or worried? Regarding emotional pain from failure, clinical psychologists, especially, have wondered why the same stressful life event, such as being divorced or being fired, can make some people clinically depressed while making others clinically anxious. Giants in the field, such as Sigmund Freud and Carl Rogers, described psychological mechanisms that underlie depression and anxiety. They did not, however, explain why the same failure or negative life event can cause depression in one person and anxiety in another. My self-discrepancy theory (Higgins, 1987) was developed specifically to address this issue.

I started with a consistent finding from several decades of psychological studies: When people experience a discrepancy between the kind of person they believe they are currently (their actual self) and the kind of person they want to be (their desired self), they feel bad. If the discrepancy is extreme and relates to a significant aspect of the desired self, then it can produce extreme negative feeling, such as depression and anxiety. Thus, the magnitude and significance of a discrepancy between an actual self and a desired self are major factors in the story of how failure or negative life events produce severe emotional distress. Clinicians have also known that the magnitude and significance of a congruency between an actual self and a desired self makes people feel good. Indeed, people's self-esteem depends on their having actual self/desired self congruencies.

Self-discrepancy theory introduced an additional factor critical for understanding the emotional impact of actual self/desired self congruencies and discrepancies—the notion that there are different types of desired states, or self-guides, that function as goals to attain or standards to be met. The theory distinguishes between two types of self-guides—an ideal self-guide, representing a person's hopes, wishes, and aspirations; and an ought self-guide, representing a person's beliefs about his or her personal duties, obligations, and responsibilities. The type of self-guide that is involved in self-regulation is the crucial factor in the differing emotional effects of the same life event on different people or on the same person at different times.

Specifically, self-discrepancy theory proposes that an actual self/desired self that is congruent or discrepant with people's ideal self-guides leads us to experiences along the cheerfulness-dejection dimension of emotions (for example, feeling happy after success and sad or even depressed after failure). In contrast, an actual self/desired self congruent or discrepant with people's ought self-guides results in emotions along the quiescence-agitation dimension (for example, feeling relaxed after success and nervous or even anxious after failure).

Most of the research on self-discrepancies and congruencies has focused on the distinction between ideal and ought self-guides. Research has shown that for self-guide discrepancies and congruencies to have emotional and motivational effects, they have to have high accessibility or high readiness to be activated. This condition could occur because some individuals have self-guides that are chronically high in accessibility. It can also occur because a situation temporarily makes people's self-guides high in accessibility. When this accessibility condition is clearly met, research has shown that, as predicted, congruencies and discrepancies from ideal self-guides produce emotions along the cheerfulness-dejection dimension, whereas congruencies and discrepancies from ought self-guides produce emotions along the quiescence-agitation dimension.

Importantly, researchers working with clinical patients (who typically have self-guides that are chronically accessible) have found that those who have mainly actual self discrepancies to their ideal self-guides suffer from clinical depression, whereas those who have mainly actual self discrepancies to their ought self-guides suffer from clinical anxiety. Applied research on clinical depression has demonstrated that interventions that reduce patients' ideal discrepancies produce a decrease in severity of their depressive disorder (Strauman et al., 2006).

Self-discrepancy theory considers congruencies and discrepancies from ideals and oughts in terms of particular types of psychological situations that people experience. An ideal congruency is experienced as the presence of a positive (that is, a gain). An ideal discrepancy is experienced as the absence of a positive (that is, a nongain). An ought congruency is experienced as the absence of a negative (that is, a nonloss). An ought discrepancy is experienced as the presence of a negative (that is, a loss). These different psychological situations underlie the different emotions associated with congruencies and discrepancies to ideals and oughts (see Figure 1). For example, when people experience the presence of a positive (ideal congruency), they feel happy; and when they experience the absence of a positive (ideal discrepancy), they feel sad. When people experience the absence of a negative (ought congruency), they feel relaxed; and when they experience the presence of a negative (ought discrepancy), they feel nervous.

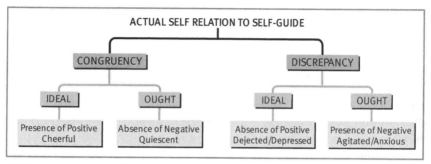

FIGURE 1 Summary of self-discrepancy theory. Congruencies and discrepancies between the actual self and the ideal or ought self-guides lead to characteristic feelings and have long-term effects.

Motivated-Cognition Consequences of Imagined Future Selves as Evaluative Standards

Research has shown that the different psychological situations associated with ideal and ought congruencies and discrepancies have implications beyond their emotional significance. These situations function like personal constructs—worldviews that influence how individuals perceive and remember the world around them (Kelly, 1955). Thus, for example, people remember better those events in a story that match their accessible self-guides (that is, they are more likely to recall story events involving the presence or absence of something positive when ideals are accessible than when oughts are accessible). People also remember better those events in their own lives that relate to whichever type of self-guide is more accessible for them.

Beyond their importance for people's emotional lives, research has shown, for example, that ideal and ought discrepancies relate to different physical problems, such as ideal discrepancies being associated with bulimia and stomach ailments and ought discrepancies being associated with anorexia and headaches. Individuals with ideal discrepancies have been found to have greater empathy for other people who suffer from dejection-related problems, whereas those with ought discrepancies have greater empathy for those suffering from agitation-related problems.

In addition, recent research has shown that self-regulation operates differently when it serves different motives in decision-making situations. Ideal self-regulation serves a promotion focus, a concern with accomplishment and advancement. In contrast, ought self-regulation serves a prevention focus, a concern with security and safety. When promotion-focus ideals are relatively more accessible (whether situationally activated or chronically accessible), people are more open to change and are more creative than when their prevention-focus oughts are more accessible. Conversely, when people's oughts are more accessible, they are more accurate and analytic than when their promotion focus ideals are more accessible (Higgins & Pittman, 2008).

Conclusion

The emotional lives of humans vary depending on the personal standards toward which we strive. We are constantly asking ourselves: Are we the type of people we aspire to be in the future (promotion-focus ideals)? Are we the type of people we believe we should be in the future (prevention-focus oughts)? These kinds of self-regulatory processes underlie our entire strategic response to and views about the world. Thus, our unique characteristic—our ability to imagine the inner states that we want to attain (or maintain) in the future and the type of person that we want to be and become—is critical to human motivation and emotion.

Suggested Further Reading

Higgins, E. T. (1987). Self-discrepancy: A theory relating self and affect. *Psychological Review, 94,* 319–340.

Higgins, E. T., & Pittman, T. S. (2008). Motives of the *human* animal: Comprehending, managing, and sharing inner states. *Annual Review of Psychology, 59,* 361–385.

References

Cooley, C. H. (1964). *Human nature and the social order.* New York: Schocken Books. (Original work published 1902)

Higgins, E. T. (1987). Self-discrepancy: A theory relating self and affect. *Psychological Review, 94,* 319–340.

Higgins, E. T., & Pittman, T. S. (2008). Motives of the *human* animal: Comprehending, managing, and sharing inner states. *Annual Review of Psychology, 59,* 361–385.

James, W. (1948). *Psychology.* New York: The World Publishing Company. (Original publication, 1890)

Kelly, G. A. (1955). *The psychology of personal constructs.* New York: W. W. Norton.

Markus, H., & Nurius, P. (1986). Possible selves. *American Psychologist, 41,* 954–969.

Oettingen, G., Pak, H., & Schnetter, K. (2001). Self-regulation of goal setting: Turning free fantasies about the future into binding goals. *Journal of Personality and Social Psychology, 80,* 736–753.

Oyserman, D., Bybee, D., Terry, K., & Hart-Johnson, T. (2004). Possible selves as roadmaps. *Journal of Research in Personality, 38,* 130–149.

Rogers, C. R. (1961). *On becoming a person.* Boston: Houghton Mifflin Company.

Strauman, T. J., Vieth, A. Z., Merrill, K. A., Kolden, G. G., Woods, T. E., Klein, M. H., et al. (2006). Self-system therapy as an intervention for self-regulatory dysfunction in depression: A randomized comparison with cognitive therapy. *Journal of Consulting and Clinical Psychology, 74,* 367–376.

Chapter 11

Development

Barbara Rogoff, Maricela Correa-Chávez, and Kalie G. Silva
Cultural Variation in Children's Attention and Learning

Carolyn Rovee-Collier
Preserving Infant Memories

Cultural Variation in Children's Attention and Learning

Barbara Rogoff
University of California, Santa Cruz

Maricela Correa-Chávez
University of California, Los Angeles, now at Clark University

Katie G. Silva
University of California, Santa Cruz

▶ *Please describe your current positions and research interests.*
Barbara Rogoff: I hold the UCSC Foundation Distinguished Professorship of Psychology at University of California, Santa Cruz. My research focuses on cultural aspects of how children learn, especially learning by observing and pitching in to family and community activities in Indigenous-heritage communities of North and Central America.

Maricela Correa-Chávez: I am currently Assistant Professor at Clark University. The focus of my research is the cultural organization of learning in communities with Indigenous North and Central American histories, cultural differences in attention and communication in learning, and tools and strengths that children from Latin American immigrant families bring to school contexts.

Katie Silva: I am a doctoral candidate at the University of California, Santa Cruz. My research is on children's learning through observation, teasing with adults, and family stories, especially in Mexican-heritage communities.

▶ *How did you get interested in the social and collaborative nature of children's learning?*
Our interest in the cultural, social, and collaborative nature of children's learning comes from each of our experiences studying children's development and living in communities that vary in their cultural organization, including a Mayan community in Guatemala; the highlands of Utah; eastern Australia; Santa Cruz and Los Angeles, California; several regions of Mexico; and a Mexican-American area in New Mexico.

▶ *What has been the real-world impact of this work?*
We hope that our research contributes to improving the well-being and learning of children, by encouraging greater opportunities for them to be present, observe, and contribute to important activities of their families and communities. In addition, we hope that the research enhances mutual understanding among people of varying cultural backgrounds.

At age 80, Caroline Pratt, a leader in education who grew up in the mid-1800s, thought back on her childhood community and the abundance of opportunities for learning through observing and participating in community activities:

> When I grew up in Fayetteville, New York, school was not very important to children who could roam the real world freely for their learning. . . . No one had to tell us where milk came from, or how butter was made. We helped to harvest wheat, saw it ground into flour in the mill on our own stream; I baked bread for the family at thirteen. There was a paper mill, too, on our stream; we could learn the secrets of half a dozen other industries merely by walking through the open door of a neighbor's shop. (Pratt, 1948, pp. xi–xii)

These experiences underline important cultural aspects of childhood that have come to interest development psychologists. Psychologists have begun to focus on the ways that social, cultural, and historical processes organize the lives of children and their communities. We focus in this essay on research on cultural variation that has taught us about differences in how children learn and pay attention.

Cultural research has inspired important innovations in the organization of children's learning opportunities. For example, the encouragement of collaboration in classrooms was prompted in large part by observations of the home community practices of native Hawaiian children. These observations sparked the inclusion of group work and other new approaches in classrooms in one innovative school, which then spread to many other schools. Such innovations are especially important for children whose community background differs from mainstream middle-class experience. At the same time, innovations based on cultural research with specific populations have also improved learning opportunities for children from other backgrounds, including "mainstream" middle-class backgrounds.

In our own research, we have studied cultural differences in how children pay attention to events going on around them and learn from those events. Our focus is on examining patterns of attention and learning that seem to be related to children's experience in two different learning traditions: One approach to learning emphasizes participation of children in a wide range of family and community activities; it is common in many Indigenous-heritage communities in North and Central America. Another approach to learning, which is common in middle-class European-heritage communities, separates children from the range of family and community activities and instead creates exercises and lessons for them to do in specialized settings such as school.

Learning Through Observing and Pitching In versus Lessons Out of the Context of Productive Activity

Studies of Indigenous communities of the Americas have documented a way of organizing learning in which children are present during family and community activities and are expected to help out as they become able (Morelli, Rogoff, & Angelillo, 2003; Rogoff, 2003); we call this learning by intent community participation (Rogoff et al., 2003; Rogoff et al., 2007).

In many traditional Indigenous communities of the Americas, children are embedded in community activities from a very young age. For example, in Zinacantán, Mexico, 8-month-old infants spend two-thirds of the day carried on a caregiver's back as she goes about her daily activities (de Leon, 2000). As children grow older, they continue to be present when adults engage in important daily activities such as buying and selling in the market, tending to fields and engaging in other work, conversing, and nearly all community activities. In such Indigenous communities, children are alert for important information even while engaged in another activity like play (de Haan, 1999; Gaskins, 2000). They keenly observe and pitch in to ongoing events, many of which are not directed toward them or designed to instruct them. For example, a child accompanying a parent to sell items in the market can see how the parent makes change and can begin to help when ready. Children are expected to observe ongoing activities and develop keen attention to events around them.

By contrast, children in middle-class European-American communities are frequently segregated from the range of community social activities and work. For example, toddlers in two middle-class European-American communities had less access to adults' work and more involvement in specialized child-focused activities than did children in two Indigenous communities—a Mayan town in Guatemala and Efe foragers of the Democratic Republic of Congo (Morelli et al., 2003). Thus, middle-class children have comparatively restricted opportunities to learn by observing the range of important community activities.

Instead, middle-class children are often involved in teachers' or parents' lessons or exercises that are separate from the productive activities of everyday life. Middle-class adults' interactions with children often involve lessons that do not include using the skill being taught in order to accomplish something important in children's lives, such as teaching vocabulary words without using them to communicate. In such lessons and exercises, the children's attention and motivation are frequently managed by adults, rather than by the children themselves. For example, in a teaching task, European-American middle-class mothers took responsibility for making their toddlers learn by trying to arouse the children's interest and focus their attention, whereas Gusii (Kenyan) mothers with little schooling seemed to expect toddlers to be able to learn by observing a demonstration of how to do the task (Dixon et al., 1984).

Cultural Comparisons of Attention

Is learning through keen observation more common in Indigenous communities of the Americas than in middle-class U.S. communities? This idea comes from research that has examined learning through observation in Indigenous communities, but without systematic comparisons with middle-class U.S. communities.

Several systematic comparisons of cultural differences in attention support the idea of more frequent use of keen attention in Indigenous communities of the Americas as compared with middle-class settings. The studies involve families from regions of Mexico and Guatemala where a family history of limited schooling may mean more (or more recent) family experience with traditional Indigenous practices such as learning through intent community participation. For example, Mexican children whose families likely had experience with Indigenous practices (and whose mothers had little schooling) more frequently observed an origami demonstration without pressing for more information, compared with European- and Mexican-heritage U.S. children whose mothers had extensive experience in Western schooling (Mejía Arauz, Rogoff, & Paradise, 2005). Children whose families likely had experience with Indigenous practices of Mexico and limited experience with school also focused their attention on several events simultaneously more often than did children from the other two backgrounds, who more often focused on one event at a time in rapid alternation (Correa-Chávez, Rogoff, & Mejía Arauz, 2005). Similarly, Guatemalan Mayan toddlers and their mothers attended simultaneously to several events more often than did middle-class European-heritage toddlers and mothers, who tended to alternate attention between events (Chavajay & Rogoff, 1999).

These differences are consistent with the idea that children from families with experience with Indigenous practices of the Americas are more likely to keenly observe events than are middle-class children (a cultural group partially defined by extensive Western schooling). The differences also suggest that families with extensive experience with schooling may encourage children to learn in ways that resemble the learning approaches used in schools.

Our work explores children's attention when, instead of being addressed, they had the chance to observe the interactions of others. This situation is common for children included in the range of their community's events—they are present but may not be directly involved when others are carrying out their work or social activities. Children with more experience of being included in a range of family and community activities, such as in communities with Indigenous-heritage practices, may be more attentive when they are not addressed than children whose families have extensive experience with contrasting practices typical of Western schools and related institutions.

Cultural Differences in Learning When Someone Else Is Addressed

All children learn from interactions that are not addressed directly to them. For example, they learn some aspects of language by overhearing others speak, and they learn to emulate violence by watching television shows that are not designed for them. However, learning from interactions that are not directed to children may be especially prevalent in communities that integrate children in a wide range of family and community events, as has been common in Indigenous-heritage communities of the Americas.

Here we present evidence from two studies that found especially keen attention and enhanced learning among children whose families had experience with Indigenous practices, when they were present at an interaction that was directed to someone else. Children from families with extensive schooling experience were less attentive and learned less.

In both studies, a research assistant showed one child how to make an interesting toy, while his or her sibling sat waiting at another table. The non-addressed sibling sat near but not facing the research assistant and the child making the toy (a foam mouse that runs). This child was shown a different toy (an origami jumping frog) that he or she would make soon and was invited to play with a distracter toy while waiting. This way, the nonaddressed child was present and could watch but was not told to observe and would not anticipate needing to observe in order to know how to make the toy he or she would soon make. We videotaped the children and coded the extent to which the nonaddressed children paid attention to the nearby event while they waited.

About a week later, we examined the children's learning from the instruction addressed to their siblings by unexpectedly inviting them to construct the toy that they previously had the opportunity to observe being constructed. When the children returned to pick up the toy they had made, the research assistant said, "Oh, it turns out we have some extra materials. Would you like to make the toy that your [brother/sister] made last week?"

The research assistant then offered the materials and sat back, seemingly occupied with some work. We videotaped the child's efforts and coded the amount of help needed from the research assistant. The research assistant followed a script that designated specific escalating steps of help they were to provide a child when he or she could not proceed alone.

In the first study, we compared the attention and learning of 120 children from three cultural backgrounds: (1) Guatemalan Mayan children whose mothers had extensive experience with traditional Indigenous practices and limited exposure to middle-class Western ways; (2) Mayan children from the same town whose mothers had more familiarity with middle-class Western ways through extensive schooling and related practices; and (3) European-American middle-class children whose families had extensive familiarity with middle-class Western ways through schooling and related practices (Correa-Chávez & Rogoff, 2009).

We found that the Mayan children of both backgrounds were more likely to sustain attention to interactions directed to their sibling than were the European-American middle-class children. The Mayan children spent most of the time watching, whereas the European-American children spent most of the time either not attending to the construction or glancing at it briefly. The differences between the Mayan children from more traditional families and the European-American children were especially pronounced; the extent of attention of Mayan children from families familiar with "Western" ways through extensive schooling and related experiences was intermediate between that of the other two background groups. When the children were given the chance to make their sibling's toy, the Mayan children from more traditional families also showed that they had generally learned more—they commonly needed less help than the children from the other two backgrounds.

The results of the second study, which involved children from two populations that were not living in an Indigenous community, were similar. The study examined the attention and learning of 80 children from two cultural backgrounds: (1) U.S. children from Indigenous-heritage regions of Mexico whose families were likely more familiar with Indigenous ways and less familiar with middle-class Western ways and (2) U.S. children from the same regions of Mexico but whose families were likely more familiar with Western ways through extensive schooling and related experience (Silva, Correa-Chávez, & Rogoff, in press).

The U.S. Mexican-heritage children whose families likely had more experience with Indigenous practices (and whose mothers had limited experience in Western schooling) engaged in sustained attention to the interactions directed to their sibling. They did so more than did U.S. Mexican-heritage children whose mothers had extensive experience in Western schooling (and related practices). They also learned how to construct the toy with less help from the research assistant.

These results support the idea that children whose families have experience with Indigenous Mesoamerican community practices—where children are often present and expected to learn from surrounding events—observe more keenly in situations when they are not directly addressed than do children from middle-class backgrounds, characterized by extensive schooling and related practices. The findings fit with prior work that found that even when Indigenous Mexican children were playing and removed from adult work, they continued to monitor nearby adult activity for moments when their presence would be needed (de Haan, 1999; Gaskins, 2000). Our findings also indicate that when children attend to events not addressed to them, they learn from observing.

Participation in Cultural Practices and Institutions

Children appear to develop patterns of attention related to the cultural practices of their families, communities, and the institutions in which they participate. The differences we found align with the idea that children whose families are from communities where children are present and expected to pitch in to a wide range of family and community activities more keenly observe a nearby interaction, even when there is no obvious need to do so. They may learn more from observing than do children from families and communities that do not have such experience and instead have extensive experience in institutions with contrasting practices of attention and learning—especially Western schooling.

Our findings indicate that involvement in the now-ubiquitous institution of schooling is a cultural experience. For those of us who have extensive schooling—almost all of the readers of this essay—it is easy to think of schooling as a "natural" feature of growing up. But mass, extensive schooling is a feature of children's lives only in some countries and has been available only for the last century or so, anywhere.

Although we refer to schooling as a key cultural experience, extent of schooling is only one part of a constellation of associated practices that fit together. Increases in experience with Western schooling in Indigenous-heritage communities are associated with many other changing practices—such as migration to urban settings or to the United States, new occupations, greater media access, reduced family size, and less involvement of extended family in children's lives (Rogoff & Angelillo, 2002; Rogoff, Correa-Chávez, & Navichoc Cotuc, 2005).

Thus, although we have examined schooling differences, we do not regard schooling as the only "active ingredient" in community differences. We see differences in the extent of families' experience with Western school practices as potentially contributing, along with many associated practices, to community differences in how children go about learning. Experiences with school practices, along with many other cultural experiences, likely foster certain ways of managing attention and provide expectations of what is considered a learning opportunity. Families with extensive experience in Western schooling—and related practices—may encourage children to depend on adults to organize their attention and to expect that the primary source of learning opportunities are adult-led lessons directed to them.

Implications of Cultural Differences in Learning by Observing

Cultural research on human development provides evidence of how children's lives often vary in accordance with the practices of their communities. Cultural research also provides inspiration for changes in current practices to make them more conducive to children's learning and well-being. In this final section, we suggest some changes to improve children's learning in schools and in the broader organization of family and community life.

We suggest that schools shift their organization to make greater use of opportunities to learn by observing. In the usual organization of classrooms, children have little opportunity to learn by observing their classmates or teachers. Students are often discouraged from watching each other, and teachers seldom actively participate in the exercises that they are teaching. Some innovative elementary schools (such as the Open Classroom in Salt Lake City and Academia Semillas del Pueblo in Los Angeles) manage to structure classroom learning in a way that allows students to learn from observing the work of adults and of other children on meaningful projects (Rogoff, Goodman Turkanis, & Bartlett, 2001).

Enhancing children's opportunities to learn by observing others would benefit all children. Middle-class children could learn to make more use of observation, and children from Indigenous-heritage backgrounds, who may often be disadvantaged in schools where they have little chance to observe, could make use of keen observation that they may be familiar with in their families and communities.

In the United States, the organization of children's out-of-school lives also provides limited opportunities to learn by observing and beginning to pitch in to a wide range of valued activities of their families and communities. The exceptions are instructive. For example, U.S. children whose parents do not speak English often accompany their parents in bureaucratic and other complex U.S. institutional settings, helping by serving as language brokers. Children in these immigrant families thereby learn a great deal about the range of community work and other activities, and they show impressive skill in handling them. Although children's work as language brokers may be challenging, it also gives them an opportunity to develop a range of skills and to make important contributions to their family (Dorner, Orellana, & Li-Grining, 2007).

On the basis of our research, we advocate decreasing the segregation of middle-class children from the range of mature activities of their communities, giving them greater opportunities to learn by observing and beginning to pitch in. When industrialized nations excluded children from working in factories about a century ago, they were working to avoid child exploitation—young children worked long hours in dangerous conditions. However, we feel that social policies and the organization of U.S. life have gone too far in excluding children from places where they can learn and from making contributions to their families and communities. Such contributions, we argue, are important not only for children's learning but also for their feeling of doing something of value as they contribute.

Of course, major structural changes in workplaces and social expectations would be needed to undo the extreme segregation that today's children often experience in middle-class settings in the United States (and around the world). However, on small scales, some families in post-industrial nations manage to integrate children more fully in their work and social lives. For example, lawyers and real estate agents who manage their own offices sometimes organize their workplaces in ways that allow children to be present. Children of parents who telecommute have a chance to be present as their parents work.

Some occupations may be more conducive to very young children's actual contributions. However, observing even in settings that have fewer openings for young children to participate allows them to learn about those occupations and about work more generally. Children can pick up far more from observing and listening in on activities than we give them credit for. Supporting this idea is the fact that one of the best predictors of children's early reading is the extent to which people around them read. If they see people reading, whether or not people read to them, they are more prepared to learn to read themselves. Relatedly, it is probably no accident that children of academics often have a relatively easy time in school, and children of doctors seem to become doctors at a level greater than chance.

If children are excluded from the range of their family's and community's activities, they have little chance to learn how to behave or contribute, but if there is a place for them to be present and begin to pitch in, they can learn how to blend with the community's social and work life. Allowing children to be present in a wide range of family and community activities permits them to develop an understanding of the valued work and other activities in their communities. On the basis of our research with families from communities where children have had wide opportunities to observe and pitch in, we argue that children everywhere deserve opportunities to be present to observe and learn how to fit in and to make meaningful contributions to their families and communities.

Author Note

Author order does not reflect relative contribution to the development of this article; authorship was constrained by editorial policy to reflect seniority; all three authors contributed equally.

Acknowledgments

We are grateful to the children, families, and teachers who participated in the research, and to our colleagues who have contributed work along related lines. The writing of this article was supported by a Postdoctoral Fellowship from the American Educational Research Association/Institute of Education Sciences to Maricela Correa-Chávez; a Fellowship from the Center for Informal Learning and Schools (NSF ESI# 0119787) to Katie Silva; and a sabbatical from UCSC, the UCSC Foundation Professorship, and a Fellowship at the Center for Advanced Study in the Behavioral Sciences to Barbara Rogoff.

Suggested Further Reading

Rogoff, B. (2003). *The cultural nature of human development.* New York: Oxford University Press.

Rogoff, B., Paradise, R., Mejía Arauz, R., Correa-Chávez, M., & Angelillo, C. (2003). Firsthand learning through intent participation. *Annual Review of Psychology, 54,* 175–203.

References

Chavajay, P., & Rogoff, B. (1999). Cultural variation in management of attention by children and their caregivers. *Developmental Psychology, 35,* 1079–1090.

Correa-Chávez, M., & Rogoff, B. (2009). Children's attention to interactions directed to others: Guatemalan Mayan and European American patterns. *Developmental Psychology, 45,* 630–641.

Correa-Chávez, M., Rogoff, B., & Mejía Arauz, R. (2005). Cultural patterns in attending to two events at once. *Child Development, 76,* 664–678.

de Haan, M. (1999). Learning as cultural practice: How children learn in a Mexican Mazahua community. Amsterdam: Thela Thesis.

de Leon, L. (2000). The emergent participant: Interactive patterns in the socialization of Tzotzil (Mayan) infants. *Journal of Linguistic Anthropology, 8*(2), 131–161.

Dixon, S. D., LeVine, R. A., Richman, A., & Brazelton, T. B. (1984). Mother-child interaction around a teaching task: An African-American comparison. *Child Development, 55,* 1252–64.

Dorner, L. M., Orellana, M. F., & Li-Grining, C. P. (2007). "I helped my mom," and it helped me: Translating the skills of language brokers into improved standardized test scores. *American Journal of Education, 113,* 451–478.

Gaskins, S. (2000). Children's daily activities in a Mayan village: A culturally grounded description. *Cross-Cultural Research, 34*(4), 375–389.

Mejía Arauz, R., Rogoff, B., & Paradise, R. (2005). Cultural variation in children's observation during a demonstration. *International Journal of Behavioral Development, 29*(4), 282–291.

Morelli, G. A., Rogoff, B., & Angelillo, C. (2003). Cultural variation in young children's access to work or involvement in specialized child-focused activities. *International Journal of Behavioral Development, 27,* 264–274.

Pratt, C. (1948). *I learn from children: An adventure in progressive education.* New York: Simon & Schuster.

Rogoff, B., & Angelillo, C. (2002). Investigating the coordinated functioning of multi-faceted cultural practices in human development. *Human Development, 45,* 211–225.

Rogoff, B., Correa-Chávez, M., & Navichoc Cotuc, M. (2005). A cultural-historical view of schooling in human development. In D. Pillemer & S. H. White (Eds.), *Developmental psychology and social change* (pp. 225–263). New York: Cambridge University Press.

Rogoff, B., Moore, L., Najafi, B., Dexter, A., Correa-Chávez, M., & Solís, J. (2007). Cultural routines and practices. In J. Grusec & P. Hastings (Eds.), *The handbook of socialization: Theory and research* (pp. 490–515). New York: Guilford Press.

Rogoff, B., Goodman Turkanis, C., & Bartlett, L. (2001). *Learning together: Children and adults in a school community.* New York: Oxford University Press.

Silva, K.G., Correa-Chávez, M., & Rogoff, B. (in press). Mexican-heritage children's attention and learning from interactions directed to others. *Child Development.*

Preserving Infant Memories
Carolyn Rovee-Collier
Rutgers University

▶ *Please tell us about your current position and research interests.*
I am Professor II of Psychology at Rutgers University. I study learning and long-term memory in 2- to 24-month-old human infants, examining how they form new associations, how their memories are prolonged, and how new information updates their memory of a prior event.

▶ *How did you come to study long-term memory in preverbal infants?*
My graduate research with newborns was ongoing in the same lab when the first study of newborn classical conditioning was being conducted. Later, when I reported that 2½-month-olds could be operantly conditioned, it made a big to-do because there was no evidence that infants could remember what they had learned longer than a few seconds to minutes at most. Without a capacity for long-term memory, how could infants' early experiences be important for their later behavior? I wondered why they had bothered to learn in the first place. This question motivated my research.

▶ *What has been the real-world impact of this work?*
First, by documenting the importance of early stimulation, enriched environments, and varied experience and their enduring impact on subsequent cognitive development, our findings have major implications for both caregivers and public policymakers. Second, our findings can inform parents, practitioners, and educators about how to introduce and program new information so that it can be learned most efficiently and remembered longer. Third, the findings make possible the formulation of personalized interventions to ameliorate the learning and memory deficits of cognitively impaired individuals of all ages, whether brain damaged or not, and have offered new insights into the elimination of undesirable behaviors.

For more than a century, scientists have believed that infants' early experiences have a lasting impact. Paradoxically, they also believe that young infants lack the capacity for long-term memory and cannot retain memories for more than a few seconds or minutes until late in the first year of life. Unless infants are able to preserve a relatively enduring record of their early experiences in some form or other, how could the impact of those experiences possibly be lasting? Our research on infant memory has not only confirmed that the effects of early experiences are relatively enduring, but it also has revealed how infants remember them.

How Long Do Infants Remember?

The short answer to this question is "longer than you think." The long answer is "it depends on how the infant acquired the memory (that is, the original parameters of training or exposure to an event), the infant's age (older infants initially remember longer), and the infant's prior retrieval experience. Specifically, the more times the infant has retrieved a particular memory in the past, the longer it will be remembered in the future, and the longer the interval between one memory retrieval and the next, the longer the infant will remember the event in the future.

To document the development of long-term memory in infancy, we studied learning and retention among infants whose ages ranged from 2 to 18 months when the target memory was first acquired. Because infants' knowledge of the world and their repertoire of behaviors change dramatically over the first year and a half of life, no single learning task could possibly be appropriate over this wide age range. We therefore developed two equivalent tasks—one to use with younger infants, and one to use with older ones. For 2- to 6-month-olds, we string a ribbon between one ankle and an overhead crib mobile, and they learn to move the mobile by kicking; for 6- to 18-month-olds, we place a large box housing a miniature train with a front lever, and infants learn to move the train by lever pressing.

Infants of these ages cannot tell us what they remember, and so their actions have to "speak" for them. During the long-term retention test, therefore, we simply show infants the same mobile or train they had seen before or one that differs in some way and "ask" them if they recognize it. If they do, then they say "yes" by kicking or lever pressing at a rate greater than their pretraining rate (baseline); otherwise, they do not respond above baseline. Because we disconnect the ankle ribbon and deactivate the lever during the test, infants' performance reflects only what they truly remember of their prior experience and not something new they might have learned at the time of testing.

Using these two procedures with infants of different ages, we tested groups of infants of each age after progressively longer delays until they finally forgot the task. Figure 1 (p. 166) shows that infants' retention increased linearly over the first year-and-a-half of life. Babies as young as 2 months of age remembered for 2 days that foot kicking activated the mobile, while 18-month-olds remembered for 13 weeks (Hartshorn et al., 1998). This pattern of results is not unique to these procedures.

Infants' retention in deferred imitation tasks also increases linearly with age, from 1 day at 6 months of age to 4 weeks at 18 months (Barr & Hayne, 2000). In deferred imitation tasks, an adult models novel actions and infants are given an opportunity to imitate those actions after a delay. In our task, the adult removes a same-colored mitten from the puppet's hand, shakes it to ring a jingle bell pinned inside, and replaces the mitten. Infants receive their first opportunity to imitate the actions during a deferred test. At that time, the puppet is presented within the infants' reach, and the number of target actions (remove the mitten, shake it, attempt to replace the mitten) that each infant reproduces within 90 to 120 seconds of first touching the puppet is his or her imitation score (range = 0–3).

Although these findings reveal that even very young infants remember what they have learned for periods that are considerably longer than researchers previously thought, they still do not tell us whether an infant can

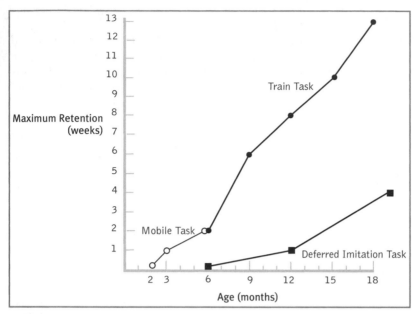

FIGURE 1 The maximum retention (in weeks) of infants who were trained in the mobile task at 2 to 6 months of age or the train task at 6 to 18 months of age and tested (only once) after increasingly longer delays until they forgot the task. Infants trained at 12 months, for example, remembered the task until they were 14 months old, or for a maximum of 8 weeks. (From Hartshorn, 1998.)

remember a prior experience long enough for it to have a lasting impact. How that occurs is the subject of this essay.

How Do Memories of Early Experiences Become Enduring?

1. Reminders restore retention of forgotten memories. We found that briefly exposing infants to a reminder after a memory has been forgotten initiates an automatic, perceptual identification process that reactivates (primes) it and restores retention to the same level that it was originally (Rovee-Collier et al., 1980). Our finding that infants' forgotten memories are not permanently lost but can be recovered by a reminder changed the dialogue about the transient nature of infant memories.

Any isolated aspect of the original event, as long as it is represented in the original memory of that event, will reactivate the memory of the entire event. We typically expose 3-month-olds to the moving mobile as the reminder, but the experimenter—not the infant—moves it. Similarly, we typically expose 6-month-olds to the moving train as the reminder, but a computer—not the infant—moves it.

When the memory is reactivated *within a week* of forgetting, infants of all ages remember the reactivated memory for the same duration that they had remembered the original one. In other words, a single reactivation *doubles the life of the memory* (Hildreth & Rovee-Collier, 2002). When the memory is reactivated after the longest delay possible (that is, at the upper limit of reactivation), a single reactivation *quadruples the life of the memory* (Hildreth & Hill, 2003). Three-month-olds initially remember the mobile task for almost 1 week after training, for example, and its forgotten memory can be reactivated 4 (but not 5) weeks afterward, while 9-month-olds initially remember the train task for 6 weeks, and its forgotten training memory can be reactivated 6 (but not 7) months afterward. Because 15- and 18-month-olds initially remember for so long, they actually outgrow the train task before they reach the upper limit of reactivation! When the forgotten memories of infants who were trained at 15 and 18 months are reactivated at approximately 2 years of age, the infants simply stop pressing when the train doesn't move and tell their mother that the train is "broken" or needs "batteries" (Hsu & Rovee-Collier, 2006).

The preceding findings are summarized in Figure 2. The bottom curve in Figure 2 depicts the maximum duration for which infants of different ages remember the task after they originally learned it. The middle curve shows how long infants of the same ages remember the task when its memory is reactivated 1 week after they had forgotten it. The top curve in Figure 2 shows how long the same ages could remember the task when its forgotten mem-

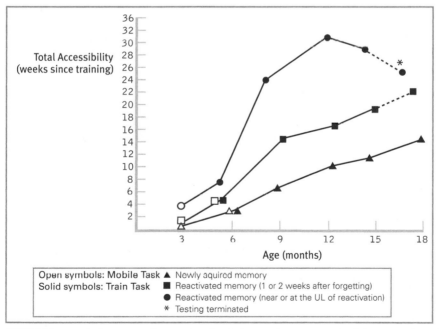

FIGURE 2 The total duration of retention for infants who were trained between 3 and 18 months of age. From bottom to top, the functions indicate how long infants remembered after original training (triangles), how long infants remembered after original training when the memory was reactivated a week after it was forgotten (squares), and how long they remembered after original training when the forgotten memory was reactivated near or at the upper limit of reactivation (circles). Dashes indicate that the verbal and operant indices of retention differed at the last data point; the asterisk indicates that further testing was discontinued.

ory was reactivated near or at the upper limit of reactivation. As you can see, the retention benefit of encountering a single reactivation reminder after a very long delay is huge at all ages.

Because exposure to a single reminder had such an impact in prolonging retention, we decided to examine the retention benefit of exposing infants to multiple reminders. We asked if exposure to multiple reminders might be the means by which early memories are maintained over significant periods of development. To answer this question, we trained 2-month-olds in the mobile task and reminded them every 3 weeks until they outgrew it. After five reminders, infants still exhibited significant retention 4½ months later, and after six reminders, all but one infant still remembered the task 5¼ months later, at 7¼ months of age. At that point, we discontinued testing because infants outgrew the task. When the study ended, all 2-month-olds except one were remembering longer than typical 2-year-olds who are trained for the first time, and the 2-month-old with the "poorest" memory had remembered almost as long as a typical 18-month-old. In contrast, infants who were not originally trained but received the same schedule of reminders exhibited no retention after any delay, confirming that the multiple reminders had not induced new learning that was mistaken for retention (Rovee-Collier, Hartshorn, & DiRubbo, 1999).

Because most infants were still remembering when the mobile study was terminated, Hartshorn (2003) repeated the study using the train task and beginning at 6 months of age. After five reminders, infants trained at 6 months still exhibited significant retention 1½ years later, when they were 2 years old! What's more, these infants had received only one reminder in the preceding year—at 18 months of age.

The successful use of multiple reminders to maintain infants' memories is not unique to conditioning procedures. The quintessential example comes from a study of deferred imitation. Recall that 6-month-olds can imitate a sequence of target actions 1 day after they are modeled. Because infants younger than 6 months lack the motoric competence necessary to perform the puppet imitation task, however, the question of whether they too are capable of deferred imitation remained unanswered. We attempted to answer this question by showing 3-month-olds the same demonstration that was shown to 6-month-olds and then using multiple reminders to maintain the memory of the demonstration until they were old enough to perform the puppet imitation task (Campanella & Rovee-Collier, 2005).

To determine whether our multiple reminder procedure even "worked," however, we first exposed 3-month-olds to two hand puppets (A, B), either simultaneously (paired) or at different times of day (unpaired), for 1 hour per day for 1 week. Next, we attempted to maintain the memory of the puppet A–puppet B association (presumably formed when the puppets were paired) by showing infants puppet A for 30 seconds as a reminder every 3 weeks (6 reminders in all) until they reached 6 months of age. At that time, an adult modeled the target actions on puppet A and, 24 hours later, tested infants' ability to imitate the actions on puppet B. Only infants who had seen the puppets paired at 3 months of age imitated the actions on puppet

B; infants who had seen the puppets unpaired did not. This result confirmed that 3-month-olds had associated the two puppets and that the multiple-reminder procedure had successfully maintained the memory of the association for 3 months.

Therefore, we repeated the prior procedure for 3-month-olds with one major difference: One day after the last exposure to the paired puppets, an adult modeled the sequence of target actions on puppet A. At 6 months of age, 1 day after the last reminder, infants successfully imitated the modeled actions on puppet B! They had not seen either puppet B or the target actions for 3 months, and infants obviously had not imitated the actions immediately after they were modeled.

Most cognitive neuroscientists argue that the rapid forgetting exhibited by very young infants is due to the immaturity of their brains, which limits their ability to maintain and retrieve memories over the long term. Obviously, such conclusions are wrong. The preceding results clearly demonstrate that the brains of even very young infants are sufficiently mature to encode, maintain, and retrieve memories of events that had occurred months earlier—in fact, the equivalent of two to three *lifetimes* earlier!

2. Reminders inoculate against forgetting. Although a reminder can recover a forgotten memory after a remarkably long delay, in the interim, individuals undergo a relatively long period of sustained forgetting. In addition to reactivating memories that were forgotten, reminders forestall forgetting. Each reminder that is encountered before the memory is forgotten will retrieve it and extend its retention longer than it was remembered before. Moreover, the longer the interval since the memory was last retrieved, the longer it will be remembered in the future (Barr, Rovee-Collier, & Campanella, 2005).

When 3-month-olds received a brief reminder immediately after learning the mobile task, for example, they remembered the task for an additional day—6 days instead of 5 days; when they received the same reminder 3 days after training (at the midpoint of their original forgetting function), they remembered the mobile task for 10 days instead of 5 days; and when they received the same reminder 5 days after training (at the end of their original forgetting function), they remembered the mobile task for 21 days instead of 5 days (Galluccio & Rovee-Collier, 2006). In other words, the duration of retention increased exponentially as a function of the retrieval delay. Retention was doubled when infants were reminded after 3 days and was quadrupled when they were reminded after 5 days. We have obtained this same result many times with both conditioned and deferred imitation tasks with infants of all ages.

Are the Memories of Infants Like the Memories of Adults?

Discussion of our research often includes the disclaimer, "Of course, the memories of infants are very different from the memories of adults." The critics are correct to the extent that the memory contents of infants and adults differ both quantitatively (for example, adults have more memories and more links between them) and qualitatively (for example, what adults encode and the cues that retrieve it are different). The basic structure of memory in infants and adults, however, is fundamentally the same.

Table 1 lists the "rules" for prolonging infant memories that our research has turned up thus far, although I did not discuss all of our research that underlies these rules in this essay. Of particular importance is the fact that these rules apply equally well to individuals of all ages. Thus, anyone can enhance his or her learning and retention by following these rules—a matter that should be of particular interest to students. Moreover, clinicians and other practitioners can apply these same rules whether they are assisting healthy individuals overcome learning disabilities or are treating individuals whose memory is impaired as a result of acute brain damage or trauma (for example, in a car accident).

TABLE 1 Rules for Prolonging Retention
1. Distribute training or study sessions
2. Increase the number of training or study sessions
3. Increase the duration the of training or study sessions
4. Enhance attention during encoding
5. Increase the number of retrievals
6. Retrieve the memory nearer the end of its forgetting function
7. Periodically remind (reactivation, reinstatement) of the event
8. Increase the number of associations into which the memory enters
9. Associate shorter-lived memories with longer-lived memories

Back to the Future . . .

Regardless of the time, place, or circumstances of birth, infants begin learning about the structure of their particular environment from the earliest moments of life. Eventually, findings from basic research on what and how young infants learn and remember will permit practitioners to detect and begin treating potential learning and memory problems long before their adverse effects have begun to snowball and become debilitating.

Resolution of the Paradox

As a result of systematic, basic research on infant learning and memory, we have finally resolved the paradox that was introduced at the beginning of this essay. Most of us had long believed that early stimulation plays a major role in cognitive development, but this belief was seriously challenged by the argument that early experiences cannot be important because infants cannot remember them. The evidence now shows that *memories of early experiences can be maintained over significant periods of development by occasional exposures to a reminder*. This evidence has major public policy implications for the funding of federal, state, and local programs that provide early stimulation and enriched environments.

Acknowledgments

Preparation of this essay and the research described in it were supported by grant MH32307 from the U.S. National Institute of Mental Health.

Suggested Further Reading

Barr, R., Rovee-Collier, C., & Campanella, J. (2005). Retrieval facilitates retrieval: Protracting deferred imitation by 6-month-olds. *Infancy, 7*, 263–283.

Rovee-Collier, C. (1995). Time windows in cognitive development. *Developmental Psychology, 31*, 147–169.

References

Barr, R., & Hayne, H. (2000). Age-related changes in imitation: Implications for memory development. In C. Rovee-Collier, L. P. Lipsitt, & H. Hayne (Eds.), *Progress in infancy research* (Vol. I, pp. 21–67). Hillsdale, NJ: Erlbaum.

Barr, R., Rovee-Collier, C., & Campanella, J. (2005). Retrieval facilitates retrieval: Protracting deferred imitation by 6-month-olds. *Infancy, 7*, 263–283.

Bjork, R. A. (2001). Recency and recovery in human memory. In H. L. Roediger, III., J. S. Nairne, I. Neath, & A. M. Surprenant (Eds.), *The nature of remembering: Essays in honor of Robert G. Crowder* (pp. 211–232). Washington, DC: American Psychological Association.

Campanella, J. L., & Rovee-Collier, C. (2005). Latent learning and deferred imitation at 3 months. *Infancy, 7*, 243–262.

Galluccio, L. D., & Rovee-Collier, C. (2006). Nonuniform effects of reinstatement within the time window. *Learning and Motivation, 37*, 1–17.

Hartshorn, K. (2003). Reinstatement maintains a memory in human infants for 1½ years. *Developmental Psychobiology, 42*, 269–282.

Hartshorn, K., Rovee-Collier, C., Gerhardstein, P., Bhatt, R. S., Wondoloski, T. L., Klein, P. J., et al. (1998). The ontogeny of long-term memory over the first year-and-a-half of life. *Developmental Psychobiology, 32*, 69–89.

Hildreth, K., & Hill, D. (2003). Retrieval difficulty and retention of reactivated memories over the first year of life. *Developmental Psychobiology, 43*, 216–229.

Hildreth, K., & Rovee-Collier, C. (2002). Forgetting functions of reactivated memories over the first year of life. *Developmental Psychobiology, 41*, 277–288.

Hsu, V. C., & Rovee-Collier, C. (2006). Memory reactivation in the second year of life. *Infant Behavior & Development, 29*, 91–107.

Rovee-Collier, C., Hartshorn, K., & DiRubbo, M. (1999). Long-term maintenance of infant memory. *Developmental Psychobiology, 35*, 91–102.

Rovee-Collier, C., Sullivan, M. W., Enright, M. K., Lucas, D., & Fagen, J. W. (1980). Reactivation of infant memory. *Science, 208*, 1159–1161.

Schmid, R. E. (2007). Infants form memories, but forget them. Associated Press, retrieved from *Yahoo! News* on February 16, 2007.

Personality

Mark Snyder

Products of Their Personalities or Creatures of Their Situations? Personality and Social Behavior Have the Answer

Products of Their Personalities or Creatures of Their Situations? Personality and Social Behavior Have the Answer

Mark Snyder
University of Minnesota

▶ *Please tell us about your current position and research interests.*
I am McKnight Presidential Chair in Psychology and Director of the Center for the Study of the Individual and Society, University of Minnesota. How individuals create their own social worlds is the overarching theme of my programs of research.

▶ *What got you interested in the influence of personality and situations on the social behavior of individuals?*
The question of whether individuals are products of their dispositions or creatures of their situations drew me into psychological research, when, as a student in psychology courses, I learned that the role of personality and situations was a matter of great debate in the psychological sciences, with strong proponents on either side of the issue. I have been especially interested in the processes by which individuals construct and enact motivational agendas for action that draw upon and integrate features of their personal identities and their social settings and that guide and direct their pursuit of relevant life outcomes in diverse domains of functioning.

▶ *What has been the real-world impact of this work?*
Much of my research, conducted within the Center for the Study of the Individual and Society, focuses on understanding how and why people become actively involved in doing good for others and for society. Such involvement can take the form of volunteerism and philanthropy, social and political activism, and participation in community and neighborhood organizations. Among the questions being addressed are: What are the consequences of such action for individuals and for society?

When the people of ancient Rome attended the theater, they watched performers wearing masks that told them what character each actor was playing. A performer who appeared behind a particular mask played a particular character, one who displayed a consistent pattern of behavior and attitudes (a villain, a hero, a friend, a foe, a wise man, a fool, and so forth). The Latin word for mask is *persona*. Originally, the term referred only to the theatrical mask. But, as time went by, it came to refer also to the character played by the wearer of the mask and eventually to the actor who played the character. Persona is also the Latin root of the psychological term *personality*. In the same way that persona referred to regularities and consistencies in the characters created by performers on the stage, so too does personality refer to regularities and consistencies in the behavior of people in the course of their lives.

For example, someone who regularly behaves in a sociable and outgoing fashion across diverse situations (at work and at play), with different partners (friends and strangers), over time (yesterday, today, and tomorrow) is said to have an extraverted personality; by contrast, someone who is shy and retiring across situations, partners, and time is described as having an introverted personality. To the extent that such consistencies do exist, they distinguish some individuals from others (for example, separating extraverts from introverts), render actions predictable (for example, allowing us to forecast who will be the life of the party and who will be the wallflower), and determine adjustments to life circumstances (for example, influencing who will best fit into an occupational role that calls for much glad-handing and back-slapping and who will cope best in a working environment of solitude and isolation).

In what ways might regularities and consistencies in behavior be reflected in the concerns of psychological scientists? If, indeed, meaningful regularities and consistencies do exist in the behavior of individuals in the course of their lives, what are their origins? And what are their consequences? What are their implications for understanding human nature? It is to questions such as these that I and many other researchers in personality and social psychology have sought answers.

Persons, Situations, and Their Interaction

In contemplating these questions, let us first reflect further on the theater, the players, their masks, their roles, and their audiences. If the mask worn by the actor and the character played by the actor are appearances—outward displays of behavior and attitude—do these outward appearances reflect inner realities? Is the actor someone with exactly that personality, as we are tempted to infer in the case of actors who always seem to play the same role and to play it so naturally as to suggest that they are simply being themselves on the stage or screen? If we see the names of these actors—the Clint Eastwoods and John Waynes of the performing world—on a theatre marquee, we immediately know exactly who they will be in the show.

Our expectations regarding this kind of actor, the one whose persona (in the sense of an underlying personality) is the same as the persona (in the sense of the part being played), has much in common with the view of human nature associated with the field of personality psychology. In defining personality, these psychologists usually include references to the quest to understand how the actions of individuals reflect stable and enduring traits and dispositions thought to reside within individuals and to move them to act in accord with their personalities. As Gordon Allport (1897–1967) defined it, "personality is the dynamic organization within the individual of those psychophysical systems that determine his unique adjustments to his environment" (1937, p. 48).

Of course, some actors simply play a role, their persona reflecting a script, with all of the demands and commands, specifications and instructions of its stage directors. These actors are chameleons, taking on the colors of their surroundings. They are highly flexible, role-playing creatures with great range and diversity, with such highly developed control of their verbal and nonverbal expressions that they literally can, in the course of their careers, become a cast of thousands, all roles played with equal conviction and equal persuasion. These actors are the Anthony Hopkinses and the Meryl Streeps of the dramatic arts; their names on a marquee assure us that they will give a great performance but don't tell us what role they will be playing.

This kind of actor, the one whose personas (that is, their public roles) are many and do not reflect an underlying persona (that is, their own personality), can serve as a metaphor for the view of human nature associated with social psychology. In characterizing personality, social psychologists view people as social animals, creatures of their situations, molding and tailoring their behavior with great flexibility and sensitivity to fit the shifting demands of their current situations, the pressures of their peers, the demands of their roles, and so forth. Thus, Allport said, ". . .with few exceptions, social psychologists regard their discipline as an attempt to understand and explain how the thought, feeling, and behavior of individuals are influenced by the actual, imagined, or implied presence of others" (1968, p. 3). In this view of human nature, to the extent that there are any consistencies in individuals' actions, they have their origin in regularities in the situations in which people find themselves. For example, people who seem forever to be the life of the party may behave that way precisely because they regularly spend time at parties and in other situations that bring out extraverted behaviors.

When faced with such different views of human nature, you might be tempted to ask: Which view is correct—that individuals are products of their dispositions or that individuals are creatures of their situations? In fact, it was this very question that drew me into psychological research, when as a student in psychology courses, I learned that the role of personality and situations was a matter of great debate in the psychological sciences, with strong proponents on either side of the issue. As is so often the case with either/or questions, the answer is that *both* views are correct, but neither view is wholly correct. For, each view captures *a part* of the truth. Dispositions are important, and so are situations. And curiously enough, dispositions are important in part because of the influence of situations, and situations are important in part because of the influence of dispositions. This intimate interplay between dispositions and situations has been revealed through the work of psychologists in a hybrid discipline that brings together both perspectives: personality and social behavior.

Personality Matters More in Some Situations Than in Others

The evidence from research in personality is unequivocal: People's traits and dispositions are linked to their behavior. The linkages between personality and behavior are, however, stronger in some situations than in others. Thus, for example, the influence of personality is especially evident in those situations that actively encourage individuals to turn to their traits, dispositions, and attitudes as guides to action (for a review, see Snyder & Ickes, 1985). William Swann and I demonstrated this effect in a study of attitudes toward affirmative action employment policies. We set up a mock courtroom in which student "jurors" had to offer verdicts in a sex discrimination case. Jurors who were given time to think about their own general attitudes and values prior to hearing the evidence were more likely to reach verdicts that reflected these attitudes and values than were jurors who did not have this opportunity. Taking time to think about their attitudes may have made deciding the court case a matter of principle for these mock jurors (Snyder & Swann, 1976). More generally, life situations that involve consciousness raising, self-disclosure, taking a stand, and matters of principle may also be ones that are likely to foster high degrees of correspondence between personality and behavior.

By contrast, personality dispositions have minimal impact on behavior in situations that place very strong demands and constraints on people and that offer little latitude for people to respond in individualized ways. (These situations are sometimes called strong situations; for a review, see Snyder & Ickes, 1985.) Moviegoers familiar with the film *The Godfather* will understand this principle. Faced with an "offer that he couldn't refuse" (a gun to his head and the choice between his signature or his brains on the contract), the reluctant opponent signs the contract he had been refusing to sign. In a strong situation, individual differences in attitudes, values, temperament, and personality pale in comparison to the strong situational demands to which everyone responds in the same way. To pick a more mundane example than the Godfather's offer, in this culture, we *all* stop at red lights, whether or not we are characteristically inclined to be rule followers or rule benders in other circumstances.

Situations Matter More for Some Personalities Than for Others

Research in social psychology provides clear evidence that individuals' behavior is sensitive to the guidelines provided by situations. However, the strength of these situational influences is greater for some people than for others. For example, the power of situations to guide behavior is especially evident for those people who characteristically turn to situational cues for guides to action; by contrast, the links between situations and behavior are considerably less pronounced for people who characteristically turn inward to their attitudes, traits, and dispositions as guides to action (for a review, see Snyder & Ickes, 1985).

Individual differences in the extent to which situations matter are captured in an aspect of personality trait known as self-monitoring, defined as the degree to which people can and do modify their behavior in response to situational pressures (see, for example, Snyder, 1987). For some people, known as high self-monitors, life is a series of public appearances molded and tailored to fit the situations in which they find themselves and the people with whom they are dealing. In a fashion not unlike the chameleon that takes on the colors of its physical surroundings, the high self-monitor takes on the social colors of his or her situations, with words and deeds carefully chosen to convey just the right image. For other people, known as low self-monitors, life is more a matter of finding ways to display and convey their

---

TABLE 1 **Sample Items from the Self-Monitoring Scale**

Items Typically Endorsed by High Self-Monitors

- When I am uncertain how to act in a social situation, I look to the behavior of others for cues.
- In different situations and with different persons, I often act like very different persons.
- In order to get along and be liked, I tend to be what other people expect me to be rather than anything else.

Items Typically Endorsed by Low Self-Monitors

- My behavior is usually an expression of my true inner feelings, attitudes, and beliefs.
- I can only argue for ideas that I already believe.
- I would not change my opinions (or the way I do things) in order to please someone or win their favor.

---

own true selves, with actions chosen to reflect their own underlying attitudes, traits, and dispositions.

Individual differences in self-monitoring are identified with the Self-Monitoring Scale (Snyder, 1974), sample items from which are provided in Table 1. Differences between high and low self-monitors manifest themselves across a wide range of life domains, including how people choose their friends, their romantic partners, their jobs, their consumer products, and their political candidates. The unifying theme across these diverse domains of life is responsiveness to the demands of social situations: The choices of high self-monitors are much more sensitive to considerations specific to particular situations than are the choices of low self-monitors (for a review, see Gangestad & Snyder, 2000). In other words, situations seem to matter more for high self-monitors than for low self-monitors.

The Interactionist View of Personality and Social Behavior

Taken together, these two propositions (that personality matters more in some situations than others and that situations have more influence on some personalities than others) have formed the basis for the interactionist view of the role of persons and situations in determining behavior. This interactionist approach to personality and social behavior makes it possible to specify *how* persons and situations work together in accounting for individual and social behavior.

In particular, the interactionist approach emphasizes the mutual interplay of persons and situations, with persons selecting situations conducive to the expression of relevant features of their personalities and with situations providing opportunities for people to act on traits and dispositions relevant to those situations (see, for example, Snyder & Cantor, 1998). That is, in some measure, situations are chosen and structured by people themselves, and people are motivated in their choices of situations by their own identities and personalities (for a review, see Ickes, Snyder, & Garcia, 1997). Thus, people with extraverted personalities may choose to spend time in situations such as parties that allow them to display their extraverted personalities; similarly, people with competitive dispositions may choose whenever possible to be in situations that provide opportunities to compete with others. More generally, through their choices of situations, people may create opportunities to act on their personalities.

Moreover, just as dispositions may influence the situations in which people live, so too can the situations in which people find themselves encourage and even enforce consistencies in people's behaviors and even in their personalities. Thus, for example, a lifetime spent in situations calling for success in public relations may produce a reliable record of sociability across situations, partners, and time—a pattern that, at a minimum, may reinforce an underlying extraverted disposition, or that may even be internalized to create an extraverted disposition to match a life spent in extraverted situations. More generally, people's personalities may be shaped and molded by regularities and consistencies in the situations in which they function (for further perspective on the influence of situations on individuals, see Kelley et al., 2003).

Conclusion

Many years ago, Kurt Lewin (1890–1947), a psychologist so influential that he is claimed as a founding parent both of social psychology and personality psychology, observed, "Every psychological event depends upon the state of the person and at the same time on the environment, although their relative importance is different in different cases" (1936, p. 12). In accord with Lewin's fundamental proposition, those of us in the hybrid field of personality and social behavior have shown that if we are to understand people, we need to know something about them as individuals *and* as social beings, to understand their personalities *and* their situations. Moreover, the power of personality and the power of situations become particularly evident in their interaction. For personality is always important, but more so in some situations than others; and situations are always important, but more so for some people than others. And personality and situations are intricately interwoven, with people choosing situations conducive to their personalities, and situations affecting the personalities displayed in them.

This appreciation of the mutual interplay of persons and situations may pay dividends when it comes to understanding how people pursue important outcomes in critical domains of their lives. Thus, when it comes to understanding how people make critical choices in their lives—whether in choosing friends and romantic partners, or in selecting a career or a profession—there may be value to looking at those choices from the perspective of the ways that those choices are guided by personality and how those choices in turn feedback on and influence their opportunities to express personality.

Suggested Further Reading

Snyder, M. (1987). *Public appearances/private realities: The psychology of self-monitoring.* New York: W. H. Freeman.

Snyder, M., & Cantor, N. (1998). Understanding personality and social behavior: A functionalist strategy. In D. T. Gilbert, S. T. Fiske, & G. Lindzey (Eds.), *The handbook of social psychology: Vol. 1.* (4th ed., pp. 635–679). Boston: McGraw-Hill.

References

Allport, G. (1937). *Personality: A psychological interpretation.* New York: Holt.

Allport, G. (1968). The historical background of modern social psychology. In G. Lindzey & E. Aronson (Eds.), *The handbook of social psychology: Vol. 1.* (2nd ed., pp. 1–80). Reading, MA: Addison-Wesley.

Gangestad, S. W., & Snyder, M. (2000). Self-monitoring: Appraisal and reappraisal. *Psychological Bulletin, 126,* 530–555.

Ickes, W., Snyder, M., & Garcia, S. (1997). Personality influences on the choice of situations. In R. Hogan, J. A. Johnson, & S. R. Briggs (Eds.), *Handbook of personality psychology* (pp. 165–195). New York: Academic Press.

Kelley, H. H., Holmes, J. W., Kerr, N. L., Reis, H. T., Rusbult, C. E., & Van Lange, P. A. M. (2003). *An atlas of interpersonal situations.* New York: Cambridge University Press.

Lewin, K. (1936). *A dynamic theory of personality.* New York: McGraw-Hill.

Snyder, M. (1974). The self-monitoring of expressive behavior. *Journal of Personality and Social Psychology, 30,* 526–537.

Snyder, M. (1987). *Public appearances/private realities: The psychology of self-monitoring.* New York: W. H. Freeman.

Snyder, M., & Cantor, N. (1998). Understanding personality and social behavior: A functionalist strategy. In D. T. Gilbert, S. T. Fiske, & G. Lindzey (Eds.), *The handbook of social psychology: Vol. 1.* (4th ed., pp. 635–679). Boston: McGraw-Hill.

Snyder, M., & Ickes, W. (1985). Personality and social behavior. In G. Lindzey & E. Aronson (Eds.), *The handbook of social psychology: Vol. 2.* (3rd ed., pp. 883–948). New York: Random House.

Snyder, M., & Swann, W. B., Jr. (1976). When actions reflect attitudes: The politics of impression management. *Journal of Personality and Social Psychology, 34,* 1034–1042.

13

Psychological Disorders

Irving I. Gottesman
Predisposed to Understand the Complex Origins of Behavioral Variation

Susan Nolen-Hoeksema
Lost in Thought: The Perils of Rumination

Predisposed to Understand the Complex Origins of Behavioral Variation

Irving I. Gottesman
University of Minnesota

▶ *Please tell us about your current position and research interests.*
I am currently semi-retired but two days a week hold the Drs. Irving and Dorothy Bernstein Professorship in the Department of Psychiatry, University of Minnesota Medical School. I am also Senior Fellow, Department of Psychology, University of Minnesota, and Sherrell J. Aston Professor of Psychology Emeritus, University of Virginia. My research interests continue to be in psychiatric and behavioral genetics, including new strategies from epigenetics, focused on schizophrenia and bipolar disorder.

▶ *What got you interested in studying and resolving psychiatry genetics?*
It was a mountain (of ignorance) needing to be climbed and a rather empty niche when I began graduate school in 1956.

▶ *What has been the real-world impact of this work?*
One concrete example can be seen in the number of times my work has been cited in Google Scholar: Both my textbooks and my journal articles have been heavily cited and that has led to numerous national and worldwide prizes for advancing my three fields (psychology, psychiatry, and genetics). The recognition comes both from scientific organizations and from organizations advocating for the mentally ill (NAMI, NARSAD). My formulations in genetic counseling for the families of the mentally ill have brought relief from exaggerated fears of mental illness "running in the family."

Had I been born two centuries ago, I might have ended up pursuing a career as a naturalist, happy enough but without the means to live well and to educate my children. The field of behavioral genetics, arising at the interfaces of the biological and behavioral sciences with essential support from medicine, mathematics, and the philosophy of science, has been very, very good to me, and satisfying. My childhood curiosity about nature took the form of collecting rocks, leaves, bird eggs, and pond water, and really escalated with birthday and Christmas gifts of junior microscopes and expansions of starter chemistry sets, supplemented by trips to the pharmacy. Before completing elementary school, my mother had to constrain my expertise at bad smells emanating from the basement as well as the potential self-harm of homemade fireworks.

The Journey to Psychology via Physics

Success in high school biology, physics, and chemistry led to the strong advice to major in physics in college, as it had a future. Reading the novel *Arrowsmith* by Sinclair Lewis about biomedical researchers also made a deep impression on my career fantasies. It only took one course in abnormal psychology for me to switch majors and to focus on psychopathology as a way to reconcile my interests. After a 3-year interlude on active duty as a naval officer during the Korean War, I was fortunate to be accepted into the scientist-practitioner-model training program in clinical child psychology at the University of Minnesota on the G.I. Bill. Mandatory core courses on the psychology of individual differences, taught by Donald G. Paterson and James J. Jenkins, exposed me to the classical twin studies of schizophrenia and other psychoses conducted by F. J. Kallmann in this country and by E. T. Slater in the United Kingdom, with their unambiguous conclusions that hereditary factors play major roles in their distal etiologies—unambiguous, that is, to those not bitten by the psychodynamic bug endemic in post–World War II psychiatry, psychology, and clinical social work.

Paterson, an eminent applied psychologist who had shaped military cognitive testing for literate and illiterate draftees during World War I and an avid civil libertarian, introduced me to his friend in the Department of Zoology, Sheldon C. Reed. The latter was a fruit fly geneticist whose interests had shifted to human psychopathology (mental retardation and the psychoses), conceptualized as continuously distributed traits, with his new appointment to head the Dight Institute for Human Genetics. He coined the term "genetic counseling," and it was one of the functions of the Dight. Conversations with him and members of the clinical program quickly gave rise to the design of my doctoral dissertation initiated in 1957: I would somehow collect a sample of adolescent identical and fraternal same-sex twins from the public high schools of Minneapolis and Saint Paul, determine their zygosity objectively, administer objective tests of their personality traits, and then delve into the "psychogenetics of personality"—not a popular topic in that day.

One instrument, of course, would be the locally invented but world-renowned Minnesota Multiphasic Personality Inventory (MMPI). This paper-and-pencil test consisting of 550 true-false questions was developed by the psychologist Starke R. Hathaway, a member of my dissertation committee, and his neuropsychiatrist friend and colleague J. C. McKinley, M.D., to assess symptoms and prodromal features of mental disorders along Kraepelinian lines in time for its deployment in evaluating the millions of draftees in World War II in a cost-effective manner. The giant intellect of Paul E. Meehl influenced and shaped the thought processes about clinical psychology of all the graduate students and faculty in the Ph.D. program.

The objective results were very reinforcing to a would-be behavioral geneticist (the term would not be used until 1960 with the publication of the textbook by J. Fuller and W. R. Thompson) in that they showed 4 of the 10 clinical scales were reliably more similar for identical than fraternal twins, even in a small sample of 68 pairs. The scales implicated to contain appreciable genetic variance had been derived from criterion groups with diagnoses of affective disorders, schizophrenia, and antisocial personality disorders. Such findings, especially when replicated a few years later in a sample twice the size and in a different locale, helped to usher in a paradigm shift in the study of psychopathology and personality two decades later, wherein genetic factors, including genes and SNPs (single-nucleotide polymorphisms, which are DNA sequence variations), would become targets of large-scale research using new tools from molecular genetics and medicine.

Escalating the Degree of Difficulty: Twin Studies of Schizophrenia

One of the major goals of psychopathologists who study people in the general population, such as the normal adolescent twins described above, is that our assumptions are correct about there being a continuum from normality into psychiatrically noteworthy disorders, and that awareness of such a dimensional approach will shed light on the causes of abnormal behavior. Studying the diseases themselves, such as schizophrenia, in adult twin samples is a demanding, time consuming, and expensive enterprise. All such studies in the literature were conducted before the use of fertility-enhancing drugs, when the overall twinning rate in this country was 12 pairs per 1,000 deliveries. The current rate of twinning overall is now about 31 per 1,000 deliveries. The older schizophrenia projects starting in 1928 allowed researchers to verify the representativeness of their samples if they came close to 12/1,000, with about 1/3 being identical twins (monozygotic, MZ, or one-egged), 1/3 being fraternal twins (dizygotic, DZ) of the same gender, and 1/3 being opposite-gender fraternal pairs.

How often might we expect to encounter a pair of identical twins in the adult population where at least one in the pair has a valid diagnosis of schizophrenia? This is the calculation: 4/1,000 multiplied by the age-adjusted base rate of schizophrenia, 1/100, yields an expectancy of 4/100,000 persons in the general population meeting our needs to locate the uranium in the pitchblende. The task of assembling a decent-sized sample of both identical and fraternal twins meeting the criteria is facilitated by having national population and twin birth registries such as those in Australia, the Netherlands, and the Scandinavian countries, or by having special records of twinships in large teaching hospitals in countries with a form of national health insurance that records treatment for mental disorders in both inpatients and outpatients.

When James Shields and I, under the guidance of Eliot Slater, commenced our London, United Kingdom, study in 1962 of schizophrenia in twins consecutively admitted to the Bethlem Royal Hospital and the Maudsley Hospital (Joint Hospital), we could identify all same-gender twin pairs from some 45,000 patients admitted between 1948 and 1965. After personal and record follow-up of the 479 patients who were twins to determine their most valid diagnoses, we accumulated a sample of 62 probands with a diagnosis of schizophrenia ascertained independently of one another in our hospital (index cases) from 57 pairs equally divided by gender. Further research showed that we had 24 pairs of MZ twins and 33 pairs of DZ.

Ninety-one of the 114 twins were seen by us for tape-recorded, semi-structured interviews and, when agreed upon, testing with the MMPI. We did not rely on either our diagnosis or that in the hospital charts; we chose to prepare case histories, without mentioning zygosity, and presented them in random order to a panel of six expert diagnosticians. The next task was to make use of the consensus diagnoses from the panel to calculate the most accurate summary rates for the MZ and DZ samples, still without an attempt to correct for age among the younger co-twins, still at risk for developing the disease in their future. The probandwise rate for a schizophrenia-related psychosis in MZ twins was 58% ±10, while that for the DZ pairs was 12% ±6. Allowing for the usual age correction would have little effect on these uncorrected rates, 62% and 15%.

The fact that these results have been replicated in more than a dozen studies across the globe means that an irrefutable foundation has been established for moving forward on an enlightened neuroscience frontier, recognizing the priority to be accorded to gene finding, gene expression, and epigenetics (heritable changes in gene function that occur without a change in the sequence of DNA), identifying endophenotypes (Gottesman & Gould, 2003; Ritsner, 2009), and probing the brain pathophysiology that can lead to new treatments. The term *endophenotype* was introduced by Gottesman and Shields (1972) to specify variables mediating the long chain of events in the complex pathways between gene expression and the precursors of psychiatric symptoms, which, in combination, usher in the disease itself. The term *enlightened* means a necessary sensitivity to probable gene by environment interactions as well as to measured environments, pre- or postnatal, that may be triggers to, or inhibitors of, varying degrees of predisposition. I am reminded of the powerful rhetoric of Sir Winston Churchill in 1942 when the tide began to turn in favor of the Allied forces against the Nazi forces, as an analogy to our war against the ignorance surrounding the causes of schizophrenia and other psychoses: "Now this is not the end. It is not even the beginning of the end. But it is, perhaps, the end of the beginning."

Variations on the Classical Twin Design

The straightforward contrasting of MZ concordance rates (or correlations) with DZ concordance rates (or correlations) for a disease or trait, while of fundamental value to advancing knowledge about causes and their proper weights, far from exhausts the other kinds of information that can be derived from the study of twins. I would caution against just searching in Google for "twins" as it would drown you in some 67 million hits; the field is narrowed to a manageable 121,000 by asking for the combination "twins, psychology, psychiatry." Contemplating variations on the classical theme will open your mind: A focus on MZ twin pairs discordant for diseases and traits generates a list of vulnerability factors and another for contributions to resistance; studying the adult offspring of twins concordant or discordant for disorders may reveal unexpressed genotypes in the healthy MZ co-twin; MZ and DZ twins reared apart (often a practice of adoption agencies) allows for the assessment of the power, or lack of power, of environmental factors/rearing styles on behavioral outcomes; and a last example, collaboration with epigeneticists will allow the exploration at the molecular genetic level for factors impacting gene regulation on behavioral outcomes for which twins are discordant or differ greatly. A serious concern for the role of epigenetics on behavioral features is relatively recent, opening a window on sources of variation in behavior not directly attributable to either environment or to DNA-sequence changes or to gene by environment interactions. An appreciation of epigenetics will perhaps be analogous to the introduction of the Hubble Space Telescope into earth orbit and its impact on our old ideas about the solar system.

Complexity, Complexity, and Complexity

No one has ever been as bold or uninformed as to believe that understanding why one human differs from another across behaviors would be easy. Even formulating the best questions to ask requires a talented, judicious, and multidisciplinary task force, as discovered when The Hastings Center and the American Association of Science garnered funding from the Ethical, Legal, and Social Implications (ELSI) division of the National Human Genome Research Institute to reconnoiter the intellectual territory. The fruits of the labors are well worth deep exploration. (See suggested readings at the end of the essay for titles and how to locate them.) A sampling of the disciplines convened to generate ideas and understanding (sometimes) in a confrontational (often) atmosphere would include several flavors of theology, philosophers of science, ethics and bioethics, law, psychology, psychiatry, molecular genetics, chemistry, human genetics, animal genetics, mathematics, sociology, neurobiology, journalism, anthropology, and the lay public— quite an assemblage of sharpened minds. But even more variety is needed to do justice to the complexities.

How can we approximate our dilemma of describing and explaining the sources of variation in human behavior, normal and deviant, to the point of requiring therapeutic interventions without obtaining, say, three different higher degrees, field experiences, and spending the majority of our adult lives in universities or medical schools? Don't answer. One suggestion I will proffer is to look for analogous questions elsewhere, tackling other complexities, and then examine partial answers that may have been discovered. For example, what causes floods or car crashes or divorce or 50 percent drops in the stock market in one year, and how could partial answers to those questions help with finding the causes of schizophrenia?

Let's start with floods such as the one that decimated New Orleans during Hurricane Katrina and see how far and where it takes us. The list of variables on our list, looked at both cross-sectionally at the time of the flood and historically, would include current local rainfall, rainfall upriver feeding into all the tributaries of the Mississippi, saturation levels of the earth from the previous season's snowfall, current wind velocities from the hurricane, the condition of the protective dikes, the presence or destruction of upriver and tributary dams, and so forth. The point is that both cross-sectional and "developmental" histories of the land, river, behavior of the Corps of Engineers and of political decisions over the previous n-years will all enter into one big prediction equation and it must be a dynamic one. I would make the same argument for understanding and predicting schizophrenia. We know less about which elements will be the puzzle pieces for schizophrenia than we do for floods, but we can begin with a schema for organizing those in which we have some confidence. Let's call the schema "an endophenotype strategy" and the cartoon/sketch could look like Figure 1 (Gottesman & Gould, 2003).

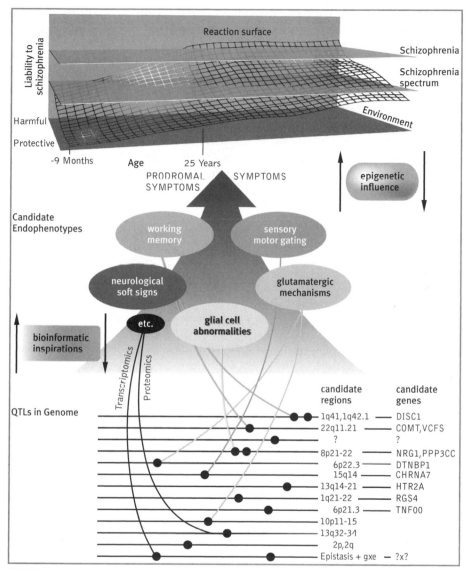

FIGURE 1 Gene regions, genes, and candidate endophenotypes are implicated in a biological systems approach to psychosis research. Endophenotypes are theoretically characterized as having simpler structural antecedents than the psychiatric phenotypes themselves. This schema (genes to endophenotypes to symptoms to disease), allowing for epigenetic, environmental, and stochastic influences, can be applied to other complex diseases as well. None of the components in the figure can be definitive; many more elements exist or await discovery. © I. I. Gottesman & T. D. Gould 2008. Used by permission.

The schema has provisions for the roles of specific genes or SNPs implicated as distal contributors to the phenotype of schizophrenia and those to be discovered; it implies just a few of the many endophenotypes already in the literature from different domains of brain functioning; it suggests the need to consider the essentiality of developmental processes over time; it allows for the interplay of genes, environments, and epigenetic factors over time coming together pre- and postnatally with the additional schema of the "reaction surface" promoted by Turkheimer, Goldsmith, and Gottesman (1995) and, in passing, reminds us of the importance of bioinformatics, proteomics, and transcriptomics for the big picture. I can only hope that I have whet your appetite for complexity with this brief essay and the clues it has provided along the trail from my own interests to examples of some of the research I have pursued for the past 52 years. Those clues and the recommended readings may lead some of you to a nontraditional career in psychology, one that has permeable borders with other disciplines and one that prepares you for working collaboratively for the betterment of our species on projects akin to those that led to the Manhattan Project and putting an astronaut on the moon.

Suggested Further Reading

Baker, C. (2004). *Behavioral genetics: An introduction to how genes and environments interact through development to shape differences in mood, personality, and intelligence.* Washington, DC: American Association for the Advancement of Science and The Hastings Center.

Carey, G. (2003). *Human genetics for the social sciences.* Thousand Oaks, CA: Sage.

DiLalla, L. F. (Ed.) (2004*). Behavior genetics principles: Perspectives in development, personality, and psychopathology.* Washington, DC: American Psychological Association.

Kaminsky Z. A., Tang, T., Wang, S. C., Ptak, C., Oh, G., Wong, A. H. C., et al. (2009). DNA methylation profiles in monozygotic and dizygotic twins. *Nature Genetics, 41,* 240–245.

Kendler, K. S., & Prescott, C. A. (2006). *Genes, environment, and psychopathology: Understanding the causes of psychiatric and substance use disorders.* New York: Guilford Press.

McGuffin, P., Owen, M. J., & Gottesman, I. I. (Eds.). (2004). *Psychiatric genetics and genomics* (Rev. ed.). Oxford, U.K.: Oxford University Press.

Parens, E. (2004). Genetic differences and human identities: On why talking about behavioral genetics is important and difficult. *The Hastings Center Report, 34,* S1–S36.

Parens E., Chapman, A. R., & Press, N. (Eds.). (2006). *Wrestling with behavioral genetics: Science, ethics, and public conversation.* Baltimore: Johns Hopkins University Press.

Plomin, R., DeFries, J. C., Craig, I. W., & McGuffin, P. (Eds.). (2003). *Behavioral genetics in the postgenomic era.* Washington, DC: American Psychological Association.

Plomin, R., DeFries, J. C., McClearn, G. E., & McGuffin, P. (2008). *Behavioral genetics* (5th ed.). New York: Worth.

References

Gottesman, I. I., & Gould, T. D. (2003). The endophenotype concept in psychiatry: Etymology and strategic intentions. *American Journal of Psychiatry, 160,* 636–645.

Gottesman, I. I., & Shields, J. (1972). *Schizophrenia and genetics: A twin study vantage point.* New York: Academic Press.

Ritsner, M. S. (Ed.). (2009). *The handbook of neuropsychiatric biomarkers, endophenotypes, and genes: Promises, advances, and challenges.* Frankfurt: Springer.

Turkheimer, E., Goldsmith, H. H., & Gottesman, I. I. (1995). Commentary (on G. Gottlieb). *Human Development, 38,* 142–153.

Lost in Thought: The Perils of Rumination
Susan Nolen-Hoeksema
Yale University

▶ *Please tell us about your current position and research interests.*
I am Professor of Psychology, Yale University. My research interests are depression, gender differences in psychopathology, and adolescent psychopathology.

▶ *What got you interested in studying the style of thinking you call rumination and its impact on mood?*
In working with depressed patients, I was impressed by their tendency to ruminate about their past and about their current problems in a way that was nonproductive and decided to study it as a causal factor in depression.

▶ *What has been the real-world impact of this work?*
The work has led to innovations in treatment for depressed people. I have also written self-help books that people who ruminate tell me have been helpful.

When something unpleasant happens—you fail a test or have an argument with a friend—do you ever find yourself going over and over what happened, questioning why it happened, how you could have prevented it, what the consequences might be, and how upset you feel? If your answer is "yes," you're like most people. We analyze unpleasant events to understand them, hoping that questioning will lead to solutions to ongoing problems, prevent bad things from happening in the future, or both. However, some people never move into a problem-solving mode. Instead, they remain stuck, rehashing events or situations, microanalyzing them, contemplating their deep meaning. They also tend to worry about future events, imagining all the ways that things could go wrong. We call this process rumination—repetitively thinking about difficult situations and all their possible causes, consequences, and meanings without moving into problem solving.

The Consequences of Rumination

Although most of us ruminate occasionally, some people—we call them ruminators—ruminate very frequently. In other words, the tendency to ruminate appears to be a stable trait in some individuals. Some years ago, colleagues and I developed a questionnaire, the Response Styles Questionnaire, to assess rumination (Nolen-Hoeksema & Morrow, 1991). Our questionnaire asks people what they tend to do when they feel sad, blue, and depressed. For examples of items from this questionnaire, see Table 1.

Respondents who endorse many items such as those in Table 1 are designated as ruminators. Ruminators tend to ruminate even when their lives are going relatively smoothly.

TABLE 1 Sample Rumination Items				
Instructions: People think and do many different things when they feel sad, blue, or depressed. Please read each of the items below and indicate whether you never, sometimes, often, or always think or do each one when you feel sad, down, or depressed. Please indicate what you generally do, not what you think you should do.				
	never	**sometimes**	**often**	**always**
1. I think "What am I doing to deserve this?"	1	2	3	4
2. I think "Why do I always react this way?"	1	2	3	
3. I think "Why do I have problems other people don't have?"	1	2	3	4
4. I think about a recent situation, wishing it had gone better	1	2	3	4
5. I think "Why can't I handle things better?"	1	2	3	4

Ruminators are at increased risk for a number of mental health problems including depression, a problem we have studied closely. In several studies, we have found that ruminators are more likely than those without this trait to experience severe and prolonged symptoms of depression after difficult events and even to be diagnosed with major depressive disorder, one of the most severe forms of depression. For example, we studied the effects of rumination on depression among people who had recently lost a loved one to cancer (Nolen-Hoeksema & Larson, 1999). Recently bereaved people often feel quite depressed, but the severity and duration of bereavement-related depression varies greatly from one person to another, with bereaved ruminators having relatively longer and more severe episodes of depression following the loss of their loved one.

Similarly, in a study of reactions to the 1989 earthquake that rocked the San Francisco Bay Area, we found that ruminators experienced more symptoms of depression and anxiety after the earthquake than did nonruminators (Nolen-Hoeksema & Morrow, 1991). In a fortuitous coincidence for our research, about 140 Stanford University students had taken the Response Styles Questionnaire 2 weeks before the earthquake. When we assessed their mental state after the quake, those students who had previously scored as ruminators were found to be more depressed and anxious 10 days after the quake and 7 weeks after the quake than those who were not ruminators, regardless of how much stress they had endured as a result of the earthquake (for example, whether they were in a safe building or a building that literally fell down around them).

In other studies, we have found that rumination predicts not only depression and anxiety but also substance abuse (for example, binge-drinking alcohol), binge-eating and bulimia nervosa, and self-harming behavior (for example, cutting) (for a review, see Nolen-Hoeksema, Wisco, & Lyubomirsky,

2008). We think that these diverse behaviors all represent maladaptive attempts to escape from the aversive self-awareness and negative emotions that rumination brings about.

Mechanisms Linking Rumination with Negative Outcomes

How does rumination lead to all these negative consequences? In laboratory studies designed to answer this question, our method has been to compare two groups: people who are experiencing depression or dysphoria and people who are not at all depressed. We ask participants to ruminate, or we distract them from any natural ruminations by requiring them to focus their attention on a series of phrases. In the rumination-induction condition, the phrases direct their attention to thoughts about themselves, how their bodies feel, and how their lives are going—for example, "think about your level of motivation right now" or "think about your character and who you strive to be." In the distraction-induction condition, the phrases direct their attention to thoughts and images that are not self-focused—for example, "think about a truckload of watermelons" or "think about the face on the Mona Lisa."

Notice that both the rumination and distraction phrases are neutral in emotional tone. We don't specifically ask participants to focus on negative aspects of themselves or negative images in the environment. Thus, we don't expect the rumination phrases to have any effect on the mood of nondepressed participants, whereas we expect the rumination phrases to *increase* the depressed mood in the short term in depressed participants because they are more likely to be thinking negatively about themselves and feeling badly. In contrast, we expect the distraction phrases to *decrease* the depressed mood in the short term because these phrases draw the attention of the depressed participants away from their negative ruminations. And this is just what we have found. In a few dozen studies using this paradigm, rumination induction has been found to increase depressed mood in depressed participants and have no effect on mood in nondepressed participants. In contrast, the distraction induction decreases depressed mood in depressed participants but does not affect mood in nondepressed participants (see Nolen-Hoeksema et al., 2008).

What's particularly interesting, however, is how rumination induction affects the quality of depressed people's thoughts, increasing negativity about the past, present, and future (see Nolen-Hoeksema et al., 2008). Specifically, we have assessed thoughts about past, present, and future events in four groups—depressed people who have ruminated, depressed people who have been distracted, nondepressed people who have ruminated, and nondepressed people who have been distracted. Depressed/ruminators on average generate more negative memories of the past and rate these negative events as having been more frequent than do those in the other three groups. When thinking about the present, the depressed/ruminators as a group focus more on their problems, engage in more self-blame for their problems, and express less self-confidence about overcoming their problems compared with the other three groups. When thinking about the future, depressed/ruminators are on average less optimistic and predict fewer happy events in their future, compared to the other three groups. In turn, these negative thoughts about the past, present, and future feed the depression of the depressed ruminators, prolonging it and worsening it.

Ruminators often tell us that they ruminate in an attempt to understand and solve their problems. But, paradoxically, rumination appears to interfere with good problem solving. In other experimental studies, we have given participants sticky, interpersonal problems to solve after they have ruminated or been distracted. The problems are typical of the kinds of interpersonal issues that arise in the life of a depressed person, such as a friend avoiding you. We find that depressed people who have been ruminating generate solutions to such problems that are significantly lower in quality (as rated by impartial judges) than the solutions generated by depressed people who were distracted or nondepressed people who either ruminated or were distracted. For example, in response to the friend-is-avoiding-you problem, individuals in the depressed/rumination group generate "solutions" such as "I guess I would avoid them, too." In contrast, members of the other three groups tend to generate solutions such as "I would ask a mutual friend if I had done anything to upset my friend, and if so, I would apologize."

Even when ruminators generate reasonable solutions to problems, rumination seems to get in the way of their implementation of these solutions. In another study, for example, we asked ruminators and nonruminators (defined by answers to our questionnaire) to generate solutions to a concrete problem, such as revising the curriculum for their school or solving the housing problem on their campus. For such noninterpersonal problems, the ruminators generated solutions that were just as good as those generated by the nonruminators. But when it came time to commit to a solution and present it to a panel of judges, the ruminators had less confidence than the nonruminators in the quality of their solution and were more likely to ask for additional time to work on it. And at the presentation, the ruminators appeared less confident in their presentations than did the nonruminators (Ward et al., 2003). Thus, ruminators may become immobilized in indecision and self-doubt and fail to implement solutions to their problems, even when those solutions are good ones.

Finally, ruminators may drive away social support, perhaps when they need it the most, because people become weary and frustrated at the ruminator's inability to let go of their concerns and move on. In our bereavement study, we found that ruminators were reaching out to others for social support even more than were nonruminators. This makes sense because ruminators were feeling more depressed and had a lot on their minds. Over time, however, the ruminators reported that others were becoming annoyed with their constant need to talk about their loss and their feelings of grief and critical of their inability to get on with their lives. In turn, this loss of social support and increase in criticism gave ruminators more to ruminate about and fueled their depression (Nolen-Hoeksema & Davis, 1999).

What Drives Rumination?

If rumination leads to such misery, why do ruminators continue to ruminate? One reason may be that rumination saps motivation. In one study using our rumination and distraction inductions in depressed and nondepressed participants, we asked how useful several pleasant, simple activities—for example, "go for coffee with a friend" or "take a walk in the hills"—would be in improving mood. The depressed/rumination group rated these activities as just as useful as the other three groups (depressed/distraction, nondepressed/rumination, and nondepressed/distraction) for lifting mood. But when we asked the four groups how likely they would be to get up immediately and actually go for coffee or take a walk, the depressed/rumination group rated themselves as less likely to do so, compared the other three groups. It was as if they said, "Yes, I know doing one of these activities would make me feel better, but I'm not going to do it." The content of depressed rumination—the focus on how tired and blue you feel, and on compelling problems in your life—may drain any motivation individuals have to do things they can intellectually acknowledge would improve their moods.

Basic cognitive deficits associated rumination may make it difficult for ruminators to pull out of rumination once it starts. Jutta Joormann (2006) has used tasks that assess participants' ability to inhibit negative information when instructed to do so; she finds that ruminators have more difficulty on these tasks compared to nonruminators. So, once ruminators get going, turning off negative thoughts may be very difficult, even if they are motivated to do so. Similarly, in a neuroimaging study, we found that ruminators showed sustained activity in areas of the brain associated with self-related thought even when given distractions. In other words, compared to nonruminators, they could not redirect their attention to the distractions and continued to show activity in brain regions associated with self-related thought (Johnson et al., 2009).

These cognitive deficits may have genetic roots. In a group of adolescent girls and their mothers, we examined the relationship between rumination and a specific gene abnormality (Val/Val genotype for BDNF) that is associated with difficulties in inhibiting information (Hilt, Sander, Nolen-Hoeksema, & Simen, 2007). We found that participants with the Val/Val genotype were more likely to be ruminators than participants with other variants of this genotype. Thus, genetic factors may play a role in who becomes a ruminator, perhaps by affecting the brain regions involved in the ability to inhibit information voluntarily.

Overcoming Rumination

Are there strategies for overcoming rumination? Our experimental studies provide some clues. We have found if depressed ruminators spend just 8 to 10 minutes engaged in a pleasant, distracting activity, their negative mood decreases and their thinking improves. A wide range of activities can break the cycle: physical exercise, engaging in hobbies such as gardening or cooking, spending time with others, or meditating on pleasant images. The key is to find activities that are engaging and distracting but that are not in themselves maladaptive or dangerous (such as binge drinking). Because depressed ruminators are not motivated to engage in pleasant activities, they may need extra encouragement. Actually scheduling such activities in their date book can increase commitment.

Distraction only has short-term effects on mood and thinking, however. People prone to ruminating also need to do something about the situations or problems they frequently ruminate about: They must engage in active problem solving around these issues once their mood has lifted and their thinking has cleared. Starting small is important; focusing on actions that are simple and relatively easy can have a positive impact on the problem. For example, if you are afraid of losing your job, a possible solution would be to increase relevant skills, so that you become a more valuable employee. This big goal could seem distant and overwhelming to a ruminator, but a small step toward that solution would be to look into community college classes. Then the next small step would be to actually enroll in a class. And so on. . . . Taking small steps toward solutions can increase a person's sense of control and counter ruminations.

Sometimes ruminators do not have a specific problem they need to solve. Instead, they need to change their perspective on a situation. For example, a woman whose parents were emotionally abusive might understandably ruminate about why they were so cruel to her, whether they loved her, how much they damaged her self-esteem, and so on. This problem cannot be solved with concrete actions. But gaining a different perspective on the emotional abuse might help this woman stop ruminating about it. How to do this? One strategy would be to imagine talking with a good friend who had the same background—that is, to try to look at the situation as if it were happening to someone else who needed helpful advice. She might say, "I'd tell my friend that you'll never know why they behaved the way they did. But you can choose to focus on your life right now, and to not let your past haunt you."

Studies show that interventions that include teaching depressed people to use positive distracting activities to break their rumination cycles, to engage in active problem solving, and to work toward different perspectives on their life situations help to reduce their ruminations and relieve their depression (Watkins et al., 2007). Even if they are not depressed, people prone to ruminate can benefit from self-help strategies involving positive activities, problem solving, and gaining new perspectives (Nolen-Hoeksema, 2003).

Conclusion

Rumination can certainly be destructive. It leads to more negative thinking about the past, present, and future. It interferes with good problem solving and carrying through with solutions to your problems. It drives friends and family away. Ultimately, it can lead to serious depression, anxiety, binge-drinking, binge-eating, and other escapist behaviors. But rumination can be overcome. The first task is to break rumination cycles through pleasant distractions. Then you must begin to solve the problems you frequently ruminate about, or try to gain a new perspective on the situations that fuel rumination.

Suggested Further Reading

Nolen-Hoeksema, S. (2003). *Women who think too much: How to break free of overthinking and reclaim your life*. New York: Holt.

Nolen-Hoeksema, S., Wisco, B., & Lyubomirsky, S. (2008). Rethinking rumination. *Perspectives on Psychological Science, 3,* 400–424.

References

Hilt, L. M., Sander, L. C., Nolen-Hoeksema, S., & Simen, A. A. (2007). The BDNF Val66Met polymorphism predicts rumination and depression differently in young adolescent girls and their mothers. *Neuroscience Letters, 429,* 12–16.

Johnson, M. K., Nolen-Hoeksema, S., Mitchell, K., & Levin, Y. (2009). Emotional distress, rumination, and medial cortex activity during self-reflection. Manuscript under review.

Joormann, J. (2006). Differential effects of rumination and dysphoria on the inhibition of irrelevant emotional material: Evidence from a negative priming task. *Cognitive Therapy and Research, 30,* 149–160.

Nolen-Hoeksema, S. (2003*). Women who think too much: How to break free of overthinking and reclaim your life*. New York: Holt.

Nolen-Hoeksema, S., & Davis, C. G. (1999). "Thanks for sharing that": Ruminators and their social support networks. *Journal of Personality and Social Psychology, 77,* 801–814.

Nolen-Hoeksema, S., & Larson, J. (1999). *Coping with loss*. Mahwah, NJ: Erlbaum.

Nolen-Hoeksema, S., Larson, J., & Grayson, C. (1999). Explaining the gender difference in depressive symptoms. *Journal of Personality and Social Psychology, 77,* 1061–1072.

Nolen-Hoeksema, S., & Morrow, J. (1991). A prospective study of depression and post-traumatic stress symptoms following a natural disaster: The 1989 Loma Prieta earthquake. *Journal of Personality and Social Psychology, 61,* 115–121.

Nolen-Hoeksema, S., Wisco, B., & Lyubomirsky, S. (2008). Rethinking rumination. *Perspectives on Psychological Science, 3,* 400–424.

Ward, A., Lyubomirsky, S., Sousa, L., & Nolen-Hoeksema, S. (2003). Can't quite commit: Rumination and uncertainty. *Personality and Social Psychology Bulletin, 29,* 96–107.

Watkins, E. R., Scott, J., Wingrove, J., Rimes, K. A., Bathurst, N., Steiner, H., et al. (2007). Rumination-focused cognitive behaviour therapy for residual depression: A case series. *Behaviour Research and Therapy, 45,* 2144–2154.

Chapter 14

Treatment of Psychological Disorders

David H. Barlow

The Development and Evaluation of Psychological Treatments for Panic

Varda Shoham and Michael J. Rohrbaugh

Looking Beyond the Patient: A Couple-Focused Intervention for Health-Compromised Smokers

The Development and Evaluation of Psychological Treatments for Panic Disorder

David H. Barlow
Center for Anxiety and Related Disorders
Boston University

▶ *Please tell us about your current position and research interests.*
I am Professor of Psychology and Psychiatry and Founder and Director Emeritus of the Center for Anxiety and Related Disorders at Boston University. I received my Ph.D. from the University of Vermont in 1969 and have published over 500 articles and chapters and 60 books, mostly in the area of the nature and treatment of emotional disorders. I have received numerous awards, including the Distinguished Scientific Award for Applications of Psychology from the American Psychological Association, and continue to attempt to develop a deeper understanding of emotional disorders as well as improved treatments.

▶ *What got you interested in studying the effectiveness of treatments of anxiety disorders?*
Following a fascination that developed in high school with why people do the things they do, I became aware that many people had fears and anxieties focused on objects or situations even though they knew there was nothing to be afraid of. This is called the "neurotic paradox," and I've been studying it ever since.

▶ *What has been the real-world impact of this work?*
Individual mental health clinicians and health services around the world have adopted our new treatments for panic and related disorders based on our deeper understanding of the nature of these chronic problems, and we hope to further improve these tools to relieve human suffering and enhance functioning.

Early in my career, a middle-aged woman called my office and asked if I would make a house call on her elderly mother who lived alone in a small flat in the middle of a medium-sized city. When I mentioned that it would be better for her mother to come to the clinic where she would get the full attention of all of our staff, the daughter replied that the mother had not been out of her apartment for 20 years. The daughter went on to say that in the early years when her mother attempted to leave her flat to go anywhere, she suffered from uncontrollable episodes of severe anxiety. After a number of years, the attempts to leave decreased and finally stopped altogether.

When I arrived at the apartment, I rang the bell, was buzzed in and, over the intercom, asked to walk up a flight of stairs. As I reached the door to the second-floor flat and knocked, I heard an elderly woman's voice asking me to let myself in. I found the woman sitting in a chair in the middle of her living room. She apologized for not greeting me at the door, but explained that she had not been near the front door of her apartment for at least 5 years, nor could she go to the back of her kitchen or the back porch beyond. She was living out her life in a portion of her living room, the front portion of her kitchen, and her single bedroom and bath.

I realized that the woman was suffering from a severe case of panic disorder with agoraphobia, a condition in which people experience sudden surges of fear for no apparent reason at unpredictable times. I knew without asking that these unexpected surges of fear would be characterized by sharply increased heart rate, blood pressure, muscle tension, and other physical signs of the flight/fight syndrome, in which the body gears up to handle an imminent threat or danger. In situations of real danger, this surge in the sympathetic nervous system prepares us to be at our physical best: We see more acutely, run faster, perform feats of incredible strength. (Newspapers occasionally feature stories of these extraordinary deeds—for example, a 90-pound woman lifting a car off of a trapped child.)

If the fear is groundless, this reaction is called a panic attack. With nothing dangerous happening, individuals who are susceptible to developing panic disorder experience the attack as a mysterious jolt out of the blue, which they attribute to a heart attack or some equally terrible bodily affliction, with death soon to follow. They believe that if somehow they survive that first attack, the next one will surely get them. Because panic attacks occur unpredictably, affected individuals soon learn not to venture far from a safe place (or safe person) where help might be available if the worst happens. This avoidant behavior is called agoraphobia. In severe cases, the individual becomes housebound, which is what had happened to the elderly woman. Limited by her fears to a small area of her apartment, she had everything delivered or brought to her by her adult daughter, who came by every few days. She wiled away the long days reading and watching television, utterly alone.

What Causes Panic Disorder?

Panic disorder seems to be caused by an interaction of three factors, referred to as triple vulnerabilities (Barlow, 2000; Suarez et al., 2009; see Figure 1).

1. A generalized biological vulnerability in the form of an inherited anxious temperament can result in a high-strung or easily stressed individual. Although this genetic vulnerability does not cause panic disorder, it does make the problem more likely.

2. A generalized psychological sense, while growing up, that the world is a potentially dangerous place can produce a pervasive belief that coping with all of the challenges and threats that come along might be difficult indeed. This sense of the unpredictability and uncontrollability of future threats does not focus on any one threat but becomes a broad-based disposition to experience the world as dangerous. This psychological vulnerability also does not cause panic disorder but can contribute to its formation.

3. A belief, developed at an early age, that physical sensations are particularly dangerous and that one must be on guard for unexplained somatic (bodily) events or illnesses. For example, when they were children, some individuals who later developed panic disorder were rushed to the doctor at the first sign of unexplained physical symptoms. Others witnessed chronic illness and were sensitized to the dangers of illnesses or injuries. That these individuals would become vigilant for any unexplained somatic symptoms is not surprising. This third factor is referred to as a *specific* psychological vulnerability because the individual learns to be anxious about a very specific set of circumstances; in this case, bodily sensations.

The three vulnerabilities, when they occur in the same individual, set the stage for the development of panic disorder.

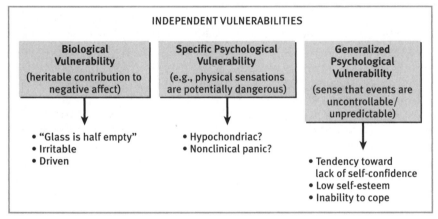

FIGURE 1 Triple vulnerabilities in the etiology of panic disorder. These three vulnerabilities, or diatheses, must all be present for an individual to develop panic disorder. (From Barlow, 2002)

Why Do Panic Attacks Initially Occur?

Stressful events trigger panic attacks in approximately 10 percent of the population. In fact, panic is a common reaction to stress, as are headaches, high blood pressure, and a "nervous" stomach. These "nonclinical" panic attacks pass quickly for most people. But in approximately 3 percent of the population, the panic attack activates the three vulnerabilities, and these individuals, believing that they are dying or losing control, may develop panic disorder and possibly agoraphobia.

Psychological Treatments for Panic Disorder

In the 1980s, a physical problem—some kind of a brain dysfunction—was thought to cause panic disorder. The leading candidate was a "chemical imbalance," which was believed to cause heightened sensitivity in the brain stem. But research in the 1990s ruled this out as the sole underlying cause

(Barlow, 2002; Gorman et al., 1990), and investigators agreed that an interacting web of biological and psychological factors, such as those just described, contribute to the onset of panic disorder.

When the cause of panic disorder was thought to be solely biological, drugs were the first choice for treatment. In the 1980s, the most popular drugs for panic disorder were high-potency tranquilizers, known by brand names such as Xanax and Klonapin. These drugs could be effective for panic disorder, but many patients developed a dependence, such that attempts to stop taking them produced serious side effects. Because of this problem with dependence and addiction, other drugs, such as selective serotonin reuptake inhibitors (SSRIs), have become the preferred drugs for treating panic disorder. These drugs include brand names such as Paxil and Prozac. Approximately 60 percent of patients with panic disorder respond at least somewhat (and some very well) as long as they continue to take the medication. But relapse rates are high once the medication is stopped (Craske & Barlow, 2008).

Around 1990, Michelle Craske and I developed a psychological treatment for panic disorder that focused directly on the sensitivity of these individuals to their own physical sensations, such as fluctuating heart rate, skin temperature, and dizziness (Barlow & Craske, 2007; Craske & Barlow, 2007). In people who are susceptible, these sensations are very frightening because they come to trigger the next panic attack through the psychological process of learning and association called conditioning (Bouton, Mineka, & Barlow, 2001).

Based on this insight, we experimented with a treatment in which individuals with panic disorder were exposed to mild versions of the physical sensations. In the protected setting of our clinic, we had them exercise vigorously to produce fluctuations in heart rate, spin around in a chair to produce slight dizziness, and so forth. We chose a person's induced symptoms based on an assessment of the mix of physical sensations that were closely associated with their panic attacks. (These vary from one person to another.)

In a psychological process called extinction, our patients—by experiencing these physical sensations repeatedly—learned that the sensations don't lead to a terrible outcome, such as a heart attack. Of course, their rational self knew this all along, but the emotional brain, where these fear responses reside, tends to override the rational brain in cases of panic or any emotional disorder. Hence, these specialized treatments reach the emotional brain.

To assist in strengthening the "rational brain," the patients' basic faulty attitudes and perceptions about the dangerousness of these sensations are also identified and modified. Patients may also be taught calming techniques such as breathing and meditation to help them cope with stress and anxiety. A number of studies subsequently demonstrated that this treatment, a cognitive-behavioral approach called panic control treatment (PCT), is effective for panic disorder (Barlow & Lehman, 1996).

Combined Psychological and Pharmacological Treatments

My colleagues and I then sought to test the hypothesis that combining drugs and psychological treatments might prove more effective than either individual treatment alone. We conducted a large clinical trial that treated 312 patients with panic disorder at four different sites. Two of these sites were known for their expertise with drug treatments, and two were known for their expertise with cognitive-behavioral treatments. Patients at all sites were administered either the psychological or drug treatment alone, or in combination, along with appropriate comparison conditions such as a drug placebo condition. The experiment was also double blind, which means that neither the therapists nor the patients knew whether they were getting the actual medication or the placebo (sugar) capsule (Barlow et al., 2000).

We found that both the drug and the psychological treatments were effective as we expected, with each better than the placebo. But, much to our surprise, the combination treatment was not any better than the individual treatments. Thus, our hypothesis was not proven, and the widespread practice of administering both treatments simultaneously for panic disorder was called into question. Furthermore, after all treatments were stopped, the psychological treatment was found to be more durable. That is, among those patients who received psychological treatment either alone or combined with placebo, fewer people relapsed in the 6 months after treatment as compared with patients who received either drug treatment alone or drug plus psychological treatment.

We concluded from this evidence that combining treatments offered no advantages and that, given a choice, the preference would be for the psychological treatment because it is more durable and less intrusive. (Drug treatments are almost always considered more intrusive than psychological treatments due to side effects or drug interactions that can occur.) Of course, some patients prefer to take a drug, or the cognitive-behavioral treatment may not be available, in which case drug treatment is a good alternative.

Keeping People Healthy

In a second study (not yet published), colleagues and I evaluated the best strategies for maintaining long-term health after treatment. We began with the working hypothesis that once patients received cognitive-behavioral therapy and were essentially cured, they would not need any further treatment sessions. We based this assumption on the view of most of our therapists that no further intervention is needed if patients have learned all the concepts that the therapists teach and have implemented them well in daily life.

Not all of our therapists agreed, however. Some argued that occasional booster sessions would prove useful in preventing relapse over the long term in this chronic condition. To test this notion, we treated 256 patients with panic disorder and agoraphobia of varying degrees of severity, using the same cognitive-behavioral therapy that we employed in our first study. Many of these patients (157, or 61.3%) did very well with treatment and were essentially cured. To evaluate the advantage of booster sessions, half of these patients (n=79) went on to receive 9 additional sessions spaced every month for 9 months, and they then were followed for another year with no further treatment. The other half of the patients (n=78) received no further treatment.

When the results were assessed after the 1-year period without any treatment, the majority view was proved wrong. That is, there *was* an advantage to having booster sessions. Among the group that did not have booster sessions, 18% had some relapse or recurrence of panic disorder during the 1-year follow-up and 82% stayed well. By contrast, only 2.7% of the group that experienced booster sessions evidenced a relapse or recurrence during that year, and fully 97.3% stayed well. This significant difference demonstrates the value of some continued attention to these patients, who are, after all, suffering from a chronic condition that waxes and wanes.

Of the remaining patients—individuals who did not meet our criteria for "responding" to treatment to the point where they were essentially cured—some dropped out along the way for a variety of reasons, such as moving away or just feeling they didn't need treatment anymore. Others finished treatment with varying responses, from just missing our criteria for being all but "cured" to having no benefit whatsoever. In this latter group, we evaluated the benefits of then giving them a medication for panic disorder, and while the results haven't been fully analyzed yet, sequencing the treatments in this way looks like a promising treatment approach.

Conclusion

Scientific discoveries about the nature of panic disorder led us to develop a specifically tailored psychological treatment. The two experiments I've described confirm that we have an effective psychological treatment for panic disorder—a treatment that has become a first-line choice based on recommendations from national health services around the world. Of course, we still have a long way to go to make our treatments powerful enough to benefit the largest number of people.

Interestingly, our studies also confirm that a number of our assumptions were incorrect. First, we proved ourselves wrong that combining drug and psychological treatments would be better than simply providing patients with one treatment or the other. Second, we now know that individuals who do well need further attention after treatment has ended to ensure that they have the best chance to stay well. Without close scientific examination of the effects of psychotherapy, we would have been unaware of these important treatment issues, and patients with panic disorder would not be getting the best care possible.

Suggested Further Reading

Barlow, D. H. (2004). Psychological treatments. *American Psychologist, 59*(9), 869–878.

Barlow, D. H. (2000). Unraveling the mysteries of anxiety and its disorders from the perspective of emotion theory. *American Psychologist, 55*(11), 1245–1263.

References

Barlow, D. H. (2000). Unraveling the mysteries of anxiety and its disorders from the perspective of emotion theory. *American Psychologist, 55*(11), 1245–1263.

Barlow, D. H. (2002). *Anxiety and its disorders: The nature and treatment of anxiety and panic* (2nd ed.). New York: Guilford Press.

Barlow, D. H., & Craske, M. G. (2007). *Mastery of your anxiety and panic: Client workbook* (4th ed.). New York: Oxford University Press.

Barlow, D. H., Gorman, J. M., Shear, M. K., & Woods, S. W. (2000). Cognitive-behavioral therapy, imipramine, or their combination for panic disorder: A randomized controlled trial. *JAMA, 283,* 2529–2536.

Barlow, D. H., & Lehman, C. L. (1996). Advances in the psychosocial treatment of anxiety disorders: Implications for national health care. *Archives of General Psychiatry, 53,* 727–735.

Bouton, M. E., Mineka, S., & Barlow, D. H. (2001). A modern learning-theory perspective on the etiology of panic disorder. *Psychological Review, 108,* 4–32.

Craske, M. G., & Barlow, D. H. (2007). Mastery of your anxiety and panic: Therapist guide (4th ed.). New York: Oxford University Press.

Craske, M. G., & Barlow, D. H. (2008). Panic disorder and agoraphobia. In D. H. Barlow (Ed.), *Clinical handbook of psychological disorders* (4th ed.). New York: Guilford Press.

Gorman, J. M., Goetz, R. R., Dillon, D., Liebowitz, M. R., Fyer, A. J., Davies, S., et al. (1990). Sodium D-lactate infusion of panic disorder patients. *Neuropsychopharmacology, 3,* 181–189.

Suárez, L., Bennett, S., Goldstein, C., & Barlow, D. H. (2009). Understanding anxiety disorders from a "triple vulnerabilities" framework. In M. M. Antony & M. B. Stein (Eds.), *Oxford handbook of anxiety and related disorders.* New York: Oxford University Press.

Looking Beyond the Patient: A Couple-Focused Intervention for Health-Compromised Smokers

Varda Shoham and Michael J. Rohrbaugh
University of Arizona

▶ *Please describe your current positions and research interests.*
Varda Shoham: I am Professor of Psychology and Director of the Clinical Psychology Graduate Program at the University of Arizona.

Michael Rohrbaugh: I am Professor of Psychology and Family Studies/ Human Development and Director of the Psychology Department Clinic at the University of Arizona.

We are a couple who studies couples: For more than a decade, we have investigated the role close relationships play in maintaining and resolving various "individual" problems ranging from alcoholism, adolescent drug abuse, and change-resistant smoking, to surviving chronic heart disease.

▶ *What drew you to studying the application of family systems treatment to health-compromising behaviors?*
Why do people continue to engage in health-compromising behaviors like smoking, drinking, or overeating when they already have health problems that these behaviors exacerbate? Do they simply lack the awareness that, say, smoking is bad for them? As family psychologists, our background in "social cybernetics" led us to question the prevailing assumption that behavior change depends primarily on understanding an individual patient's motivations or "disorder" and on teaching better coping or health-management skills. Instead, we think that repetitive, circular cycles of interaction involving the patient and intimate others play a key role in maintaining such behavior, and more importantly, that identifying and interrupting such interaction cycles can be sufficient to initiate sustainable behavior change.

▶ *What has been the real-world impact of this work?*
The main real-world impact of our work has been to encourage health professionals to look beyond the patient when promoting health behavior change. For example, although prevailing conceptualizations cast nicotine addiction almost exclusively as an "individual" problem, our work adds credence to alternative, more contextual avenues of intervention. Because close relationships have clear prognostic significance for many health problems and most health-compromising behaviors, their relevance to intervention—especially for patients who don't benefit from conventional individually focused treatments—is undeniable.

How are family relationships relevant to treating health problems and addictions? It is easy to see how a chronic physical illness or a loved-one's addiction can burden or disrupt family relations, but causal arrows can actually go both ways. For more than a decade, we have investigated the role close relationships play in maintaining and resolving various "individual" problems ranging from alcoholism, adolescent drug abuse, and change-resistant smoking, to surviving chronic heart disease. Reflecting our shared background as family psychologists, we assume that these problems rarely occur in a vacuum, but rather persist as an aspect of current close relationships in which "causes" and "effects" are inextricably interwoven, with one person's behavior setting the stage for what another does, and vice versa, in ongoing, circular sequences of interaction. Such an interpersonal-systems view attaches more importance to problem maintenance than to etiology: Indeed, we find that what keeps a problem going is usually more relevant to the outcome of an intervention than what may have caused the problem in the first place. A crucial flip side of this view is that *positive* relationships not only confer health benefits but also provide a powerful resource for helping people change health-compromising behavior.

To illustrate these ideas, we describe the rationale, procedures, and preliminary outcomes of a couple-focused intervention for patients with heart or lung problems who continue to smoke cigarettes. Despite increasing societal prohibitions, many adults continue to smoke; relapse rates are high for those who try to quit; and smoking remains the health behavior most strongly associated with health outcomes. Although effective cessation treatments exist, their overall success rates are modest, and they rarely reach the high-risk, health-compromised smokers who need them most (Fiore et al., 2000). Change-resistant smoking poses a special challenge for family-oriented researchers: Although a partner's smoking status and support for cessation predicts whether a smoker will be able to quit and stay quit (Roski, Schmid, & Lando, 1996), most research on why people smoke—and on ways to help them quit—has focused almost exclusively on biological, cognitive, and motivational factors residing in the individual smoker. A final reason to study smoking, both attractive and intimidating to treatment researchers, is that the outcomes are biologically verifiable and clear-cut: Participants either quit or they don't!

Why Look Beyond the Individual?

As the root word *psyche* suggests, psychology has long been preoccupied with events and processes occurring inside the skin—and more recently, the brain—of the individual. Perhaps ironically, recent developments in the emerging field of social neuroscience now encourage psychologists to look outward, at least as far as the close relationships in which individuals (and their brains) participate. As psychologist Daniel Goleman (2006) puts it in *Social Intelligence: The New Science of Human Relationships*, "We are wired to connect." Neuroscience is showing that our brains are fundamentally social, such that our interactions with others (particularly those we care about most) have far-reaching biological consequences, with brain-to-brain links triggering hormones that regulate, among other things, how our cardiovascular and immune systems function.

A compelling illustration of the power of close relationships comes from our research on couples coping with chronic heart failure. In a study of

189 heart-failure patients (139 men and 50 women) and their spouses, we found that interview and observational measures of marital quality predicted all-cause patient mortality over the next 8 years, independent of how well the patient's heart functioned at baseline (Rohrbaugh, Shoham, & Coyne, 2006). Marital quality was a substantially better predictor of survival than individual (patient-level) risk and protective factors such as psychological distress, hostility, neuroticism, self-efficacy, optimism, and breadth of perceived emotional support. In addition, the overall statistical effect of marital quality was greater for female patients than males. These results suggest that relationship factors may be especially relevant to managing heart failure, which makes stringent and complex demands on patients and their families.

To understand better how marital processes "get under the skin," we are now following additional samples of couples coping with this difficult chronic condition. Although other researchers have documented direct (physiological) pathways between marital conflict and neuroendocrine systems related to cardiovascular and immune function (Kiecolt-Glaser & Newton, 2001), our current work focuses on indirect (behavioral) pathways through which marital interaction facilitates or undermines health *behavior*, such as a patient's adherence to dietary, exercise, medication, and stress-management regimens that, in turn, influence the course of heart disease. For example, we find diminished patient adherence associated with patterns of demand-withdraw couple interaction in which one partner (usually the spouse) criticizes, complains, and pressures for change, while the other resists, avoids, and withdraws. This pattern is also common in couples where one partner smokes against the other's wishes—hence the connection to our work with health-compromised smokers, for whom smoking is an indirect (behavioral) pathway to poor cardiac health.

Thinking Outside the (Individual Smoker) Box

Why focus on close relationships and smoking? One reason is that at least a dozen studies link the success of a smoker's cessation efforts to positive partner (usually spousal) support for quitting and the absence of criticism. Unfortunately, early "social support" interventions based on teaching partners better support skills had disappointing results—perhaps because giving up such a well-entrenched habit requires more than knowledge and skill acquisition. Another problem may be that teaching one-size-fits-all support skills and problem-solving strategies within group formats detracts attention from how particular support behaviors fit (or don't fit) particular couple relationships. For example, it would make a difference if a spouse's refusal to allow smoking in the house provokes resistance in some smokers but actually helps others stay quit.

Another reason to focus on close relationships is that having a spouse or partner who smokes is a major risk factor for continued smoking and failure in future quit attempts (Homish & Leonard, 2005). A pattern we call "symptom-system fit" occurs when a problem such as drinking or smoking appears to have adaptive consequences for a relationship, at least in the short run

(Rohrbaugh, Shoham, & Racioppo, 2002). Thus, in couples where both partners smoke, shared smoking might create a context for mutually supportive interactions by providing soothing joint experience or helping partners stay positive, even when they disagree. In a laboratory demonstration of this phenomenon, 25 couples, in which one or both partners smoked, discussed a health-related disagreement before and during a period of actual smoking. Immediately afterward, while watching themselves on video, the partners used independent joysticks to recall their continuous emotional experience during the interaction. Participants in dual-smoker couples reported increased positive emotion contingent upon lighting up, while in single-smoker couples both partners (nonsmokers and smokers alike) reported the opposite (Shoham et al., 2007). The affective experience of partners in dual-smoker couples also became more synchronous during laboratory smoking (as if they were dancing to the same emotional tune), while affective coordination in single-smoker couples tended to decrease (Rohrbaugh et al., 2009).

A problem-maintaining pattern more common among single-smoker couples involves interpersonal ironic processes, which occur when well-intentioned but persistent "solutions" to a problem feed back to keep the problem going or make it worse (Shoham & Rohrbaugh, 1997). For example, a partner's nagging may lead to more smoking, which leads to more nagging, and so on. This pattern and its complement (which involves *avoiding* direct influence attempts) can be seen across a range of health problems and health behaviors, as illustrated by our studies of heart patients mentioned above.

The Family Consultation (FAMCON) Approach

Family systems theory provides a useful perspective on how close relationships can both maintain, and be maintained by, change-resistant smoking—and why including family members can enhance treatment outcome (Doherty & Whitehead, 1986). The intervention we developed for health-compromised smokers assumes that (1) smoking is inextricably interwoven with the family and social relationships in which it occurs; (2) these relationships can play a key (albeit inadvertent) role in maintaining change-resistant smoking; and (3) partners and important family members should be involved in treatment, not merely as adjunct therapists or providers of social support, but as full participants with a stake in the process of change (Rohrbaugh et al., 2001). Consistent with these ideas, FAMCON focuses on two types of interpersonal problem maintenance—symptom-system fit and ironic processes—and aims to mobilize communal coping as a relational resource for change. An overarching guideline is to maximize clients' *choice* in the consultation process. Accordingly, presenting FAMCON as "consultation," a term connoting collaboration, seems to arouse less resistance than calling it "counseling" or "treatment."

Procedurally, the family-consultation (FAMCON) approach provides up to 10 "consultation" sessions for single- or dual-smoker couples, ideally proceeding through a preparation phase (sessions 1 through 3), a quit phase (sessions 4 and 5), and a consolidation phase (session 6+). The treatment typically unfolds over 2 to 6 months, with sessions 1 through 3 conducted during the first month in a structured format, and subsequent sessions allocated according to each couple's quit plan and progress. The preparation phase includes detailed assessment of smoking-related interaction patterns, past quit attempts (and how they failed), and couple strengths. In session 3, the consultant presents a carefully tailored "opinion," providing specific observations and feedback about how smoking fits the couple's relationship; why/how quitting will be difficult; reasons to be optimistic about success; and issues for the couple to consider in developing a quit plan. The opinion session then concludes with an invitation for the couple to consider a quit date.

Specific couple dynamics are relevant throughout, both as sources of smoking maintenance targeted for intervention and as resources for successful cessation. To understand problem maintenance, the therapist-consultant pays close attention to ironic interpersonal cycles fueled by well-intentioned attempts to control or protect a smoker, as well as to the functions smoking appears to serve in the couple's relationship (for example, providing a basis for cohesion when both partners smoke or maintaining distance when only one does). To interrupt an ironic pattern in which one partner persistently attempts (without success) to control the other partner's smoking directly, the consultant looks for ways to help the spouse back off. Alternatively, when an ironic solution pattern entails *avoiding* the problem, the consultant would encourage a more direct course of action, such as gently taking a stand.

The aim of addressing symptom-system fit is to help couples realign their relationship in ways not organized around tobacco use. For example, if partners anticipate relational difficulties likely to accompany cessation attempts, they can practice exposing themselves to such situations before attempting to quit and work toward establishing substitute rituals and activities that do not involve smoking—in this way, they begin to make nonsmoking fit the system. Finally, regardless of whether one or both partners smoke, the consultant encourages them to view this as a communal problem ("ours" rather than "yours" or "mine") and work together toward solving it.

Preliminary Results

We tested FAMCON with 20 couples in which one partner (the primary smoker) continued to smoke despite having or being at significant risk for heart or lung disease. In 8 couples the other partner smoked as well.

On average, couples participated in eight FAMCON sessions and had quit outcomes that compare favorably with benchmarks in the literature. For example, the 50 percent rate of stable abstinence achieved by primary smokers at 6 months is approximately twice that cited in Fiore et al.'s (2000) meta-analysis involving other, comparably intensive interventions. As you can see in Figure 1, for the entire sample of 28 smokers, stable cessation rates were 54 percent and 46 percent over 6 and 12 months, respectively (Shoham, Rohrbaugh, et al., 2006).

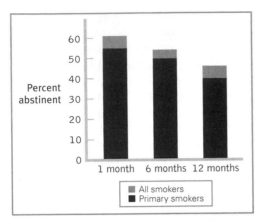

FIGURE 1 FAMCON cessation rates by follow-up interval

Encouragingly, the FAMCON intervention appeared well suited to female smokers and smokers whose partner also smoked—two subgroups at high risk for relapse. Although the number of female participants was small, virtually all cessation, health, and client satisfaction indices were in the direction of better outcomes for women than men, which could reflect the fact that FAMCON, more than most other cessation interventions, explicitly takes relationship dynamics into account. Similarly, the fact that dual-smoker couples were at least as successful as single-smoker couples is consistent with the possibility that FAMCON's emphasis on relational functions of smoking (symptom-system fit) helped to neutralize the spousal-smoking-status risk factor.

Although we could not document with quantitative rigor how FAMCON helped smokers quit and stay quit, our process observations were generally consistent with the family systems principles on which the intervention is based. For example, cessation tended to be most successful when partners worked together and accepted the "communal coping" frame for doing so. In fact, among the three couples in which primary smokers failed to abstain at all (even for 2 days), nobody bought the communal coping idea, and all resisted suggestions to view smoking as "our" problem (rather than just the individual smoker's problem). Cessation seemed most successful when couples found satisfactory ways to protect their relationship during the quit phase, and when the partners freely and conjointly chose and prepared for a quit date without explicit or implicit pressure from the therapist-consultant. Rather different patterns of couple interaction served to maintain smoking in different ways for different couples, and correspondingly different intervention strategies (for example, encouraging a spouse to back off versus take a stand) helped to facilitate constructive change.

Open Questions, Future Directions

The results of this small, treatment-development study highlight the potential value of a couple-focused social support intervention informed by family-systems theory—an approach that is different in concept and format from social-support interventions tested in the past.

Nevertheless, our study has obvious limitations—most notably its small sample size and lack of a control group. Only a randomized clinical trial can unambiguously rule out the possibility that other, individually focused interventions would have worked just as well, or that a substantial proportion of our health-compromised smokers would have somehow managed to quit on their own. Questions also remain about FAMCON's applicability to different subgroups of health-compromised smokers and its exportability to other settings. A key limitation, for example, is that smokers must have a committed partner willing to participate fully in the program, regardless of whether that partner also smokes.

Where do we go from here? Scientific development of psychosocial interventions progresses through three stages, and FAMCON is ready to move from the Stage 1 preliminary study summarized here to Stage 2 clinical trials (sometimes called efficacy studies) with control conditions ranging from measurement only to comparably intensive individual treatments in which family members do not participate. The third stage, which surprisingly few psychosocial treatments actually reach, consists of effectiveness research testing an intervention's exportability and applicability in real-world (community) settings. Along the way, we will aim to test more rigorously hypotheses about *how* FAMCON works (does it interrupt ironic interaction patterns? accommodate symptom-system fit?) and *for whom* it works best (women? double smokers?) relative to other treatments.

Acknowledgments

This project was supported by National Institute on Drug Abuse grant R21-DA13121, as well as grants R01-DA17539 and U10-DA15815.

Suggested Further Reading

Goleman, D. (2006). *Social intelligence: The new science of human relationships.* New York: Random House.

Fiore, M. C., Bailey, W. C., Cohen, S. J., Dorfman, S. F., Goldstein, M. G., Gritz, E. R., et al. (2000). *Treating tobacco use and dependence.* Clinical Practice Guideline. Rockville, MD: U.S. Department of Health and Human Services, Public Health Service. (See http://www.surgeongeneral.gov/tobacco/treating_tobacco_use.pdf for the 2008 update.)

References

Doherty, W. J., & Whitehead, D. (1986). The social dynamics of cigarette smoking: A family systems perspective. *Family Process, 25,* 453–549.

Homish, G. G., & Leonard, K. E. (2005). Spousal influence on smoking behaviors in a US community sample of newly married couples. *Social Science and Medicine, 61,* 2557–2567.

Kiecolt-Glaser, J. K., & Newton, T. L. (2001). Marriage and health: His and hers. *Psychological Bulletin, 127,* 472–503.

Rohrbaugh, M. J., Shoham, V., Butler, E. A., Hasler, B. P., & Berman J. S. (2009). Affective synchrony in dual- and single-smoker couples: Further evidence of "symptom-system fit"? *Family Process, 48,* 55–67.

Rohrbaugh, M. J., Shoham, V., & Coyne, J. C. (2006). Effects of marital quality on 8-year survival of patients with heart failure. *American Journal of Cardiology, 98,* 1069–1072.

Rohrbaugh, M. J., Shoham, V., & Racioppo, M. W. (2002). Toward family-level attribute x treatment interaction research. In H. Liddle, D. Santisteban, R. Levant, & J. Bray (Eds.), *Family psychology: Science-based interventions,* pp. 215–237. Washington, DC: American Psychological Association.

Rohrbaugh, M. J., Shoham, V., Trost, S. E., Muramoto, M., Cate, R., & Leischow, S. (2001). Couple-dynamics of change resistant smoking: Toward a family-consultation model. *Family Process, 40,* 15–31.

Roski, J., Schmid, L. A., & Lando, H. A. (1996). Long-term associations of helpful and harmful spousal behaviors with smoking cessation. *Addictive Behaviors, 21,* 173–185.

Shoham, V., Butler, E. A., Rohrbaugh, M. J., & Trost, S. E. (2007). System-symptom fit in couples: Emotion regulation when one or both partners smoke. *Journal of Abnormal Psychology, 116,* 848–853.

Shoham, V., & Rohrbaugh, M. J. (1997). Interrupting ironic processes. *Psychological Science, 8,* 151–153.

Shoham, V., Rohrbaugh, M. J., Trost, S., & Muramoto, M. (2006). A family consultation intervention for health-compromised smokers. *Journal of Substance Abuse Treatment, 31,* 395–402.

Chapter 15

Stress and Health

Peter Salovey

Framing Health Messages

Shelley E. Taylor

Positive Illusions: How Ordinary People
Become Extraordinary

Framing Health Messages
Peter Salovey
Yale University

▶ *Please tell us about your current position and research interests.*
I am the Chris Argyris Professor of Psychology and Provost at Yale University. I also have joint appointments on the faculty of the School of Public Health, School of Management, and Institution for Social and Policy Studies. Previously I served as Dean of the Graduate School of Arts and Sciences and Dean of Yale College. The research conducted by my collaborators, students, and me concerns two general themes: The first is the impact of mood and emotion on cognition and social behavior. We developed a broad framework called *emotional intelligence*, the theory that just as people have a wide range of intellectual abilities, they also have a wide range of measurable emotional skills that profoundly affect their thinking and action. The second area of research concerns the relation between health communication and health behavior. In particular, we investigate the effectiveness of health-promotion messages in persuading people to change risky behaviors relevant to cancer and HIV/AIDS. Much of this work has focused on the framing of health messages in gain or loss terms and the tailoring of messages to the psychological characteristics of recipients.

▶ *What got you interested in applying principles from social and personality psychology to persuasive health-promoting messages?*
In graduate school I was very influenced by the writings of "action researchers" such as Kurt Lewin and Chris Argyris, who argue that the best way to test social science theories is to attempt interventions that change real-world behaviors in ecologically complex contexts. I completed both the clinical and social psychology programs as a way of getting a graduate education that would allow me to conduct research of this kind. Although I value laboratory experiments that explore basic principles in social and personality psychology, I worry about small effect sizes and, generally, findings that can only be obtained in special populations and in environments relatively free of sources of error and noise. I think the ideas contributed by social and personality psychologists are so important that it is incumbent on us to show that they generalize to more "realistic" contexts.

▶ *What has been the real-world impact of this work?*
I have spoken about our work to many different audiences, including government public health officials, advertising agencies, and community health centers. We always try to articulate a set of health communication principles that derive from our research. It is very gratifying to see a television public service announcement or pick up a brochure at a hospital or read a government publication that encourages healthy behaviors in ways that reflect our research findings. By combining our results with those from other laboratories, it is possible to design health messages that have a greater chance (than earlier strategies) to be effective in promoting desired behaviors.

The effectiveness of interventions designed to promote healthy behaviors often depends on the persuasiveness of a public service announcement, brochure, print advertisement, government letter, educational program, or communication from a health professional. Indeed, we are surrounded by such health appeals in newspapers and magazines, radio and television, billboards along the highway, and on the Internet. In schools and workplaces, we are bombarded further with information urging us to adopt healthier lifestyles. Although much of this information is helpful, it is likely that some has no value at all. Some messages that are designed to encourage healthy behaviors could even have a negative impact, promoting just the wrong behaviors or encouraging just what the designers of such messages intended to discourage.

The only way to know whether health messages are having the desired influence on our behavior is to test their effectiveness. A first step is to see if such messages are more effective than nothing at all. More sophisticated approaches to the study of health communication explore whether some kinds of messages are more persuasive than other kinds of messages. The most exciting research in this area also attempts to address the following questions: Why *are* certain kinds of messages especially powerful? What are the mechanisms by which such messages affect our behavior?

For about two decades, my collaborators and I have been attempting to address these and other questions. We have focused primarily on behaviors that are relevant to preventing or detecting various kinds of cancer and HIV/AIDS, illnesses with relatively high prevalence and a global reach. We have studied cigarette smoking, diet, physical exercise, mammography, Pap testing, sunscreen use, condom use, and HIV testing, among other health behaviors. Typically, our experiments compare messages in real-world settings rather than in the laboratory; often we recruit participants from especially vulnerable populations where we believe we can have the greatest public health impact.

Our goal is not merely to identify strategies that make certain kinds of health messages especially effective but to have an impact on the actual behavior of at-risk individuals along the way. In this manner, our research addresses theoretical questions while also being immediately relevant to the health of a community. In many of our experiments, the participants are more likely to adopt a salubrious behavior than if they had not been in the experiment, a benefit to them as individuals and to their communities.

Responding to Framed Messages

Imagine for a moment that you are commissioner of public health in the state where you live and that a dreaded, contagious disease is headed your way. This epidemic is expected to affect 600 of your citizens. To combat the epidemic, you are offered two options: If you select Program A, you will save the lives of 200 people. If you select Program B, you have a one-third chance of saving everyone. Which do you prefer? If you are like most people, Program A sounds a lot better. Why take a chance when saving 200 lives is a sure bet?

However, imagine that the options are presented differently: Program A is described as costing the lives of 400 people, while Program B is described as having a two-thirds chance that everyone will die. Now which option sounds better? If you are like most people, Program B is more attractive. Why select an option where many people are certain to die when, instead, you can select one in which there is only a chance that everyone will die (and a chance, albeit a smaller one, that no one will die)?

Of course, all four options are arithmetically the same: In principle, 200 people live and 400 people die no matter which alternative is chosen. What varies is the certainty of the outcome: A is always a sure thing, while B involves uncertainty or risk. More importantly, what also varies is the description of the problem itself: The first pair of options is framed in terms of the benefits of selecting a program (lives saved), and the second pair is framed in terms of the costs (lives lost). And preferences for a sure bet versus a risky option—perhaps *your* preference for a sure bet versus a risky option—are affected by the way in which the information is framed. People prefer sure bets when thinking about positive outcomes (gains) and risky options when thinking about negative outcomes (losses). This phenomenon is called a preference reversal (Kahneman & Tversky, 1979, 1982; Tversky & Kahneman, 1981).

For a number of years, my colleagues in Yale University's Health, Emotion, and Behavior Laboratory and I have looked at how the framing of health information influences the way people think about health and, more significantly, how framing affects their decisions to engage in behaviors that protect their health. Our message-framing technique involves highlighting either the positive or negative consequences of an action while keeping factual information essentially equivalent (Rothman & Salovey, 1997). Our gain-framed messages usually present the benefits of adopting a behavior (for example, "Eating more fruits and vegetables can keep you healthy"). Loss-framed messages generally convey the costs of not adopting the behavior (for example, "Not eating fruits and vegetables can lead to illness").

In general, the hypothesis guiding our work is derived from a theory of how people choose among options that vary in how risky they are. This framework is called "prospect theory." The basic framing hypothesis is that when alternatives involve some risk or uncertainty, individuals will be more likely to take these risks when information is framed in terms of the relative disadvantages (that is, losses or costs) of the behavioral options—in other words, when the downside of a situation is made obvious. Alternatively, when alternatives involve little risk or uncertainty, individuals are more likely to prefer these options when information is framed in terms of relative advantages (that is, gains or benefits)—in other words, when the upside of a situation is made obvious (Kahneman & Tversky, 1979, 1982; Tversky & Kahneman, 1981).

A tricky but critical distinction in studying the impact of health-related messages is between illness-detection behaviors and illness-prevention behaviors. Detection behaviors involve some kind of test or screening that tells us if we are sick or have some kind of problem or warning sign. Good examples are taking an HIV test (for HIV/AIDS) or a Pap test (for cervical cancer) or a mammogram (for breast cancer). Prevention behaviors reduce the likelihood of an illness or health problem and include using sunscreen at the beach (to prevent skin cancer), eating fruits and vegetables (to prevent cancer), or using a condom when having sex (to prevent sexually transmitted diseases). Notice that prevention behaviors have little associated risk or uncertainty, whereas detection behaviors do—a disease might be found. For example, in seeking a mammogram, a woman who thinks she is healthy is risking discovering that she is not.

From a prospect theory point of view, the perceived risk (of finding an abnormality) could make loss-framed messages more persuasive in promoting detection behaviors. However, prevention behaviors may not be perceived as risky at all; they are performed to deter the onset or occurrence of a health problem. Choosing to perform prevention behaviors is a low-risk option; they maintain good health. Because low-risk options are preferred when people are considering benefits or gains, gain-framed messages might be more likely to facilitate performing prevention behaviors.

Does the match between a message frame (gain or loss) and the function of the required health behavior (prevention or detection) motivate behavior change? In our studies, we have explored this issue, offering different groups of people opportunities to receive alternatively framed health information and then engage in various kinds of health behaviors. Let's look at some of our findings.

Loss-Framed Messages Promote Illness-Detecting Behaviors

Because most people who pursue screening believe that they are healthy, obtaining a mammogram is a psychologically risky behavior. Mammography involves a probabilistic, uncertain outcome and therefore should be better motivated by loss-framed messages than gain-framed messages.

Our first field experiment on mammography screening was conducted as part of a health-promotion program at a large telephone company (Banks et al., 1995). Any woman who had obtained fewer than 50 percent of the suggested number of mammograms for someone her age (that is, one every other year between age 40 and 50, and then one annually after age 50) was invited to view a 15-minute videotape on breast cancer and mammography. One hundred thirty-three women were assigned randomly to view a video in which most of the information was presented either in gain-framed terms (for example, "The Benefits of Mammography") or in loss-framed terms (for example, "The Risks of Neglecting Mammography"). The gain-framed video emphasized positive results like finding out that you are healthy, whereas the loss-framed video emphasized negative consequences like discovering you have cancer too late to do anything about it.

The two groups did not differ in their liking for the videos or knowledge about breast cancer. However, after 12 months, we found that the loss-framed video had been more persuasive: 66.2 percent of its viewers had obtained a mammogram compared to 51.5 percent of the gain-frame viewers.

Some years later, we repeated this experiment in a much different population of women (Schneider et al., 2001). We recruited 752 women from two inner-city health clinics and several public housing developments in the same neighborhoods. About 43 percent were African American, 27 percent white, and 25 percent Latina. Most of the participants were from low-income families. The women viewed 15-minute videos about breast cancer and mammography that were gain- or loss-framed and that differed in the ethnicity of the actors. One pair of videos emphasized the problem of breast cancer for all women; the others were targeted for either black, white, or Latina women and provided statistics and pictured models drawn only from the respective groups. We labeled these pairs of videos "multicultural" versus "targeted." The videos for Latina women could be viewed with either an English or Spanish soundtrack.

Six months later, we looked for the advantage of loss- over gain-framed messages seen in the telephone company study, and found it—but only with the multicultural messages, which were most like those we had used at the phone company (Banks et al., 1995). Fifty percent of women who viewed the loss-framed multicultural message received a mammogram as compared with only 36 percent in the gain-framed version. When the messages were targeted to the specific ethnicity of the participants, however, neither version of the targeted video was as effective as the loss-framed, multicultural one. Apparently, the targeted loss-framed messages were simply too threatening to be effective.

Gain-Framed Messages Promote Prevention Behavior

In comparison to early-detection behaviors such as screening mammography, the use of sunscreen at the beach, like most prevention-oriented health behaviors, involves few uncertainties and little psychological risk. Using sunscreen is a low-cost way to reduce skin cancer risk. Individuals should prefer options with certain outcomes (to options with probabilistic or uncertain outcomes) after considering potential gains—that is, when the advantages of the option are made obvious. So, we would expect gain-framed messages to be more effective in promoting prevention behaviors like using sunscreen.

We have conducted several experiments in which we manipulated the framing of messages about sunscreen and the opportunity to acquire it. In one study, 146 undergraduates read gain- or loss-framed pamphlets about skin cancer and sunscreen use and then received postage-paid postcards addressed to our laboratory requesting sunscreen samples and more information about skin cancer prevention (Rothman et al., 1993). Interest in the pamphlet was high and did not differ across the two framing conditions. As prospect theory led us to predict, the gain-framed pamphlet motivated more requests for sunscreen. Interestingly, the advantage of gain-framed messages over loss-framed ones was small for men, but quite sizable for women, who, in general, were more concerned about skin cancer than were the men. For instance, 79 percent of the women who read a gain-framed pamphlet subsequently requested sunscreen, as compared with 45 percent who read the loss-framed pamphlet. For men, request rates were 50 percent and 47 percent, respectively.

Thinking that skin cancer might be relatively more worrisome for men and women sunning themselves on a public beach, we recruited 217 sunbathers to read either gain- or loss-framed brochures about sunscreen and the prevention of skin cancer. After reading the brochure, they received a coupon that could be exchanged later for a free bottle of sunscreen. When a sunscreen "vendor"—actually a graduate student from our laboratory—appeared on the beach about half an hour later, we could count those beachgoers who turned in their coupon. Seventy-one percent of those who read a gain-framed pamphlet, but only 53 percent of those who read a loss-framed pamphlet, subsequently turned in their coupon (Detweiler et al., 1999).

The sunscreen experiments suggest that prevention behaviors might be best promoted with gain-framed messages. This was exactly the pattern of effects predicted, and this pattern was obtained across very different experiments targeting very different behaviors. However, more convincing data require observing both the loss-frame and gain-frame advantages within the same study, and I will turn to these kinds of experiments next.

Behaviors That Can Be Presented as Either Detection or Prevention

Taking health-promoting behaviors that can be described as serving both a prevention function and an early detection, or screening function, we conducted experiments to encourage, in one instance, the use of mouth rinse and, in the other, an annual Pap test (for women).

Mouth Rinse

In an experiment promoting mouthwash, we described a product to 120 University of Minnesota undergraduates (Rothman et al., 1999). Half of the students heard about "prevention mouthwash," a typical product that removes plaque from teeth and thus prevents tooth decay and gum disease. The other half heard about "disclosing mouthwash," a slightly unusual product that detects plaque buildup by leaving red discoloration on teeth. As usual, arguments in favor of either the prevention mouthwash or the disclosing mouthwash were framed in gain or loss terms, and participants were assigned randomly to receive one set or the other. Ratings of the quality of the pamphlet were unaffected by either the behavior-type or framing manipulations, although participants reported having more positive emotional reactions to the gain-framed pamphlet.

When asked whether they planned to buy the mouthwash in the next week, students' responses were as predicted: Intentions to purchase the product were strongest when the prevention mouthwash was described in terms of benefits (gain frame) and when the disclosing (detection) mouthwash was described in terms of costs (loss frame). For the prevention mouthwash, 67 percent of participants planned to purchase it after reading the gain-framed pamphlet, but only 47 percent planned to purchase it after reading the loss-framed pamphlet. In the detection condition, 73 percent of the participants said they would buy the disclosing mouthwash after reading the loss-framed pamphlet, but only 37 percent said they would purchase it after reading the gain-framed pamphlet.

Pap Tests

Although we generally think of Pap testing as a detection behavior, test descriptions can emphasize either an early-detection function, which is typical of most Pap test messages, or a preventive function—for example, detecting and then treating precancerous abnormalities in order to *prevent* a more serious condition.

We developed four different videotape programs: gain- and loss-framed versions emphasizing the early detection of cervical cancer, and gain- and loss-framed versions emphasizing the prevention of cervical cancer through the detection of treatable precancerous lesions (Rivers et al., 2005). Although the latter message is not exclusively focused on prevention, it does include more information about cancer prevention than the more typical Pap test–promoting communications.

We showed one of the four videos to each of 497 women over age 18 attending a community health clinic. Most women were from relatively poor families; 59 percent were African American, 26 percent were Latina, and 12 percent were white. Six months later, percentages of women who obtained a Pap test were higher in the prevention-gain and detection-loss conditions than in the other two groups, as illustrated in Figure 1.

Behaviors That Individuals Might Think About in Different Ways

Prevention and early detection behaviors differ in terms of the risk or uncertainty typically associated with them. Prevention behaviors are usually construed as safe, low-risk choices. However, the decision to pursue a detection behavior often involves uncertainty and risk because the outcome (health/illness) is not known in advance. Being tested for HIV would seem to be a typical detection behavior with attendant psychological risks and uncertainty, and thus should be better motivated by loss-framed messages. However, because HIV, unlike many other medical conditions, is tied in large part to behavior, some individuals might reasonably believe that they are not at risk for HIV. For them, HIV testing is psychologically safe (little chance of testing positive), with a relatively certain outcome, and therefore gain-framed messages might be more persuasive.

We completed a field experiment designed to test whether individuals with different views of HIV-testing outcomes would also differ in the type of message that would most effectively motivate them to undergo the test (Apanovitch, McCarthy, & Salovey, 2003). Participants were 480 women (most either African American or Latina) from a low-income neighborhood of New Haven, Connecticut, who either lived in public housing or attended a community health center to obtain an HIV test. We expected that women who viewed HIV testing as a risky behavior with uncertain outcomes would

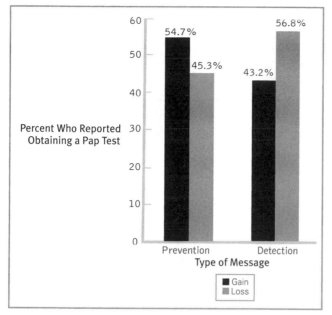

FIGURE 1   Percent of women who obtained a Pap test after 6 months. Gain-framed messages emphasizing the benefits of preventing cervical cancer and loss-framed messages emphasizing the costs of not detecting cervical cancer early were most persuasive in motivating women to obtain a Pap test. (Data from Rivers et al., 2005)

be more persuaded by a loss-framed message, whereas women who viewed HIV testing as a safe behavior with certain outcomes would be more persuaded by gain-framed messages.

Six months after they viewed the videos, testing rates were higher among women who considered HIV testing to have a certain (low-risk) outcome and who saw the gain-frame video compared with those who saw a loss-framed video (testing rates, 38% versus 26%, respectively). Testing rates among participants who considered HIV testing a risky behavior with uncertain outcomes showed a trend in the other direction, with loss-framed messages being more persuasive than the gain-framed video (testing rates, 47% versus 40%, respectively).

HIV seems unique among diseases in the extent to which individuals can assess their risk without reference to a medical test (although we strongly recommend testing to be sure). Differences in perceptions of the risk naturally follow, with those people engaging in high-risk behavior (for example, sex without condoms, multiple sexual partners) having more uncertainty as to their HIV status and test outcome, and those not engaging in high-risk behavior (for example, using a condom every time one has sex) perceiving the test as an opportunity to confirm their present health status. Loss-framed messages appear more persuasive to the high-risk group, while gain-framed messages are more effective for the low-risk group.

Conclusion

Research on the framing of health messages provides a systematic way of thinking about the kinds of advertisements, public service announcements, brochures, posters, and videos that are likely to be effective for promoting different kinds of health-enhancing behaviors. The basic pattern (gain-framing for prevention, loss-framing for detection (screening) behaviors) seems robust across different kinds of health behaviors and in different populations. The magnitude of these differences is not only statistically significant, in most cases, but also represents an increase in desired health behaviors that would have public health impact.

Aknowledgements

The research reported in this chapter was supported by grants to Peter Salovey from the American Cancer Society (RPG-93-028-05-PBP), the National Cancer Institute (R01-CA68427), the National Institute of Mental Health (P01-MH/DA56826), the National Institute of Drug Abuse (P50-DA13334), and the Donaghue Women's Health Investigator Program at Yale University.

The studies described in this essay are presented in more detail in: Salovey, P. (2005). Promoting prevention and detection: Psychologically tailoring and framing messages about health. In R. Bibace, J. D. Laird, K. L. Noller, & J. Valsiner (Eds.), *Science and medicine in dialogue: Thinking through particulars and universals* (pp. 17–42). Westport, CT: Greenwood Publishing; and Salovey, P., & Williams-Piehota, P. (2004). Field experiments in social psychology: Message framing and the promotion of health protective behaviors. *American Behavioral Scientist, 47,* 488–505.

Suggested Further Reading

Rothman, A. J., & Salovey, P. (1997). Shaping perceptions to motivate healthy behavior: The role of message framing. *Psychological Bulletin, 121,* 3–19.

Tversky, A., & Kahneman, D. (1981). The framing of decisions and the psychology of choice. *Science, 211,* 453–458.

References

Apanovitch, A. M., McCarthy, D., & Salovey, P. (2003). Using message framing to motivate HIV testing among low-income, ethnic minority women. *Health Psychology, 22,* 60–67.

Banks, S. M., Salovey, P., Greener, S., Rothman, A. J., Moyer, A., Beauvais, J., et al. (1995). The effects of message framing on mammography utilization. *Health Psychology, 14,* 178–184.

Detweiler, J. B., Bedell, B. T., Salovey, P., Pronin, E., & Rothman, A. J. (1999). Message framing and sunscreen use: Gain-framed messages motivate beach-goers. *Health Psychology, 18,* 189–196.

Kahneman, D., & Tversky, A. (1979). Prospect theory: An analysis of decision under risk. *Econometrica, 47,* 263–292.

Kahneman, D., & Tversky, A. (1982). The psychology of preferences. *Scientific American, 247,* 160–173.

Rivers, S. E., Pizarro, D. A., Schneider, T. R., Pizarro, J., & Salovey. P. (2005). Message framing and pap test utilization among women attending a community health clinic. *Journal of Health Psychology, 10,* 65–77.

Rothman, A. J., Martino, S. C., Bedell, B. T., Detweiler, J. B., & Salovey, P. (1999). The systematic influence of gain- and loss-framed messages on interest in and use of different types of health behavior. *Personality and Social Psychology Bulletin, 25,* 1355–1369.

Rothman, A. J., & Salovey, P. (1997). Shaping perceptions to motivate healthy behavior: The role of message framing. *Psychological Bulletin, 121,* 3–19.

Rothman, A. J., Salovey, P., Antone, C., Keough, K., & Martin, C. (1993). The influence of message framing on health behavior. *Journal of Experimental Social Psychology, 29,* 408–433.

Schneider, T. R., Salovey, P., Apanovitch, A. M., Pizarro, J., McCarthy, D., Zullo, J., et al. (2001). The effects of message framing and ethnic targeting on mammography use among low-income women. *Health Psychology, 20,* 256–266.

Tversky, A., & Kahneman, D. (1981). The framing of decisions and the psychology of choice. *Science, 211,* 453–458.

Positive Illusions: How Ordinary People Become Extraordinary

Shelley E. Taylor
University of California, Los Angeles

▶ *Please describe your current position and research interests.*
I am Distinguished Professor of Psychology at UCLA. My research concerns antecedents of responses to stress, such as early environment and psychosocial resources, and their impact on psychological and biological stress responses.

▶ *What got you interested in studying positive illusions and the factors that regulate them?*
My interest in positive illusions was sparked by seeing how cancer patients often hold positive, though erroneous, beliefs about their illnesses that nonetheless help them to cope successfully.

▶ *What has been the real-world impact of this work?*
Research on positive illusions tells researchers that the errors and biases commonly seen in human thought often serve vital functions, and so one must look beyond their risks to understand why they occur. For clinicians, the message underscores the realization that false beliefs may, nonetheless, be adaptive and that human beings have deep capacities for self-restoration and renewal.

Our investigations of stress and health began in the 1970s when I was invited to participate in a cancer conference to address social psychology's contribution to understanding psychological responses to breast cancer. My first reaction was that social psychologists had little to say, but I soon realized that there were many bases for hypotheses, especially in the social cognition literature. Accordingly, in 1980, Rosemary Lichtman, Joanne Wood, and I conducted an investigation with breast cancer patients in an attempt to understand what factors helped them to cope with the stress of their illness and get back to normal (Taylor, Lichtman, & Wood, 1984). Initially, we were operating with a homeostatic concept in mind. That is, our implicit thinking was that stress temporarily disturbs psychological functioning, which is then restored by coping efforts that help people return to their previous psychological state.

We were quickly disabused of this naive idea. In account after account, we heard not how these women had gotten back to normal but how their lives had changed, often for the better. Many women told us that the experience had forced them to develop or draw on strengths they did not know they had (Taylor, 1983). Many also told us that the experience had forced them to identify what was truly of value in their lives, and that relationships, especially with children, were chief among those discoveries. Other women expressed the feeling that they had discovered what was meaningful in life and expressed regret that anyone would have to go through such a stressful experience to achieve those insights.

But there was a disturbing component to these stories as well. In many cases, the women were exhibiting what we came to call positive illusions, namely, falsely positive beliefs about their abilities to stave off a recurrence of the illness or to combat an advancing metastatic condition. We asked a clinician whether these false beliefs were worrisome and were assured that they were normal and not indicative of an underlying psychological problem. However, it was this aspect of coping with illness—positive illusions—that captured our enduring interest.

These insights were first published in a 1983 paper on cognitive adaptation to illness (Taylor, 1983). I suggested that the ability to successfully cope with cancer depended heavily on restoring a sense of mastery, gaining a sense of meaning, and restoring self-enhancing self-perceptions. All of these beliefs typically suffer during the acute illness experience, and so coping efforts seem to focus heavily around these three themes.

Subsequent to our work with breast cancer patients, Jonathon D. Brown and I investigated whether positive illusions could be identified in ordinary people not going through intensely threatening health experiences, and, if so, whether the illusions are similarly adaptive. And, indeed, we did document the existence of very similar positive beliefs in normal people (Taylor & Brown, 1988). We reported evidence that people hold self-aggrandizing self-perceptions, an illusion of control, and unrealistic optimism about the future. Far from being maladaptive, we argued, these positive illusions are associated with the criteria normally associated with mental health: the ability to be happy or contented; the ability to care for and about others; the capacity for creative and productive work; and the ability to meet setbacks, challenges, and stressors of everyday life with equanimity and adaptive coping efforts. Our theoretical perspective generated many dozens of empirical investigations, and the article proved to be highly influential: More than 1,800 researchers have cited it in their publications to date.

The significance of positive illusions and their beneficial effects stems in part from the challenges they pose to traditional models of mental health. In these models, departures from rationality were regarded primarily as errors to be corrected. We showed that certain forms of irrationality have their functions and can be adaptive, leading to better outcomes than more realistic perceptions would afford.

Our initial findings prompted us to undertake several lines of empirical work. We identified the conditions under which positive illusions are most likely to exist and how they exert beneficial effects on motivation and performance (for example, Taylor & Gollwitzer, 1995). We uncovered how social comparison activities under threat are motivated to maximize both their informational value and their ability to restore or maintain positive self-perceptions (Taylor & Lobel, 1989). We also showed not only how unrealistic optimism is associated with positive outcomes but how it can be reconciled with the need to monitor reality effectively (Armor & Taylor, 1998).

Critiques of Positive Illusions

Nonetheless, the concept of positive illusions came under considerable fire. Some of the criticisms stemmed from misinterpretations. For example, the idea that more illusion is better is not a part of the positive illusions perspective. We argue that positive illusions typically stay within quite modest bounds largely because the feedback of the world is corrective. Illusions that are too extreme will be corrected into more modest proportions by feedback from the environment.

A particularly surprising paper reported evidence that people who have overly positive views of the self can be considered maladjusted when clinical interviews are the adjustment criteria (Shedler, Mayman, & Manis, 1993). The researchers also suggested that people with "illusory mental health" (that is, who claim psychological health that is contradicted by clinical evidence) have comparatively stronger biological responses to stress, suggesting potential health risks of positive illusions. This evidence contradicted pilot data from our cancer investigation, which suggested that people who held positive illusions about their ability to keep the cancer from coming back, in fact, lived longer, controlling for initial prognosis (although these data had remained unpublished due to a small sample size).

Accordingly, we replicated the Shedler et al. (2003) procedures and doubled the sample size. Contrary to their findings, we showed that self-enhancers were evaluated as well-adjusted and well-liked by clinicians, peer judges, and friends (Taylor et al., 2003b) and that self-enhancing cognitions were associated with healthier biological responses to stress (Taylor et al., 2003a).

The realization that self-enhancement, feelings of mastery, and unrealistic optimism not only have psychological effects on well-being but actually influence biological processes to affect health makes you realize how truly meaningful the act of psychological construal is and how important the psychological and biological effects of beliefs can be.

Origins of Positive Illusions

In recent years, we have explored the origins of positive illusions—that is, the factors that lead people to see themselves, the world, and the future in a positive, optimistic manner. At least some of the variance in positive beliefs is accounted for by genetic factors, although the specific genes have not yet been identified. This is an area of our current work. The origins of positive beliefs also lie in early family environment (Taylor & Stanton, 2007). Early nurturant experience helps to shape children's responses to stress, conferring the ability to respond to stress with positive beliefs and low biological reactivity. Correspondingly, a conflict-ridden, neglectful, or harsh family environment in childhood has been linked to a high rate of mental and physical health disorders in adulthood (Repetti, Taylor, & Seeman, 2002).

To examine these processes, we undertook a series of studies focusing on the interaction between family background and response to stress. We assessed participants' socioeconomic status (a contributor to chronic stress during childhood) and, to determine whether aspects of their early environment put participants at risk for later health problems, we interviewed them and asked them to complete questionnaires about their childhood family experience. We also examined their psychosocial functioning as adults (looking at the quality of their social contacts and their emotional health and distress), and we obtained data on the functioning of their biological stress regulatory systems (for example, blood pressure). Our work to date has shown that our model has predictive power for explaining health outcomes. Specifically, we find that high socioeconomic status and a positive family environment lead to the development of positive resources, such as optimism and social support, which are, in turn, tied to lower autonomic and neuroendocrine stress responses—that is, for example, lower heart rate and slower breathing in stressful situations and lower production of such stress hormones as cortisol (Taylor et al., 2004), lower risk for metabolic syndrome (which is a risk factor for heart disease and diabetes, among other conditions) (Lehman et al., 2005), and lower levels of C-reactive protein (which is prognostic for heart diseases and depression, among other conditions) (Taylor et al., 2006).

Current Directions

Our current work explores the genetic, early environmental, and neurocognitive origins of these resources in conjunction with their beneficial consequences. Specifically, we examine genes related to the serotonin and dopamine neurotransmitter systems; childhood socioeconomic status and early family environment as indicators of childhood environment; and neural mechanisms (anterior cingulate cortex, amygdala, hypothalamus, prefrontal cortex) that link socioemotional resources to low psychological and biological (cardiovascular, immunological, and neuroendrocrine) stress responses. As such, our current work integrates perspectives from genetics, psychoneuroimmunology, health psychology, and social neuroscience.

We have also shown that variations in the nurturance of early family environments can lead to dramatically different expressions of a common genotype. Specifically, people with the s/s variant of the serotonin transporter gene *5-HTTLPR* who were in early or are in current environments that are intensely stressful, experience an elevated risk for depressive symptoms; however, those with the s/s variant of the *5-HTTLPR* who experienced early or current nurturant environments actually have a reduced risk for depressive symptoms as compared with those who have s/l or l/l variants of the *5-HTTLPR*. Thus, the impact of the social environment can completely reverse the effects of a genetic risk factor (Taylor et al., 2006).

Implications

We believe that our work helps scientists and clinicians to understand how ordinary people become extraordinary. The most powerful aspect of our findings, at least to me, has been to see how people hold within themselves the abilities to construe circumstances that would seem to be inherently threatening, even traumatic, and not only adjust to them successfully but achieve a degree of heroism. We have used our research program of the past 25 years to try to identify the very best of human attributes and the power that those attributes have for achieving extraordinary human outcomes.

Acknowledgements

Preparation of this manuscript was supported by grants from the National Institute of Mental Health (MH056880) and the National Institute of Aging (AG30309).

Suggested Further Reading

Creswell, J. D., Welch, W. T., Taylor, S. E., Sherman, D. K., Gruenewald, T., & Mann, T. (2005). Affirmation of personal values buffers neuroendocrine and psychological stress responses. *Psychological Science, 16*, 846–851.

Taylor, S. E., & Stanton, A. (2007). Coping resources, coping processes, and mental health. *Annual Review of Clinical Psychology, 3*, 129–153.

References

Armor, D. A., & Taylor, S. E. (1998). Situated optimism: Specific outcome expectancies and self-regulation. In M. P. Zanna (Ed.), *Advances in experimental social psychology* (Vol. 30, pp. 309–379). New York: Academic Press.

Lehman, B. J., Taylor, S. E., Kiefe, C. I., & Seeman, T. E. (2005). Relation of childhood socioeconomic status and family environment to adult metabolic functioning in the CARDIA study. *Psychosomatic Medicine, 67*, 846–854.

Repetti, R. L., Taylor, S. E., & Seeman, T. E. (2002). Risky families: Family social environments and the mental and physical health of offspring. *Psychological Bulletin, 128*, 330–366.

Shedler, J., Mayman, M., & Manis, M. (1993). The illusion of mental health. *American Psychologist, 48*, 1117–1131.

Taylor, S. E. (1983). Adjustment to threatening events: A theory of cognitive adaptation. *American Psychologist, 38*, 1161–1173.

Taylor, S. E., & Brown, J. D. (1988). Illusion and well-being: A social psychological perspective on mental health. *Psychological Bulletin, 103*, 193–210.

Taylor, S. E., & Gollwitzer, P. M. (1995). The effects of mindset on positive illusions. *Journal of Personality and Social Psychology, 69*, 213–226.

Taylor, S. E., Lehman, B. J., Kiefe, C. I., & Seeman, T. E. (2006). Relationship of early life stress and psychological functioning to adult C-reactive protein in the Coronary Artery Risk Development in Young Adults Study. *Biological Psychiatry, 60*, 819–824.

Taylor, S. E., Lerner, J. S., Sherman, D. K., Sage, R. M., & McDowell, N. K. (2003a). Are self-enhancing cognitions associated with healthy or unhealthy biological profiles? *Journal of Personality and Social Psychology, 85*, 605–615.

Taylor, S. E., Lerner, J. S., Sherman, D. K., Sage, R. M., & McDowell, N. K. (2003b). Portrait of the self-enhancer: Well-adjusted and well-liked or maladjusted and friendless? *Journal of Personality and Social Psychology, 84*, 165–176.

Taylor, S. E., Lichtman, R. R., & Wood, J. V. (1984). Attributions, beliefs about control, and adjustment to breast cancer. *Journal of Personality and Social Psychology, 46*, 489–502.

Taylor, S. E., & Lobel, M. (1989). Social comparison activity under threat: Downward evaluation and upward contacts. *Psychological Review, 96*, 569–575.

Taylor, S. E., & Stanton, A. (2007). Coping resources, coping processes, and mental health. *Annual Review of Clinical Psychology, 3*, 129–153.

Taylor, S. E., Way, B. M., Welch, W. T., Hilmert, C. J., Lehman, B. J., & Eisenberger, N. I. (2006). Early family environment, current adversity, the serotonin transporter polymorphism, and depressive symptomatology. *Biological Psychiatry, 60*, 671–676.

16

Social Psychology

Elliot Aronson

Reducing Prejudice and Building Empathy in the Classroom

Harry T. Reis

When Good Things Happen to Good People: Capitalizing on Personal Positive Events in Relationships

Reducing Prejudice and Building Empathy in the Classroom

Elliot Aronson
University of California, Santa Cruz

▶ *Please tell us about your current position and research interests.*
I am Professor Emeritus at the University of California, Santa Cruz. My long-standing research interests include social influence and attitude change, cognitive dissonance, research methodology, and interpersonal attraction. My experiments are aimed both at testing theory and at improving the human condition by influencing people to change dysfunctional attitudes and behaviors.

▶ *What got you interested in studying and resolving social conflict?*
Social psychology has always thrilled me because it is such a wonderful blend of art and science. I believe that with sufficient ingenuity, almost any phenomenon can be tested in the laboratory. But I don't want simply to observe. I want to determine precisely what's causing a phenomenon, and if it's a situation that is impacting people's lives negatively, I want to take the next step and create an intervention that makes things better.

▶ *What has been the real-world impact of this work?*
Schools all over the country have adopted the jigsaw classroom process described in this essay. By encouraging listening, engagement, and empathy, and by giving each member of a student group an essential part to play in its activity, the process creates an environment in which racial, gender, and socioeconomic divisions can be overcome.

Prejudice is ubiquitous. In our own country, it has existed at least since the Puritans emigrated from England in 1620 to escape intolerance and eventually began practicing intolerance against everybody else in sight. It is not easy to change. In this essay, I will tell you a story about one successful attempt to reduce prejudice among elementary school children.

My story begins in 1954, when the United States Supreme Court outlawed school segregation. At that time, most social psychologists believed that when youngsters from various ethnic and racial backgrounds came to share the same classroom, negative stereotypes would gradually be reduced and cross-ethnic friendships would develop under the glow of face-to-face contact. Ultimately, these young people would grow into adults who would be relatively free of racial and ethnic prejudice.

The decision reversed the 1896 ruling (*Plessy* v. *Ferguson*), which had held racial segregation permissible as long as equal facilities were provided for both races. In 1954, in *Brown* v. *Board of Education*, the Court held that, psychologically, there could be no such thing as "separate but equal" education because the forced separation, in and of itself, implied to the minority group in question that its members were inferior to those of the majority. To quote from the 1954 decision:

> Does segregation of children in public schools solely on the basis of race, even though the physical facilities and other "tangible" factors may be equal, deprive the children of the minority group of equal educational opportunities? We believe that it does. . .to separate [Negro school children] from others of similar age and qualifications solely because of their race generates a feeling of inferiority as to their status in the community that may affect their hearts and minds in a way unlikely ever to be undone. . . . We conclude that in the field of public education the doctrine "separate but equal" has no place. Separate educational facilities are inherently unequal.

The implication of the ruling is that, because segregation *lowers* self-esteem, desegregation would produce an increase in the self-esteem of minority students. Furthermore, because segregation was depriving minorities of equal educational opportunities, the implication is that desegregation would lead to improved education for these students. Thus, the Court's decision was not only a humane interpretation of the Constitution, it was also the beginning of an exciting social experiment with three clear hypotheses: Desegregation will (1) reduce prejudice, (2) raise the self-esteem of minority students, and (3) improve the classroom performance of minority students.

Unfortunately, things did not work out exactly as supporters of the ruling had hoped. For example, in the 15 years following the implementation of the 1954 ruling, not a single study showed an increase in the self-esteem of minority children following desegregation; in fact, several studies showed that desegregation was followed by a significant *decrease* in their self-esteem. Moreover, if anything, according to the early studies, desegregation produced an increase rather than a decrease in racial prejudice, and the academic performance of minority students did not improve (Stephan, 1978).

In short, the results were incredibly disappointing. What went wrong? Why was desegregation failing to have the positive effects that most social psychologists had predicted?

What We Observed in Desegregated Classrooms

As luck would have it, I got a chance to find out first hand what was happening in the newly desegregated schools. In 1971, I was teaching at the University of Texas at Austin when the Austin public schools were finally desegregated—and all hell broke loose. Because Austin had been residentially segregated, youngsters of various ethnic and racial groups were encountering one another for the first time. A lot of suspicion and stereotyping existed prior to this contact, and it seems to have exacerbated the problem. In any case, taunting frequently escalated into fistfights. The situation was both ugly and dangerous.

The school superintendent knew that I had some experience in resolving social conflict, and he asked for my help. All he really wanted was for me to find a way to end the violence. But I had a more ambitious agenda: My students and I entered the system, not to smooth over the unpleasantness but rather to see if there was anything we might do to help desegregation achieve some of the positive goals originally envisioned for it. The first thing we did was to systematically observe the dynamics taking place in various classrooms. By far, the most common process we observed was typified by this scenario in a fifth-grade class:

> The teacher stands in front of the room and asks a question. Most frequently, seven or eight youngsters strain in their seats and raise their hands—some waving them vigorously in an attempt to attract the teacher's attention. Several other students sit quietly with their eyes averted, as if trying to make themselves invisible. When the teacher calls on one of the students, there are looks of disappointment, dismay, and unhappiness on the faces of those students who were eagerly raising their hands but were not called on. If the student comes up with the right answer, the teacher smiles, nods approvingly, and goes on to the next question. This is a great reward for that student. At that moment, however, an audible groan can be heard coming from the youngsters who were striving to be called on but were ignored. It is obvious they are upset.

Through this process, students learn several things in addition to the material being covered. First, they learn there is only one expert in the classroom: the teacher. The students also learn that the payoff comes from pleasing the teacher by actively displaying how smart they are. There is no payoff for consulting with their peers. Indeed, many learn that their peers are their enemies—to be defeated.

In this highly competitive dynamic, if you are a student who knows the correct answer and the teacher calls on one of your peers, chances are you will hope that he or she will come up with the wrong answer so you will have a chance to show the teacher how smart you are. Those who fail when called on, or those who do not even raise their hands and compete, usually resent those who succeed. The successful students, for their part, often hold the unsuccessful students in contempt; they consider them to be stupid and uninteresting. This process discourages mutual understanding. Indeed, it tends to create enmity, even among students of the same racial group. When this competitive classroom dynamic is added to a situation already strained by interracial distrust, it sets the stage for the kind of turmoil we encountered in Austin. We began to understand why desegregation was not producing the desired consequences.

Although competitiveness in the classroom was nearly universal, as social psychologists, we realized that alternative dynamics were possible. We reasoned that a cooperative process might be precisely what was needed in this situation.

Our Jigsaw Classrooms

Within a few days, my students and I had invented a simple, cooperative method for the classroom. We designed it so that, in order to learn the material and do well on an upcoming exam, students had to work *with* each other and not pull against each other. Trying to win at the expense of your class-mates became dysfunctional. We called our method the "jigsaw classroom" because it works very much like a jigsaw puzzle.

An example will clarify: In a fifth-grade classroom, the children were study-ing biographies of famous Americans. The upcoming lesson happened to be a biography of Joseph Pulitzer, the famous journalist. First, we divided the stu-dents into groups of six—making certain that each group was as diverse (in terms of race and gender) as possible. We then constructed a biography of Pulitzer consisting of six paragraphs. Paragraph one was about Pulitzer's an-cestors and how they came to this country; paragraph two was about Pulitzer as a little boy and how he grew up; paragraph three was about Pulitzer as a young man, his education, and his early employment, and so forth.

Each major aspect of Joseph Pulitzer's life was contained in a separate paragraph. We mimeographed our biography of Joseph Pulitzer, cut each copy of the biography into six one-paragraph sections, and gave every child in each of the six-person learning groups one paragraph about Pulitzer's life. Thus, each learning group had within it the entire biography of Joseph Pulitzer, but each student had no more than one-sixth of the story. In order to get the whole picture, each student needed to listen carefully to the other students in the group as they recited.

The teacher informed the students that they had a certain amount of time to communicate their knowledge to one another. She also informed them that they would be tested on their knowledge at the end of that time period.

The students eventually learned that none of them could do well without the aid of each person in the group. They learned to respect the fact that each member (regardless of race, gender, or ethnicity) had a unique and essential contribution to make to their own understanding and subsequent test per-formance. Now, instead of only one expert (the teacher), each student was an expert on his or her own segment. Instead of taunting each other, they began encouraging each other—because it was in each student's own best interest to make sure that the youngster reciting was able to communicate his or her material in the clearest possible way.

It wasn't easy. During their previous years in school, the students had grown accustomed to competing. For the first few days, most of them tried to compete against each other—even though competitiveness was now dys-functional. Let me illustrate with an actual example, typical of the way the children stumbled toward the learning of the cooperative process. In one of our groups there was a Mexican-American boy, whom I will call Carlos. Car-los's task was to report on Joseph Pulitzer's young adulthood. He knew the material, but he was very nervous and was having a very hard time. During the past few weeks, some of the Anglo students had taunted him about his accent, and he was afraid that this might happen again.

He stammered, hesitated, and fidgeted. Sure enough, the other kids in the circle were not very helpful. Well versed in the rough-and-tumble tactics of the competitive classroom, they knew what to do when a kid stumbled—especially a kid whom they believed to be stupid. They ridiculed him. During our experiment, a girl we'll call Debbie was observed to say: "Aw, you don't know it, you're dumb, you're stupid. You don't know what you're doing."

The groups were being monitored by a research assistant who was floating from group to group. When this incident occurred, our assistant made one brief intervention, saying: "Okay, you can do that if you want to. It might even be fun for you. But it's *not* going to help you learn about Joseph Pulitzer's young adulthood. By the way, the exam will take place in about 20 minutes."

Notice how the reinforcement contingencies had shifted. No longer did Debbie gain much from rattling Carlos; in fact, she now stood to lose a great deal.

After a few similar experiences, the students in Carlos's group realized that the *only* way they could learn about the segment Carlos was trying to teach them was by paying attention to what Carlos had to say. Gradually, they began to develop into good listeners. Some even became pretty good interviewers. Instead of ignoring or ridiculing Carlos when he was having a little trouble communicating what he knew, they began asking gentle, probing questions—the kinds of questions that made it easier for Carlos to communicate what was in his mind.

Carlos began to respond to this treatment by becoming more relaxed; with increased relaxation came an improvement in his ability to communicate. After a couple of weeks, the other children realized that Carlos was a lot smarter than they had thought he was. Because they were paying attention, they began to see things in him they had never seen before. They began to respect him. For his part, Carlos began to enjoy school more and began to see the Anglo students in his group not as tormentors but as helpful and responsible people. Moreover, as he began to feel increasingly comfortable in class and started to gain more confidence in himself, his academic performance improved. The vicious cycle had been reversed; the elements that had been causing a downward spiral were changed—the spiral now began to move upward. Within a few weeks, the entire atmosphere in that classroom had changed dramatically. We then randomly assigned several classrooms in Austin to the jigsaw condition and compared them with classrooms using traditional methods. The results were clear and consistent. Children in jigsaw classrooms performed better on objective exams, grew to like each other better, and developed a greater liking for school and greater self-esteem than children in traditional classrooms. The increase in liking among children in the jigsaw classroom crossed ethnic and racial barriers, resulting in a sharp decrease in prejudice and stereotyping. We replicated the same experiment in dozens of classrooms in several cities—always getting similar results (Aronson et al., 1978; Aronson & Goode, 1980; Aronson & Patnoe, 1997).

What Are the Benefits of the Jigsaw Classroom?

Over the years, dozens of experiments have shown that the jigsaw method's effectiveness is not limited to either Americans or to young children. Jigsaw has been used with great success in Europe, Africa, the Middle East, and Australia—with students at all levels, from elementary schools to universities.

We speculated that one of the processes underlying the success of the method is empathy—the ability to experience what your group member is experiencing. In the competitive classroom, the primary goal is simply to show the teacher how smart you are. You don't have to pay much attention to the other students. But the jigsaw situation is different. In order to participate effectively in the jigsaw classroom, each student needs to pay close attention to whichever member of the group is reciting. In the process, the participants begin to learn that great results can accrue if each of their classmates is approached in a way that is tailored to fit his or her special needs. For example, Alice may learn that Carlos is a bit shy and needs to be prodded gently, while Phyllis is so talkative that she might need to be reigned in occasionally. Peter can be joked with, while Serena responds only to serious suggestions.

If our analysis is sound, then it should follow that working in jigsaw groups would lead to the sharpening of a youngster's general empathic ability. To test this notion, Diane Bridgeman (1981) conducted a clever experiment with 10-year-old children. Prior to her experiment, half of the children had spent 2 months participating in jigsaw classes; the others spent that time in traditional classrooms. Bridgeman showed the children a series of cartoons aimed at testing a child's ability to empathize—to put themselves in the shoes of the cartoon characters. For example, in one cartoon, the first panel shows a little boy looking sad as he waves good-bye to his father at the airport. In the next panel, a letter carrier delivers a package to the boy. In the third panel, the boy opens the package, finds a toy airplane inside, and bursts into tears. Bridgeman asked the children why they thought the little boy burst into tears at the sight of the airplane. Nearly all of the children could answer correctly—because the toy airplane reminded him of how much he missed his father. Then Bridgeman asked the crucial question: "What did the letter carrier think when he saw the boy open the package and start to cry?"

Most children of this age make a consistent error; they assume that everyone knows what they know. Thus, the youngsters in the control group thought that the *letter carrier* would know the boy was sad because the gift reminded him of his father leaving. But the children who had participated in the jigsaw classroom responded differently. Because of their experience with jigsaw, they had developed the ability to take the perspective of the letter carrier; they realized that, not having witnessed the farewell scene at the airport, he would be confused at seeing the boy cry over receiving a nice present.

Schools are conservative organizations. As such, they are slow to change. In spite of jigsaw's success, it is being used in approximately 15 percent of the schools in this country. In those schools, desegregation works the way it was supposed to work.

Suggested Further Reading

Aronson, E. (2008). *The social animal* (10th ed.). New York: Worth.

Aronson, E. (2000, May/June). Nobody left to hate: Developing the empathic schoolroom. *The Humanist, 60,* 17–21.

References

Aronson, E., Bridgeman, D. L., and Geffner, R. (1978). The effects of a cooperative classroom structure on students' behavior and attitudes. In D. Bar-Tal and L. Saxe (Eds.), *Social Psychology of Education: Theory and Research.* Washington, DC: Hemisphere.

Aronson, E., & Goode, E. (1980). Training teachers to implement jigsaw learning: A manual for teachers. In S. Sharan, P. Hare, C. Webb, R. Hertz-Lazarowitz (Eds.), *Cooperation in Education* (pp. 47–81). Provo, UT: Brigham Young University Press.

Aronson, E., & Patnoe, S. (1997). *Cooperation in the classroom: The jigsaw method.* New York: Longman.

Aronson, E., Stephen, C., Sikes, J., Blaney, N., & Snapp, M. (1978). *The jigsaw classroom.* Beverly Hills: Sage.

Bridgeman, D. L. (1981). Enhanced role taking through cooperative interdependence: A field study. *Child Development, 52,* 1231–1238.

Stephan, W. G. (1978). School desegregation: An evaluation of predictions made in *Brown* v. *Board of Education. Psychological Bulletin, 85,* 217–38.

When Good Things Happen to Good People: Capitalizing on Personal Positive Events in Relationships

Harry T. Reis
The University of Rochester

▶ *Please describe your current position and research interests.*
I am a professor of psychology at the University of Rochester. My research concerns the factors that lead people to perceive that their partners are responsive to them. More broadly, I am interested in the ways in which relationships affect human behavior in nearly all domains of activity.

▶ *How did you get interested in positive factors that influence the quantity and closeness of social interactions?*
I felt that the clinic-inspired psychology of relationships was much too heavily focused on conflict. People don't seek out relationships because they are low in conflict or because they can "fight well" with this person; they seek out partners who help them feel good about themselves, who make them feel listened to and supported, and who inspire them. That is what we are trying to get at.

▶ *What has been the real-world impact of this work?*
My hope is that from this work people will pay more attention when their partner tells them about good news and that they will make their appreciation more evident. This is a very modest goal but in my mind it is one with great potential.

A happiness shared is a happiness doubled.

—*Navajo proverb*

Whenever a friend succeeds, a little something in me dies.

.   —*Gore Vidal*

Let's consider two friendships. In the first, Jacques has just won a prestigious, all-expenses-paid fellowship to a major university. His friend Jules is excited and enthusiastic, giving him high fives, asking questions about the details, and suggesting a celebratory dinner. Another friend, Jalen, has won the same fellowship. However, when he informs his friend Jon, he gets a half-hearted response. "That's nice," Jon says and quickly changes the topic to a concert they plan to attend that evening. What's the difference between these two reactions, and why does it matter?

For the past several years, my colleagues and I have investigated the process embodied in these examples. We call it "capitalization." The term refers to the attempt to get the most out of a positive happening—that is, to capitalize on good news. There are many ways in which this might be done.

One of the most common is sharing the news with a relationship partner (Langston, 1994). You've probably had this experience: Something good happens, and your first impulse is to call, e-mail, or text message a friend, significant other, or family member. How the news is received, our research has shown, turns out to be important to the quality of the relationship and to how the sharer feels about the news.

Our involvement in this line of research grew out of our interest in the difference between what we call "appetitive" and "aversive" processes in close relationships. For many years, researchers and practitioners alike had viewed responses to potentially undesirable outcomes as critical in determining relationship success. In the arena of social life, these aversive phenomena include rejection, insecurity, rudeness, criticism, jealousy, loneliness, and conflict. Many relationship researchers, in fact, have viewed conflict and its management as the defining attribute of relationship success.

Psychological research on aversive processes has far outweighed consideration of the impact of appetitive processes on relationship functioning. Appetitive processes refer to desired outcomes and goals, such as intimacy, love, shared fun, and a feeling of meaningful connection. For my colleagues and me, the capitalization situation has been a natural prototype for our broader interest in these appetitive processes. Ideas about capitalization derive directly from research on the importance of self-disclosure and social support in close relationships. But there is a key difference. Social support, which is characterized by some researchers as an appetitive process, is usually sought when people are in a negative state—that is, when they are distressed or worried and need assistance, guidance, or comfort to help diminish their distress. By contrast, when capitalizing on good news, the goal is to savor and otherwise maximize the positive aspects of that news.

First Studies on Capitalization

We began our research with a daily diary study (Gable et al., 2004). For one week, 154 college students reported the most important positive and negative event or experience of each day and whether or not they had told someone about the event. They then rated the event's importance. Approximately 70 percent of the positive events were recounted to another person. We applied to the data multilevel analysis, a statistical procedure that controls for differences between people who are inclined to share and people who are not. After further controlling for the importance of the positive event and for whatever negative events had occurred during the day, we found that on days in which the most positive event had been related to another person, our respondents' positive affect and life satisfaction were significantly higher than on days in which those positive events were left untold. In plain language, relating a positive event to another person was strongly associated with having a better day.

Correlation is not causality, of course, and this important distinction led us to develop an experimental paradigm for examining the capitalization process. We first ask participants in our experiments to describe and rate the three best things "that have happened to you in the past 2 years." We then randomly select either the second- or third-most positive event and ask participants to spend about 8 minutes describing it to an interviewer trained to respond enthusiastically and supportively. (For example, the interviewer smiles, makes eye contact, uses a lively tone of voice, and says things like "Your friends must be really proud of you.") After these conversations, participants are asked again to rate all three of their best-in-2-years events. The results of one experiment are shown in Figure 1. We found that ratings of the event discussed increased significantly, whereas ratings of the event not discussed stayed steady (Reis, Smith, & Carmichael, 2009, study 1).

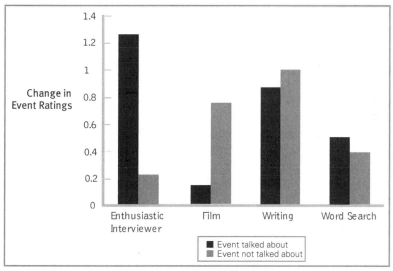

FIGURE 1 From pre to post in four experimental conditions. Change in ratings of best-in-2-years events. (From Reis, Smith, & Carmichael, 2009, study 1)

To rule out other possible causes of the capitalization effect, this study included other conditions asking participants for ratings of their best-in-2-years events after they had undergone one of three different experiences. In one condition, participants wrote an essay describing their thoughts and feelings about the target event. (Other researchers have shown that this kind of expressive writing can help people cope with traumatic events [Pennebaker, 2003]). In a second condition, participants watched a humorous clip from the film *Austin Powers: International Man of Mystery* to see if similar results might be obtained from being in a good mood (Fredrickson, 1998). The final control condition involved doing word-search puzzles. As Figure 1 shows, none of these conditions yielded differential increases for the event discussed over the event not discussed, suggesting that the *act of recounting* an event with an enthusiastic listener is responsible for the benefits of capitalization.

Does capitalization depend on an enthusiastic listener? To find out, in another experiment we compared a condition in which the listener was enthusiastic (as in the previous study) with one in which the listener adopted a more passive, disengaged, but not hostile orientation (Reis et al., 2009, study

2). For example, throughout the participant's recounting, the listener slouched and fidgeted, mostly avoided eye contact, maintained a steady and fairly dry tone of voice, and said things like "Oh yeah, that's nice." Enthusiastic listening again led to a significant capitalization effect; passive responses yielded no significant findings. This result dovetails with research showing that inattentive, distracted listening (but not attentive, responsive listening) may undermine people's ability to find personal meaning in oral narratives (see, for example, Pasupathi & Rich, 2005).

The Interpersonal Benefits of Capitalization

Capitalization is not only about savoring good news; it also contributes to the well-being of relationships. We theorize that this occurs because enthusiastic responses demonstrate emotional engagement, and such responsiveness is at the core of close relationships. For example, when one person discloses personal thoughts and feelings, responses seen as understanding, validating, and caring foster warm, supported feelings in the speaker and intimacy between the partners (Reis & Shaver, 1988).

Psychologists have tended to study responsiveness in terms of negativity—for example, after disclosures of fears, anxieties, and embarrassing moments, or in conflict-laden communications. But perceived responsiveness can also be revealed in responses to a person's aspirations, goals, and ideals. For example, romantic partners' behavioral and psychological support has been found to foster movement toward personal goals and aspirations and thereby to promote individual growth and the well–being of the relationship, a phenomenon dubbed the "Michelangelo phenomenon" (Rusbult et al., 2005).

Of course, friends, relatives, and even romantic partners do not always respond to a retelling of personal good fortune with visible pride and enthusiasm. Researchers have delineated circumstances when partners are likely to respond with envy or distance (Beach & Tesser, 1995). For example, when good news has meaning that is personally relevant for the partner, it may provoke anxiety. Imagine hearing about something that threatens your self-esteem or security in a relationship or that involves new activities or responsibilities that potentially compete with the relationship for time or attention. You'd have to put your personal feelings aside for the good of the relationship to respond with great enthusiasm.

Ironically, relationship-threatening good news from a romantic partner can create more ambivalence and make it harder to respond enthusiastically than if the same news were being related by an acquaintance. Capitalization attempts may also be hampered by the third-party experience. All other things being equal, close friends expect to learn each other's news firsthand. Thus, learning about a close friend's good fortune from a less close other (the third party) may undermine closeness and the capitalization process. Learning the same news about the same person from a third party who is closer to the target than oneself does not have this effect (Tsai, 2006).

My colleagues and I have examined the benefits of capitalization in both correlational studies and experiments. We do so for several reasons. One reason is methodological: Experiments are better for asking questions about causality, whereas correlational studies are better for examining these processes from the perspective of the individuals involved. Another, more general reason is that we believe that capitalization applies not only to transitory interactions among strangers but also to ongoing relationships, including friendship, marriage, and families. To examine these processes in romantic relationships, some of our studies have used a questionnaire that looks at the way capitalization attempts are perceived. Are they experienced as active and constructive ("My partner usually responds to my good fortune enthusiastically"), passive ("My partner says little but I know he/she is happy for me"), or destructive ("Sometimes I get the impression that he/she doesn't care much" or "He/she points out the potential downsides of the good event"). Correlations consistently reveal that the active-constructive responses are associated with higher levels of well-being in both partners and in the relationship. (These associations are obtained after controlling for general levels of satisfaction with the relationship, indicating that perceived responsiveness to capitalization attempts represents something more particular than general happiness.)

In one study conducted with 89 heterosexual couples who had been married between 1 and 43 years, we asked spouses to keep daily records of their interactions with each other. Spouses who perceived their partners' responses as active-constructive reported higher levels of daily satisfaction than did couples who perceived passive or negative feedback, and they reported more shared fun and relaxing activities, higher intimacy, and fewer conflicts. Interestingly, passive responses, which nominally might not seem destructive, were associated with *worse* outcomes (Gable et al., 2004). Another study, using carefully controlled laboratory observations, similarly showed that active-constructive responses to capitalization attempts (as rated by the individual or independent observers) were associated with higher relationship well-being and stability (Gable, Gonzaga, & Strachman, 2006).

Providing an enthusiastic response to a partner's effort to capitalize on good news may also benefit the responder. In a recent experiment, we trained listeners to provide enthusiastic feedback as research participants recounted positive experiences. In a different condition, we provided an opportunity for "fun"; this involved the participant describing in words a series of ambiguous pencil drawings that the trained listener had to draw without seeing. In both conditions, the confederate was liked equally well, but in the capitalization condition, trust was higher and participants were more willing to self-disclose.

Enthusiastic positive feedback even affects brief encounters between strangers, as we found when our lab assistants, posing as interviewers, approached people on the street and asked them to describe (for 1 dollar) the best thing that had happened to them during the previous week (Reis et al., 2009, study 3). As before, we set up three response conditions—enthusiastic, passive, and disparaging—and we also added a fourth: the interviewer offered a piece of candy from a box that she said she had just received from her grandmother. After the interviews, participants received an envelope containing 2 dollars and a receipt (hidden from the interviewer's vision). If capitalization builds social resources, we would expect that participants in the enthusiasm condition would be more likely than those in the other groups to return the unexpected additional dollar. And indeed they did. Sixty-eight percent of the enthusiastic response group returned the extra money, significantly more than in the candy (51%), neutral (48%), and disparaging (36%) conditions.

Translating Capitalization Research to Everyday Relationships

What can we learn from our findings that can be applied in everyday relationships? Most apparent is the insight that relationships benefit when partners respond with enthusiasm and visible pride to each other's good fortune. We believe that two general processes are operative. First, enthusiasm signals people's genuine appreciation for the event in question, as well as high regard for the other person. As hundreds of studies have shown, we humans are inherently social creatures whose attitudes, beliefs, and self-evaluations are profoundly influenced by the feedback we receive from others, especially from valued others. A positive response from a valued partner allows one to savor the event, makes it seem more memorable, and enhances its meaningfulness—all likely parts of the upward cycle in well-being that positive emotions induce (Fredrickson, 1998).

The second process is relational in nature and involves a defining feature of close relationships—cognitive interdependence. When we are really close to someone, attributes of the other person become linked cognitively and emotionally to our own attributes; in a psychological sense, we include the other in the self (Aron et al., 1991). By responding with pride rather than envy and with enthusiasm rather than disengagement, one partner signals mental inclusion of the other in their own self-representation and enhances their feelings of closeness. "Basking in reflected glory," or displaying pride in the accomplishments of relationship partners, is associated with closeness and the desire for continued closeness (Beach & Tesser, 1995). An enthusiastic response, then, is a sign of closeness and appreciation.

In conclusion, recounting one's personal good fortune is not just a strategic attempt to brag; it creates an opportunity for friends, relatives, and romantic partners to support and affirm, or alternatively to undermine or disparage. Although we have not yet identified the numerous personal and situational factors that encourage partners to share good news in relationship-promoting ways and to provide enthusiastic responses, a few brief principles from the social psychological literature suggest promising possibilities. For example, traits that foster responsiveness and genuine openness toward others, such as attachment security, high self-esteem, and agreeableness, would seem relevant, as would skills such as empathic accuracy (the ability to accurately perceive how others are thinking and feeling) and perspective-taking. Traits only tell part of the story (and a small part at that); situational factors are also important, suggesting that people can learn to do better. Some situational factors that are likely to be relevant include other-focused (as opposed to self-focused) attention and the absence of threats to the security of the relationship. Moreover, we see these processes as promising candidates for intervention. We suspect that in long-term relationships, the failure to engage in capitalization may reflect mindlessness and inattention to a greater extent than malign intent, processes that occur commonly as partners become habituated to their relationships and instead direct attention to stresses and strains. If so, interventions that foster mindful attention to what is transpiring within our relationships and other responsive listening skills may have merit.

Finally, our work to date suggests that fostering the positive aspects of close relationships merits as much attention as is typically devoted toward repairing the negative side. A large majority of therapies and interventions teach skills for talking about negative emotions and resolving conflicts constructively, and these are certainly important. But people do not engage in friendships and close relationships to avoid their destructive potential. They enter relationships for positive reasons, including the desire to share life's many wonderful moments with another person. Maintaining and expanding that desire represents a new opportunity for capitalizing not just on good news, but on our rewarding connections with others.

Suggested Further Reading

Gable, S. L., & Reis, H. T. (2001). Appetitive and aversive social interaction. In J. Harvey & A. Wenzel (Eds.), *Close romantic relationships: Maintenance and enhancement* (pp. 169–194). Mahwah, NJ: Erlbaum.

Reis, H. T., Clark, M. S., & Holmes, J. G. (2004). Perceived partner responsiveness as an organizing construct in the study of intimacy and closeness. In D. Mashek & A. Aron (Eds.), *The handbook of closeness and intimacy* (pp. 201–225). Mahwah, NJ: Erlbaum.

References

Aron, A., Aron, E. N., Tudor, M., & Nelson, G. (1991). Close relationships as including other in the self. *Journal of Personality and Social Psychology, 60*, 241–253.

Beach, S. R. H., & Tesser, A. (1995). Self-esteem and the extended self-evaluation maintenance model: The self in social context. In M. H. Kernis (Ed.), *Efficacy, agency, and self-esteem* (pp. 145–170). New York: Plenum Press.

Frederickson, B. (1998). What good are positive emotions? *Review of General Psychology, 2*, 300–319.

Gable, S. L., Gonzaga, G. C., & Strachman, A. (2006). Will you be there for me when things go right? Supportive responses to positive event disclosures. *Journal of Personality and Social Psychology, 91*, 904–917.

Gable, S. L., Reis, H. T., Impett, E., & Asher, E. R. (2004). What do you do when things go right? The intrapersonal and interpersonal benefits of sharing positive events. *Journal of Personality and Social Psychology, 87*, 228–245.

Langston, C. A. (1994). Capitalizing on and coping with daily-life events: Expressive responses to positive events. *Journal of Personality and Social Psychology, 67*, 1112–1125.

Pasupathi, M., & and Rich, B. (2005). Inattentive listening undermines self-verification in personal storytelling. *Journal of Personality, 73*, 1051–1086.

Pennebaker, J. W. (2003). Writing about emotional experiences as a therapeutic process. In P. Salovey & Alexander J. Rothman (Eds.), *Social psychology of health*. New York: Psychology Press.

Reis, H. T., & Shaver, P. (1988). Intimacy as an interpersonal process. In S. Duck & D. F. Hay (Eds.), *Handbook of personal relationships: Theory, research, and interventions* (pp. 367–389). New York: John Wiley & Sons.

Reis, H. T., Smith, S. M., & Carmichael, C. L. (2009). Capitalization increases personal and social resources. Manuscript under editorial review.

Rusbult, C. E., Kumashiro, M., Stocker, S. L., & Wolf, S. T. (2005). The Michelangelo Phenomenon in close relationships. In A. Tesser, J. V. Wood, & D. Stapel (Eds.), *On building, defending and regulating the self: A psychological perspective* (pp. 1–29). New York: Psychology Press.

Tsai, F. F. (2006). Why didn't you tell me first?: The third-party experience. Unpublished doctoral dissertation, University of Rochester.

Chapter 17

Work

John P. Campbell

Individual Occupational Performance:
The Blood Supply of Our Work Life

Benjamin Schneider

Organizational Climate: Theory and Evidence

Individual Occupational Performance: The Blood Supply of Our Work Life

John P. Campbell
University of Minnesota

▶ *Please describe your current position and research interests.*
I am Professor of Psychology and Director of Graduate Studies, Department of Psychology, University of Minnesota.

▶ *What drew you to applied psychology and particularly to the study of work performance?*
I originally went to Iowa State University to study engineering, which I did for 3 years, only to find it not very interesting. However, I took a course from an industrial/organizational psychologist, which was much more interesting. That got me into psychology and to a Ph.D. from the University of Minnesota. Individual job performance is I/O psychology's most important dependent variable, but for many decades the specifications for what performance is and for what constitutes a measure of performance were treated in a very cavalier and helter-skelter fashion. I decided to try and change that and make modeling performance itself as important as modeling abilities, personality, or attitudes.

▶ *What has been the real-world impact of this work?*
Since 1990, the basic tenets of the model described in this essay have been accepted and acted upon by most investigators doing applied psychological research on ways to improve performance. Its operational effects on everyday life in organizations (for example, performance appraisals of teachers, doctors, managers, equipment operators) is difficult to document, and it may be too soon to expect very widespread effects. Such issues are not covered in Psychology 101, or Management 101, so far. My grandiose dream is for every citizen to think in terms of such a model when making judgments about someone else's performance (or their own).

Our performance at work influences the people we meet and grow to respect or disrespect, and where we live. Our performance enables us to feed, clothe, and house our families and ourselves. It literally defines who we are. And whether we like it our not, all of us will have our performance assessed frequently. Unfortunately, specifying what performance means and how it should be measured is not as easy as it sounds. Applied psychology has a long and painful history of trying.

If our science has taught us anything, it is that in all things psychological there are individual differences, and performance in an occupation is no exception. Are assessments of performance differences reliable, accurate, and fair? What are the "determinants" of individual differences in work performance? Is it the quality of people's education? The amount of effort they invest? Their personality? Basic abilities? Their boss's ability to teach them new things? Situational constraints that inhibit performance? All of the above?

These issues have concerned industrial/organizational (I/O) psychologists for a century. Can we use what we know to better select people for jobs? Train them more effectively? Evaluate them fairly? Motivate them to do their best work? Provide better information for career guidance? For example, the "performance" of public school teachers has never been a more critical topic than it is today. Should teachers be paid for performance (a.k.a. merit), or shouldn't they? How can consumers spend their health care dollars wisely if they can't evaluate the "performance" of health care providers? Does the "performance" of CEOs merit the sums of money they are paid? What is the meaning of the word *performance* in these contexts?

Both the science of studying individual differences in performance and the fair and accurate use of the word in daily life suffer if there are no agreed upon specifications for what it means. The major objective of this essay is to give you such a specification, as well as a framework for thinking about the issues that pertain to it. There are also implications for the assessment of student performance. Is GPA all there is?

In general, over the history of applied psychology, relevant, reliable, and fair measures of individual performance have been hard to come by—a dilemma that became known as the criterion problem. The dilemma was made even worse when Robert L. Thorndike (1910–1990) introduced the notion of the ultimate criterion (Thorndike, 1949). He defined "ultimate criterion" rather grandiosely as a measure of the individual's *total* contribution to the goals of the organization over the entire course of his or her job tenure. Consequently, applied psychology's task was to use performance criterion measures that approximated the ultimate criterion as closely as possible. But close approximations never seemed to turn up, and the criterion problem was lamented for many decades (Austin & Villanova, 1992).

Turning a Corner

The first real opportunity to model job performance as a scientific construct, rather than as the best available objective indicator that could be found lying around, came with a series of research studies conducted in the U.S. Army between 1982 and 1994, that were and collectively known as Project A (Campbell & Knapp, 2001). During that period, the Army hired approximately 120,000 new people each year from approximately 400,000 applicants, and assigned each new hire to one of approximately 275 different jobs. Although the 275 military occupational specialties did not mirror the activities of the entire labor force, they covered a broad spectrum of occupations, ranging from electronics, to media and communications, to medical technologists, to military police officers. My colleagues and I developed multiple measures of many different aspects of performance for 20 occupations sampled representatively from the population of 275 jobs.

The performance measures ranged from archival records of both commendations and disciplinary actions, to supervisory and peer ratings on a set of carefully defined performance dimensions, to simulations of how well the individual could perform the job's major tasks (for example, treat a broken bone, troubleshoot an electrical or mechanical problem, or conduct a disciplinary meeting with a subordinate). Data on each measure were obtained from two cohorts of 10,000 people each (approximately 500 per job), and each individual's performance was assessed three times: (1) after completion of technical training, (2) after being "on the job" for 2 to 3 years, and (3) 5 to 6 years out, after the individual had begun to take on supervisory/leadership responsibilities. By orders of magnitude, this effort produced the largest single research database on occupational performance and its determinants in the history of applied psychology. The database is still being used to address many different kinds of questions.

Given this much data, we were able to hypothesize what underlying "model" of performance might best explain the pattern of observed correlations among all the different performance indicators (over 150 of them). That is, what are the fundamental, substantive components of performance (that is, its basic parts) that best explain the pattern of empirical relationships among the 150+ measures? We could also put competing alternative models to an empirical confirmatory test and find out which portrayal of the basic parts fit the data best.

Without going into the details, the result was that Project A produced a five-component model of performance in entry-level jobs and a six-component model of supervisory (that is, noncommissioned officer [NCO]) performance (Campbell & Knapp, 2001). The additional factor dealt with the leadership component of NCO positions. These findings generated a renewed look at past research on performance in *non*military occupations, and the result was an attempt to offer a model of performance that was relevant for the entire labor force.

A Model of Occupational Performance

Performance is defined as behavior at work that is judged to be relevant for the organization's goals. Also, such behaviors, or actions, can be scaled in terms of how much they contribute to the attainment of such goals. By this model, performance assessment must focus on observable actions (for example, writing a proposal) that are under the control of the individual. The consequences of such actions (that is, results, the bottom line, and so forth) are not synonymous with individual performance if they also depend on other sources of variation that are not under the control of the individual. For example, differences in total sales could also be a function of differences in sales territories or product lines. Performance measurement should assess the individual's contribution in as pure a way as possible. This is *not* an argument that the bottom line (that is, total sales, value of contracts won) is not important. It represents organizational effectiveness, and we would hope that individual performance has a direct influence on it. If not, the job needs redesigning.

What's underappreciated about this specification is that whether a specific action constitutes a performance behavior, and if so, whether it represents a high level or low level of performance, is very much a value judgment on someone's part. This centrality of goals means that goal-conflict and goal-ignorance become very relevant issues. Whether or not a president (or plumber) is judged to be a high performer or low performer is very much a function of the goals for the position. This is not a cop-out. There can be very legitimate alternative views of what an organization's goals should be.

The Major Components of Performance

Given these considerations, my colleagues and I proposed an eight-component model for describing the basic composition of work performance in the entire labor force (see Table 1). The components are intended to be substantively distinct and should not be aggregated further. That is, useful distinctions would be covered up if we simply added them up and called the total "overall performance." For any given occupation, not all components are operative (for example, supervision/leadership might not be part of the job of taxi driver), but very frequently more of the eight are relevant than you might anticipate. Think of the management and supervisory responsibilities imposed on research scientists. In addition to scientific proficiency (component 1), they frequently must lead and manage a research group (components 7 and 8).

TABLE 1 A Taxonomy of Higher-Order Performance Components

1. **Job-specific task proficiency:** Reflects the degree to which the individual performs the core substantive or technical tasks that are central to his or her job.

2. **Non-job-specific task proficiency:** In virtually every organization, individuals are required to perform tasks that are not specific to their particular job (for example, all faculty must teach).

3. **Written and oral communication:** Proficiency at making oral or written presentations to audiences of any size, independent of subject matter expertise.

4. **Demonstrating effort:** The frequency with which people expend extra time when required, and their willingness to keep working under adverse conditions.

5. **Counterproductive work behavior:** Characterized by the degree to which negative behavior, such as substance abuse at work, law or rule infractions, and excessive absenteeism, is avoided.

6. **Facilitating peer and team performance:** The degree to which the individual supports his or her peers, helps them with job problems, acts as a de facto trainer, and facilitates group functioning.

7. **Supervision/leadership:** Influencing the performance of subordinates through face-to-face interaction and influence (for example, setting goals, teaching more effective methods, modeling appropriate behaviors, being supportive in appropriate ways).

8. **Management/administration:** The major elements of management that are distinct from direct supervision (for example, articulating unit goals, organizing people and resources to work on them, monitoring progress, helping to control expenditures, representing the unit in dealings with other units).

The eight components emerged from performance analyses in many different civilian occupations, from our work in Project A, and from decades of research on supervision, leadership, and management (Borman & Brush, 1993; Yukl, 1998). The factors are meant to be consistent with the entirety of the research literature on these matters. For example, during the last 20 years, component 5 has generated dozens of studies, and excellent portrayals of its subfactors have been developed (see, for example, Gruys & Sackett, 2003). Models of subfactors for peer and team support, supervision/leadership, and management have also been developed.

Now, you might ask, how can this sound so normative if the organization's value judgments play such a big role? Don't different organizations have different ideas about what constitutes performance in different jobs? An answer is that *at this level of factor generality* a consensus does, in fact, exist. Some of it was hard-won, and some stakeholders still may not buy into certain notions, such as the value of some of the subfactors of leadership and management that research has delineated. For example, over 60 years of research shows that such things as showing consideration for subordinates and providing employees opportunities for development and achievement contribute to organizational effectiveness in a positive way. The managers who still believe that CEOs must be dictatorial and ruthless might disagree, but they are simply wrong.

The Determinants of Performance

This model of performance goes a bit further and proposes two levels of performance determinants: The independent variables that account for individual differences on a particular performance dimension can be sorted into direct determinants and indirect determinants. The latter can affect performance *only* through their effects on the former, no ifs, ands, or buts. Further, there are only three direct determinants: specific job knowledge, specific job skills, and specific choices about how you want to allocate your effort (some would call that your "motivation"). Everything else must influence performance by working through these three (that is, by changing an individual's specific job knowledge and/or skill level or their effort allocation choices).

The indirect determinants of performance are legion (for example, abilities, personality, interests, pay level, knowledge and skill acquired in school or on previous jobs, self-efficacy, and so forth); however, they can only affect performance by influencing job-specific knowledge and skills or choice behavior. People with higher cognitive ability might acquire more job-specific knowledge and skill, or certain personality types might be more likely to choose to work harder for longer periods. The available research is quite supportive of these causal sequences (Campbell, Gasser, & Oswald, 1996). Also, the summative effects of the direct determinants could result from a variety of combinatorial rules. For example, the more expert your knowledge and skill levels become, the more likely you may be to choose more difficult work assignments.

Some Important Implications

The model has some important implications that, if forgotten, invite confusion and mistaken judgments about individual work performance. First, never use the word in the singular. Performance is not one thing and although the correlations among the factors are not zero, they are far from 1.0. Pay close attention to an individual's relative performance on the various factors. This admonition applies to (1) research on performance prediction (that is, how do predictions vary across factors), (2) the development of education and training programs (for example, how to best train the technical factors versus how to best train peer leadership), and (3) the implementation of performance appraisals.

Second, always maintain the distinction between performance itself and the consequences, or results, of performance. We want measures of performance to reflect the knowledge, skill, and motivational choices of the individual and not be contaminated by differences in available resources, the mistakes of higher management, or other factors that are not under the individual's control. For example, should the performance of public school teachers be assessed via computing the average scores of their students on standardized national tests of achievement in basic skills? Not if such scores are also influenced (as they most certainly are) by characteristics that the teacher cannot control, such as the percent of native English speakers in the classroom and the quality of the students' home environment. Should we assess the performance of physicians by attaining bottom-line data on such things as death rates, number of patients seen per hour, or per patient cost of treatment? Not if the most serious cases are taken on by the most expert physicians nor if the death rates are influenced by any of a number of other factors not under the physician's control. Should the performance of a municipal bus driver be assessed via the number of stops that are made on time? Not if different drivers on different routes must deal with differences in traffic demands.

If results are so often a function of factors beyond the individual's control, then how should performance be assessed? Performance assessment must be an evaluation of how well the individual carries out the critical behaviors or actions that the performance factors require. How well does a teacher utilize appropriate instructional methods? How expertly does a physician investigate the symptoms presented by the patient? Sometimes such assessments can be made using simulations and work samples, but more often they must be made using the expert judgments of peers or supervisors who have had ample opportunity to observe the individual's performance.

Something you might think about is the use of student evaluations as indicators for instructor performance. What are the major factors that make up instructor performance? Which factors are assessed by student evaluations? Which are not? Whose value judgments are critical here?

Models of Undergraduate Performance

To get even closer to home, suppose we raise these same issues with regard to undergraduate performance. What are the major factors comprising undergraduate performance? Does GPA say it all? Is there a distinction between student performance and its outcomes? Whose value judgments are relevant?

Although there has always been pressure to go beyond GPA as the sole indicator of student performance, only a few investigators have tried to do so in any systematic way. Frederick L. Oswald and his colleagues (2004) took the faculty/administrator perspective and used published statements of goals and missions by colleges and universities to distill a summary taxonomy of performance capabilities the institutions wanted undergraduates to have when they finished their degree. Nathan R. Kuncel and his colleagues (2005) adopted the student perspective and asked several samples of students from three different universities to describe several specific examples of what they considered to be good performance and also several examples of what they considered to be poor performance on the part of undergraduates. This is the critical incident method of performance analysis. Each incident represents an example of either good or poor performance, given the operative value system of the person describing the incident. Several panels of judges then independently sorted the several hundred examples into categories, such that the categories (now called dimensions, or components, of performance) contained incidents that were judged similar in content within a category but dissimilar between categories (for example, critical incidents reflecting conventional classroom performance versus critical incidents reflecting social relationship performance outside the classroom).

The critical incident method was used extensively in Project A to develop a picture of the performance requirements for enlisted personnel. Here the goal is to develop a multidimensional picture of undergraduate performance requirements. The results, in terms of the performance dimensions, or components, that best seem to represent all the good and bad critical incidents that students described in the Kuncel et al. study, are shown in Table 2. In effect, this portrayal says that the job of a student is to excel on each of the dimensions. It is the value judgments of students that determined which performance behaviors are critical and the degree to which each incident reflects effective or ineffective undergraduate performance within each of the dimensions.

Again, the dimensions portrayed in Table 2 constitute the full array of distinguishable components of undergraduate performance, as judged by students themselves. Components 1, 2, 4, 5, 6, 7, 9, and 10 have direct analogies in the model of occupational performance my colleagues and I developed (Campbell et al., 1993). Components 3, 8, and 11 seem relatively unique to the role of student.

If Table 2 represents student performance, what then are the consequences of performance? Again, the answer depends on goals, but the bottom line could be accomplishments like getting a particular job, being admitted to a particular graduate or professional school, or establishing a life-long commitment to a specific person. Keep in mind that many other things can determine the bottom line in addition to performance as a student. Do not make them synonymous.

Finally, if you are interested in learning more about the specifications for undergraduate performance requirements that were produced by examining the goals and mission statements written by university faculty and administrators, read the Oswald article referenced at the end of this essay. Considering the different sources for the Kuncel and Oswald models, their similarity is amazing. The only differences are that faculty and administrators (Oswald model) make the requirement to learn leadership skills a bit more explicit

---

TABLE 2 Components of Undergraduate Student Performance

(From critical incidents described by students)

1. **Traditional classroom success**: Doing well (or poorly) in coursework.

2. **Self-discipline/counterproductive behavior**: Like its occupational counterpart, this factor reflects substance abuse, poor attendance, being too distracted by other activities.

3. **Studying and learning proficiency**: The expertise with which the student goes about finding information, deciding what is important, and using good strategies to master the knowledge and skill judged to be important.

4. **Goal-directed effort**: The sheer amount of time and energy the student invests.

5. **Self-management of financial resources and career progress**: Planning the academic program, seeking advice, staying within a budget.

6. **Interpersonal and social skills**: Being able to establish friendships, work in teams, resolve conflicts with other students, be supportive of students who are experiencing difficulties.

7. **Written and oral communication**: The capability to speak effectively to audiences and groups or classes and to communicate effectively in writing.

8. **Nonclassroom performance**: Volunteer or club activities, internships, tutoring, etc.

9. **Openness**: Practicing tolerance for, and openness to, new ideas, alternative opinions and beliefs, different cultures and languages. Staying informed about current events.

10. **Determination of one's academic/career path**: Exploring occupations and careers using many sources, changing goals when it best serves newly developed interests, seeking to do what you really want to do.

11. **Extra learning**: Engaging in learning activities independent of class or college requirements, with the goal of learning more about a topic.

---

and also isolate development of an appreciation for art and culture as a separate performance component. It's not all GPA from either point of view.

Conclusion

I am suggesting in this essay that individual performance at work is a critical dependent variable in the study of human behavior and that the more clearly we can "model" this domain of behavior the better. Such modeling will lead to better prediction of future performance, better performance training, and better policy decisions (for example, how to pay teachers for performance). These kinds of performance issues are addressed within I/O psychology, and the field has reached some degree of consensus about how performance should be defined and measured, what the basic components of occupational performance are, and why (1) performance itself, (2) the results of performance, and (3) the determinants of performance should be carefully distinguished. Finally, the similarities between the components of occupational performance and the components of student performance in higher education invite the following assertion: One really is preparation for the other, on several dimensions, literally.

Suggested Further Reading

Campbell, J. P., Gasser, M.B., & Oswald, F. L. (1996). The substantive nature of job performance variability. In K. R. Murphy (Ed.), *Individual differences and behavior in organizations* (pp. 258–299). San Francisco: Jossey-Bass.

Vey, M. A., & Campbell, J. P. (2004). In-role versus extra-role organizational citizenship behaviors. *Human Performance, 17,* 119–135.

References

Austin, J. T., & Villanova, P. (1992). The criterion problem: 1917–1992. *Journal of Applied Psychology, 77,* 836–874.

Borman, W. C., & Brush, D. H. (1993). More progress toward a taxonomy of managerial performance requirements. *Human Performance, 6,* 1–22.

Campbell, J. P., Gasser, M. B., & Oswald, F. L. (1996). The substantive nature of job performance variability. In K.R. Murphy (Ed.), *Individual differences and behavior in organizations* (pp. 258–299). San Francisco: Jossey-Bass.

Campbell, J. P., & Knapp, D. (2001). *Exploring the limits of personnel selection and classification.* Hillsdale, NJ: Erlbaum.

Campbell, J. P., McCloy, R. A., Oppler, S. H., & Sager, C. E. (1993). A theory of performance. In N. Schmitt & W. C. Borman (Eds.), *Frontiers in industrial /organizational psychology: Personnel selection and classification* (pp. 35–71). San Francisco: Jossey-Bass.

Gruys, M. L., & Sackett, P. R. (2003). Investigating the dimensionality of counterproductive work behavior. *International Journal of Selection and Assessment, 11,* 30–42.

Kuncel, N. R., Drasgow, F., Klieger, D. M., & Seiler, S. N. (2005). *Report on measuring student performance: Development of a computer adaptive rating system.* Department of Psychology, University of Illinois at Urbana-Champaign.

Oswald, F. L., Schmitt, N. Kim, B. H., Ramsay, L. J., & Gillespie, M. A. (2004). Developing a biodata measure and situational judgment inventory as predictors of college student performance. *Journal of Applied Psychology, 89,* 187–207.

Thorndike, R. L. (1949). *Personnel selection: Test and measurement techniques.* New York:Wiley.

Yukl, G. (1998). *Leadership in organizations* (4th ed.). Englewood Cliffs, NJ: Prentice-Hall.

Organizational Climate: Theory and Evidence
Benjamin Schneider
Valtera Corporation and University of Maryland

▶ *Please describe your current position and research interests.*
I am currently Senior Research Fellow at Valtera Corporation, an international human resources consulting firm located in Rolling Meadows, Illinois. I am simultaneously Professor Emeritus in Psychology at the University of Maryland. My research interests are in (1) organizational climate and culture, (2) employee engagement, and (3) the role of personality in organizational life.

▶ *How did you get interested in organizational climates?*
I learned early in my graduate training (Ph.D., Maryland) that industrial/organizational (I/O) psychology is basically all about individual differences, especially as it is applied to personnel selection. Yet, I was interested in the effects of environments on people and looked for ways to integrate both the environmental piece and the individual differences piece. For the environment, I discovered the work of Kurt Lewin on social climates and thought it a useful construct around which to integrate the environment into I/O research while still retaining a focus on people.

▶ *What has been the real-world impact of this work?*
Numerous practitioners have adopted the climate construct as a basis for their work. For example, Warner Burke, both an academic and a practitioner, uses climate as a basic construct in his work with companies on organizational change. In addition, at Valtera we are doing several projects with clients who are trying to become more competitive through improving customer satisfaction via improvements in service climate.

People in work environments share a sense of what's important and what the focus of their energy and talent should be. We call that shared perception "organizational climate." On a production-line factory job, for example, is the focus on safety or productivity, or both? In a retail store, is the focus on fighting to make the most sales, providing high-quality service to customers, or both? The answers to such questions become evident through the policies, practices, and procedures under which people work and the kinds of behaviors that are rewarded, supported, and expected.

In applied psychology, especially in industrial and organizational psychology, we are interested in understanding what leads employees to behave in the ways they do. In particular, we are concerned with employee behaviors that help the organization compete successfully in the marketplace so that the firm's employees, the customers, and shareholders can all benefit. Making all of these partners ("stakeholders") to organizations feel good about the company is difficult but doable when the right kind of organizational climate is created.

A Brief History of the Study of Organizational Climate

In the late 1930s, Kurt Lewin (1890–1947) and his colleagues undertook experimental research on group behavior that had a profound impact on theory and practice in the field of organizational psychology. Their study of the "social climate" of boys' groups demonstrated that boys who worked under a democratic leadership style were as productive as those who were taught under authoritarian conditions. Of considerable interest was the finding that under democratic leadership conditions, the boys behaved more cooperatively with each other and more openly with the teacher (leader), experienced less stress, and appeared to have more positive feelings about their experience. The researchers saw the different leadership styles as tactics for creating a sense in the boys of how they should behave—cooperatively versus competitively—and feel—positive versus negative. The democratic leader accomplished this without telling the boys how to behave or what to feel; they sensed it based on the leader's behavior (Lewin, Lippitt, & White, 1939).

Lewin's background as a Gestalt psychologist enabled him to predict that the experimentally induced social climate would have this effect. *Gestalt* literally means "whole," and the theory says that every detail need not be present for us to get a sense of what the whole is and means. When we undergo experiences, we "fill in the blanks." Thus, we only need to hear a few notes from a familiar song to be able to "hear" the rest, even though it has not, in fact, been played. Similarly, when we see only a part of a picture, we fill in what is missing to make the picture a "whole."

Although Lewin was interested in how young boys behave and feel when confronted with a specific leadership style, applied psychologists saw great potential in his notion of social climate as an avenue leading to increased understanding of the behavior and attitudes of people in the workplace. In fact, most of the early studies of organizational climate focused on social climate—that is, on the degree to which people cooperate with each other and their leaders and the degree to which they feel more or less positive about their work and workplace. But, unfortunately, findings from this early climate research shed little light on the researchers' main interest: how to improve organizational effectiveness.

Several conceptual and methodological problems were implicated in the failure of the early research. First, from a conceptual standpoint, applied psychologists imagined that by creating a positive social climate, employees would naturally behave more effectively in pursuit of organizational goals. Although employees did feel more positively about their workplace and their colleagues, they did not work harder nor were they more productive. In thinking about this issue, I reasoned that the lack of focus on important organizational outcomes was critical; more than a social climate was needed if employees were to get a sense of the workplace issues on which they should be focusing. I proposed that climates had to be climates *for* something (for example, service, safety, or innovation). Messages telling workers to feel positive about their company and feel less stress were not enough to engender appropriate performance (Schneider, 1975).

Second, numerous methodological flaws compromised the early research. Perhaps most important, organizational climate experiences were collected from *individual* employees, and those perceptions were used as correlates of *individual* performance. This methodological decision carried with it the implicit assumption that the basis for employees' organizational climate perceptions is their individual attitudes and opinions rather than their observations of what actually is happening to them and to their colleagues and what is going on around them. If climate perceptions are simply individual attitudes and opinions, then they are useful for understanding individual behavior but not organizational performance.

In an influential discussion of climate attributes, a crucial distinction was proposed between individual perceptions of climate, called "psychological climate," and perceptions in the aggregate, called "organizational climate" (James & Jones, 1974). In the aggregate, it was argued, organizational climate would have a significant relationship to organizational outcomes. The researchers presented some evidence to support this idea, but it was not very strong because their assessment device focused primarily on social climate. Thus, although their assessment was at the appropriate level of analysis, it still did not have the kind of focus that I had indicated was necessary.

Levels-of-Analysis Issues

The issue of levels of analysis is an interesting one in psychology in general and in I/O in particular. People, including psychologists, usually think of psychology as the study of individual behavior. But in I/O, we are also concerned with the behavior of teams, bank branches, hospital units, and sales units, and indeed, whole organizations. This is not to say that I/O is not interested in individuals. Most of I/O research and practice focuses on personnel selection and performance management of individuals.

Individuals as collectives, however, dominate performance outcomes in organizations. And, interestingly, the leader (manager, supervisor) to whom a group of employees report typically defines those collectives. In banks, we find branch managers; in retail stores, sales managers; in supermarkets, department managers; in hospital units, head nurses; and so forth. When we use the term *organizational climate* to describe the experience of employees in these kinds of work groups, we are dealing with a unit of analysis smaller than a whole organization but not so small as the individual worker.

Shared Climate Perceptions

You may be saying to yourself: Isn't this a fairly fruitless task? If researchers ask employees to report on what happens in a unit and what the focus is, won't there be a high level of disagreement? Can the researchers really aggregate across people's differing perceptions? If individuals are asked questions about their own activities and focus, then little agreement across people in a unit can be expected. However, if respondents are asked to report on what happens to the *team* and *its focus*—that is, what happens on the frontlines of the unit—typically, there is good agreement (Bliese, 2000), and aggregation of views across people in a unit is methodologically meaning-ful. Good agreement across respondents is likely for several reasons:

1. People who work together talk about what happens to them and what happens around them; they share similar experiences and ob-servations. Few people work alone, and few fail to schmooze about their work place. Instead, people often share and agree about their perceptions. The sharing of perceptions has been called "social con-struction" (Berger & Luckman, 1966) and "team mental models" (Rentsch & Klimoski, 2001). Whatever the term, it refers to agree-ment (not total agreement, but considerable similarity) in percep-tions of the setting.

2. People who work in the same job tend to share common interests, personality, and competencies, so a shared view of their work world is not surprising. People self-select into settings where other people are similar to them, where people share occupational interests (Hol-land, 1997), and where people share personality characteristics (Schneider, Smith, Taylor, & Fleenor, 1998).

People tend to share numerous characteristics when they arrive at a set-ting, and they talk about their experiences in the setting. It follows therefore that they will provide similar reports about what the setting is like—and about the focus of the setting.

A Focused Climate: Service Climate

Imagine that you own a theme park or a department store, and you want to create an environment in which customers will have a very positive experi-ence. You might decide to visit a Disney theme park and Nordstrom depart-ment store to see what they do and how they create positive experiences. You learn from talking to employees of these companies that the firms do many things that emphasize service quality: They hire service-oriented people; they reward and recognize high-quality service to customers; they track and measure customer experiences; they provide employees with the resources they need to deliver high-quality service; and so forth. Then, returning to your firm, you're curious about how your employees rate your firm's focus on service quality: You want to know the level of a service climate that exists for your employees.

Employers have been asking their workers to report on the level of serv-ice-focused polices and routines for more than 25 years (Schneider & White, 2004). Significantly, these surveys show that service climate is associated with customer satisfaction in branch banks, hotels, supermarkets, retail or-ganizations, restaurants, and other kinds of service organizations. Recently, colleagues and I, working with companies representing finance, retail, air-lines, information technology, and two other service industries, found that service climate is associated with a national customer satisfaction index called the American Customer Satisfaction Index (Schneider, Macey, Lee, & Young, 2009). In other words, based on what *employees* report about their company's focus on service quality, we can predict what their *customers* will say about their satisfaction in dealing with the company. Table 1 shows some sample items from a service climate survey (Schneider, White, & Paul, 1998).

TABLE 1 Service Climate Survey Items

- How would you rate the job knowledge and skills of employees in your business to deliver superior quality service?

- How would you rate efforts to measure and track the quality of service in your business?

- How would you rate the recognition and rewards employees receive for the delivery of superior service?

- How would you rate the overall quality of service provided by your business?

- How would you rate the leadership shown by management in your business in supporting the service quality effort?

- How would you rate the effectiveness of our communications efforts to both employees and customers?

- How would you rate the tools, technology, and other resources provided to employees to support the delivery of superior quality service?

Note: Respondents rate each item on a 1 to 5 scale of excellence for how things are in their unit or company: 1=Excellent, 2=Very Good, 3=Good, 4=Fair, and 5=Poor. A service climate score comes from averaging the responses to this collection of items. From Schneider, White, and Paul (1998, p. 154), slightly modified. © American Psychological Association.

Note that the items in Table 1 do not cover *everything* that could inform employees to focus on service quality. However, from Gestalt psychology we know that people fill in the blanks when they observe only part of the picture. Seven or so questions about a variety of policies and routines produce a reliable index of service climate. Note also in Table 1 that all but one of the survey items contains the words *service* and *quality*, so we know that employees are reporting about routines and rewards related to service quality and not about something else. My colleagues and my research on service climate is only one example of such research.

A Focused Climate: Safety Climate

Dov Zohar has been studying safety climate for many years and has shown that when employees report a positive safety climate, their units have low accident rates (see, for example, Zohar, 2000). Like Lewin, Zohar developed a model for the study of climate in which leadership behavior is key. Table 2 shows a sample of items he has used to study safety climate. As can be seen, in contrast to Lewin's focus on leadership *style* (democratic, authoritarian), Zohar asks about leadership *focus*.

TABLE 2 Safety Climate Survey Items
• My supervisor says a good word whenever he sees a job done according to the safety rules.
• My supervisor seriously considers any worker's suggestions for improving safety.
• My supervisor approaches workers during work to discuss safety issues.
• My supervisor gets annoyed with any worker ignoring safety rules, even minor rules.
• My supervisor watches more often when a worker has violated some safety rule.
• As long as there is no accident, my supervisor doesn't care how the work is done (R).
• Whenever pressure builds up, my supervisor wants us to work faster, rather than by the rules (R).
• My supervisor pays less attention to safety problems than most other supervisors in this company (R).
• My supervisor only keeps track of major safety problems and overlooks routine problems (R).
• As long as work remains on schedule, my supervisor doesn't care how this has been achieved (R).

Note: The letter R after an item indicates that it was reverse-scored such that a low score is positive. Respondents rate each item on a 1 to 5 agree–disagree scale: 1=Completely Disagree, 2=Disagree, 3=Neither Agree or Disagree, 4=Agree, and 5=Completely Agree. A safety climate score comes from averaging the responses to this collection of items. From Zohar (2000, p. 591), slightly modified. © American Psychological Association.

Note in Table 2 that Zohar's safety climate survey, like the service climate survey, does not ask about *everything* that might send the safety message; employees fill in the blanks to make sense about what is important based on activities like those in the items. Zohar's research is only one example of safety climate work.

Conclusion

Employees obtain a sense of what is important in organizations based on the focus of their organization's routines and rewards and the behavioral goals their leaders target. Consistency in the focus or target sends employees a message, and agreement with that message is likely when employees have opportunities to talk with one another and if their attributes are similar.

Employees, when asked to report on what happens in their workplace, provide reliable and valid responses about the place, not "opinions" or "attitudes" that are unique to them. We know they report reliably because others in the same setting report similarly, and we know the reports are valid because they relate to customer satisfaction and accident rates—two kinds of data that are independent from the employees' reports on climate.

Employee reports provide useful input into changes organizations can make to improve their effectiveness. Just as the employer in our example compared information from visits to Disney and Nordstrom with survey data from the home company's employees, so analyses of survey data clarify issues that can raise climate scores and, thus, increase an organization's effectiveness.

Although business organizations frequently use employee opinion or attitude surveys (sometimes called climate surveys), these surveys tend not to focus on important organizational outcomes and, therefore, are not always as useful as they could be. In addition, opinion or attitude surveys are not as strongly related to organizational effectiveness as are focused climate surveys. The key to having a useful employee survey is to ask about routines and rewards that focus on an important outcome—like customer satisfaction and safety.

Suggested Further Reading

Schneider, B., Ehrhart, M. G., & Macey, W. H. (2009). Perspectives on organizational climate and culture. In S. Zedeck (Ed.), *Handbook of industrial and organizational psychology*. Washington, DC: American Psychological Association.

Ostroff, C., Kinicki, A. J., & Tamkins, M. M. (2003). Organizational culture and climate. In W. C. Borman, D. R. Ilgen, & R. J. Klimoski (Eds.), *Handbook of psychology, Vol. 12: I/O psychology* (pp. 565–593). New York: Wiley.

References

Berger, P. L., & Luckman, T. (1966). *The social construction of reality: A treatise in the sociology of knowledge*. Garden City, NY: Doubleday.

Bliese, P. D. (2000). Within-group agreement, non-independence, and reliability implications for data aggregation and analyses. In Klein, K. J., & Kozlowski, S. W. J. (Eds.), *Multilevel theory, research, and methods in organizations: Foundations, extensions, and new directions* (pp. 349–381). San Francisco: Jossey-Bass.

Holland, J. L. (1997). *Making vocational choices: A theory of vocational personalities and work environments* (3rd ed.). Odessa, FL: PAR.

James, L. R., & Jones, A. P. (1974). Organizational climate: A review of theory and research. *Psychological Bulletin, 81*, 1096–1112.

Lewin, K., Lippitt, R., & White, R. K. (1939). Patterns of aggressive behavior in experimentally created "social climates." *Journal of Social Psychology, 10*, 271–299.

Rentsch, J. R., & Klimoski, R. (2001). Why do "great minds" think alike? Antecedents of team member schema agreement. *Journal of Organizational Behavior, 22*, 107–120.

Schneider, B. (1975). Organizational climates: An essay. *Personnel Psychology, 28*, 447–479.

Schneider, B., Macey, W. H., Lee, W. C., & Young, S. A. (2009). Organizational service climate drivers of the American Customer Satisfaction Index (ACSI) and financial and market performance. *Journal of Service Research, 12* (1), 3–14.

Schneider, B., Smith, D. B., Taylor, S., & Fleenor, J. (1998). Personality and organizations: A test of the homogeneity of personality hypothesis. *Journal of Applied Psychology, 83*, 462–470.

Schneider, B., & White, S. S. (2004). *Service quality: Research perspectives*. Thousand Oaks, CA: Sage.

Schneider, B., White, S. S., & Paul, M. C. (1998). Linking service climate and customer perceptions of service quality: Test of a causal model. *Journal of Applied Psychology, 83,* 150–163.

Zohar, D. (2000). A group-level model of safety climate: Testing the effects of group climate on micro-accidents in manufacturing jobs. *Journal of Applied Psychology, 85,* 587–596.

QUESTIONS FOR DISCUSSION

Chapter 1: Introduction

James R. Pomerantz and Morton Ann Gernsbacher
Psychology and the Real World: An Introduction

The editors chose the contributors to this volume because the contributors' work demonstrates that critical thinking and a scientific approach can solve real-world problems. What other qualities of mind are important in an effective researcher?

What drew you to psychology, and how do you expect what you learn to influence your personal goals, skills, values, and development?

Chapter 2: Methods of Psychology

John H. Krantz
Can the World Wide Web Be Used for Research?

What does John Krantz mean by the term *validity,* and how does his use of the term compare with standard textbook definitions?

The Psychological Research on the Net Web site is a rich source of data for participants as well as for researchers. Visit the site and become a subject. Afterward, ask yourself what you learned about psychological research and about yourself.

Paul R. Sackett
Integrity Testing for Personnel Selection:
The Role of Research Methods

The research that Paul Sackett describes took place in the field and in researchers' laboratories. What are the advantages and disadvantages of each type of setting?

A premise underlying pre-employment integrity testing is that paper-and-pencil test results can predict real-world behavior. Think of arguments to support and contradict that notion.

Chapter 3: Neuroscience

Bruce S. McEwen
Neurobiology of Stress and Adaptation: Implications for
Health Psychology, Behavioral Medicine, and Beyond

Explain the paradox implicit in Bruce McEwen's "allostatic load" concept. How is the concept useful in understanding certain health outcomes?

Compared with friends and family, how intense is your response to stress? What factors in your life trigger stress?

Michael I. Posner and Mary K. Rothbart
Applying the Mechanisms of Self-Regulation

How does Michael Posner's and Mary Rothbart's research add to our understanding of the interaction of genes and environment in determining human behavior?

Explain the connection between good self-regulatory abilities and successful school performance.

Chapter 4: Sensation and Perception

Donald D. Hoffman
Human Vision as a Reality Engine

Donald Hoffman uses illusions to illustrate his argument that vision is a species-specific survival tool. Look back at Figures 1 and 2; think of other familiar illusions our reality engine creates. How do they contribute to human survival?

People in virtual-reality environments begin to act as if they are experiencing the real world. To what kinds of therapeutic and educational interventions might this tendency lend itself?

Jeremy M. Wolfe
Visual Search: Is It a Matter of Life and Death?

How does Jeremy Wolfe's notion of a "prevalence effect" explain errors made by people trained to be accurate screeners?

You're searching for a lost possession, something unusual—say, a bottle of hot sauce in a crowded refrigerator or a volume of poetry among a pile of books. Unlike an airport baggage screener, your search will be made *easier* by the item's low prevalence. Why?

Chapter 5: Learning

Elizabeth L. Bjork and Robert Bjork
Making Things Hard on Yourself, But in a Good Way:
Creating Desirable Difficulties to Enhance Learning

What is the difference between a "desirable difficulty" and an "undesirable difficulty," and how do Elizabeth Bjork and Robert Bjork demonstrate that the former aids learning?

Reflect on undesirable difficulties typical of your own study habits. What kinds of learning do they impede? What might you substitute?

Henry L. Roediger, III, Kathleen B. McDermott,
and Mark A. McDaniel
Using Testing to Improve Learning and Memory

Henry Roediger, Kathleen McDermott, and Mark McDaniel have shown that testing and retesting is a more effective way to learn than is studying and restudying. Why is that so?

Can you imagine *ever* asking an instructor for more tests? In what subjects do you think it would be helpful?

Chapter 6: Memory
Fergus I. M. Craik
Levels of Processing in Human Memory

What evidence supports Fergus Craik's theory that a deeper level of processing is associated with better memory performance?

Imagine yourself learning a foreign language or the vocabulary of a scientific discipline. What methods of elaboration would you use to enrich your memory for the new words?

Elizabeth F. Loftus
Crimes of Memory: False Memories and Societal Justice

Elizabeth Loftus has said, "[W]hat we think we know, what we believe with all our hearts, is not necessarily the truth." What is her evidence that misinformation can invade our memories?

Think of a distorted memory in your own life. What led to its creation? How did you learn it was false? What has been its impact on you and on others?

Chapter 7: Language and Thought
Susan Goldin-Meadow
Creating and Learning Language by Hand

How do Susan Goldin-Meadow's findings support the idea that humans are born with an innate capacity to learn language?

Why might hearing parents *not* want their deaf children to learn sign language?

Herbert S. Terrace
Thinking Without Language

Why did Herbert Terrace choose macaques for his experimental subjects, and what cognitive-perceptual capacities underlie their remarkable ability to engage in high-level tasks without the aid of language?

The issue of ape language remains a controversial topic in psychology. Where do you stand, and what piece of evidence most persuaded you to take this stance?

Chapter 8: Consciousness

Bernard J. Baars
Thinking About Consciousness

For decades, Bernard Baars has argued that the scientific study of consciousness is possible. Why does he think mainstream psychology resisted his argument?

Imagine driving your car on a familiar route and on one that's unfamiliar. To what extent is consciousness involved in each task and what is its function?

Daniel M. Wegner
When You Put Things Out of Mind, Where Do They Go?

Explain why Daniel Wegner in his technical writings calls the strategies that people use to control their own minds "ironic processes."

What lessons does research on unwanted thoughts have for people who are concerned about their weight and are considering dieting?

Chapter 9: Intelligence

Howard Gardner
The Theory of Multiple Intelligences

Resistance to Howard Gardner's theory of multiple intelligences has focused on the absence of statistical supporting data. What other kinds of data support his ideas?

You and seven other people get lost on a day-long trip. Imagine that you each excel in one of Gardner's intelligences. What methods would you use to find your way home?

Robert J. Sternberg
The Rainbow Project: Using a Psychological Theory of Intelligence to Improve the College Admissions Process

Robert Sternberg has said, "[A]bilities are not fixed but rather flexible . . . and anyone can transform their abilities into competencies, and their competencies into expertise." How is his point of view reflected in his theory and research?

Think of situations in which analytic abilities might actually interfere with successful functioning.

Chapter 10: Emotion and Motivation

Paul Ekman and David Matsumoto
Reading Faces: The Universality of Emotional Expression

In the course of his long career, response to the work of Paul Ekman has shifted from rejection to widespread acceptance. What changes in the field of psychology and in the social world are responsible for this change?

What are some practical advantages that result from emotions and their expression being the same for everyone everywhere?

E. Tory Higgins
Human Self-Regulation and Emotion

What is Tory Higgins's evidence that evaluating ourselves against inner standards can produce emotional states that have long-term consequences?

Experiencing discrepancies between how we see ourselves and how we want to be creates problems for most people. What have you learned that could be helpful in dealing with such difficulties?

Chapter 11: Development

Barbara Rogoff, Maricela Correa-Chávez, and Katie G. Silva
Cultural Variation in Children's Attention and Learning

What evidence do Barbara Rogoff, Maricela Correa-Chávez, and Katie Silva have that cultural and educational differences affect parenting styles?

How have practices in your own cultural community influenced your personal development?

Carolyn Rovee-Collier
Preserving Infant Memories

What is Carolyn Rovee-Collier's evidence that memories are preserved even in very early infancy?

What is your earliest true memory, and what age were you when the event occurred? Can you think of reasons why earlier memories are not accessible?

Chapter 12: Personality

Mark Snyder
Products of Their Personalities or Creatures of Their Situations? Personality and Social Behavior Have the Answer

Explain how Mark Snyder's research supports Kurt Lewin's famous statement, "Every psychological event depends upon the state of the person and at the same time on the environment, although their relative importance is different in different cases."

Consider an important choice that you recently made. How was it influenced by personal dispositions and how was it influenced by the situation in which you found yourself?

Chapter 13: Psychological Disorders

Irving I. Gottesman
Predisposed to Understand the Complex Origins of Behavioral Variation

In his classic study with James Shields, what evidence did Irving Gottesman develop that genetics influences people's susceptibility to schizophrenia?

How has psychiatric genetics brought relief to people worried about mental illness "running in their family?"

Susan Nolen-Hoeksema
Lost in Thought: The Perils of Rumination

Susan Nolen-Hoeksema's research explores the dangers of thinking too much. What keeps people in a cycle of rumination, and what can they do about it?

How does rumination affect people's relationships with others?

Chapter 14: Treatment of Psychological Disorders

David H. Barlow
The Development and Evaluation of Psychological Treatments for Panic Disorder

How does David Barlow's research on panic disorder demonstrate the value of science in directing effective treatment interventions for emotional disorders?

How serious are panic attacks? What are the consequences for those who have them?

Varda Shoham and Michael J. Rohrbaugh
Looking Beyond the Patient: A Couple-Focused Intervention for Health-Compromised Smokers

Explain the theory that underlies Varda Shoham and Michael Rohrbaugh's approach to smoking-cessation treatment and how it informs their exploration of new intervention strategies.

What other health-compromising behaviors might be amenable to their therapeutic approach?

Chapter 15: Stress and Health

Peter Salovey
Framing Health Messages

Explain what "framing" is and how Peter Salovey has exploited its power in his research on health-protecting behaviors.

Think of circumstances in which a carefully framed message enticed you into behavior that, in retrospect, seems risky.

Shelley E. Taylor
Positive Illusions: How Ordinary People Become Extraordinary

What is Shelley Taylor's evidence for the psychological benefits of positive illusions in people dealing with stressful life problems?

Are you superstitious? Do you check an astrology column when times are tough? Do you engage in any kind of "magical" thinking? Explain how beliefs that others might describe as illusions have had an impact on your life.

Chapter 16: Social Psychology

Elliot Aronson
Reducing Prejudice and Building Empathy in the Classroom

As Elliot Aronson demonstrated, cooperation can reduce intergroup conflict. What conditions did he set up in his experiment that made cooperation work?

Interdependence reduced prejudice and improved performance in jigsaw classrooms. Can you think of other real-world contexts in which cooperation can break down social barriers?

Harry T. Reis
When Good Things Happen to Good People: Capitalizing on Personal Positive Events in Relationships

How does Harry Reis's approach to understanding relationship issues differ from traditional ways researchers have looked at relationships?

Do you think active-constructive responding is likely to be easy or difficult? Try it for a few days, and then evaluate its impact on you and those close to you.

Chapter 17: Work

John P. Campbell
Individual Occupational Performance: The Blood Supply of Our Work Life

How does John Campbell define the term *occupational performance*, and why is it a plural noun in his model?

Develop your own list of components of good and poor undergraduate performance. How do yours differ from the performance components shown in Table 2?

Benjamin Schneider
Organizational Climate: Theory and Evidence

Why does Benjamin Schneider focus on service quality and safety in his research on organization climate?

Think back on places you have worked. Assess their organizational climate and its impact on your job performance.